A Different Kind of Assassin . . .

Mac was down, the beast upon him once again, jaws snapping for his neck, Mac's hands on the creature's throat, struggling with the thing, trying to keep its jaws from snapping over his jugular.

Dannie was up before she realized it, wielding the sword Mac had given her in both hands. She hauled the sword up from the floor, in a wide, ragged arc from behind her right shoulder, smashing it downward into the creature's back and through fur and flesh. She felt the blade catch in bone. There was a shriek, the beast spinning away from Mac, the sword torn from Dannie's hands. The sword flew across the room, impaling itself into the floor, vibrating.

Now on all fours, the beast began to howl, and the howl became an almost human scream as the creature sagged in the middle and collapsed.

The wolf's muzzle began to shrink. Dannie heard a crackling sound as bone seemed to shrink before her eyes and matted hair withdrew into pink human skin. Hunched shoulders raised, only to slump forward into a man writhing for an agonizingly long few seconds.

Finally he was still, dead on the floor.

WEREWOLVES

JERRY AND SHARON AHERN

PINNACLE BOOKS
WINDSOR PUBLISHING CORP.

PINNACLE BOOKS

are published by

Windsor Publishing Corp.
475 Park Avenue South
New York, NY 10016

First printing: April, 1990

Printed in the United States of America

For the memory of Stuart McGowan, a friend of brief duration but lasting remembrance who, after a lifetime of the extraordinary, tragically met something deadly and ordinary. To his family, and especially young Stuart and their friend, Jasim, remember his hopes for you all and take strength from this.

Authors' Note

When writing a novel, the idea, of course, is to enable the reader to share the experiences of the characters. Accuracy of detail is often the key to this hoped-for empathetic response. But there are some experiences which cannot be researched in ordinary ways. Such was the case with that portion of this book written from the perspective of a man about to undergo quadruple bypass surgery, that medical procedure which, although it is almost commonplace these days, is no less miraculous.

To achieve our goal, we went to our good friend Blake Breitenhirt. Indeed, we are especially fortunate that open heart surgery has such a high success ratio because Blake would have been dearly missed. So it is that the experiences of "Evan Hardy" as he is about to go under the knife are in part Blake's, in part those of Evan. And there any resemblance ends.

To get a firmer grasp on the structural nuances of Hitler's SchutzStaffel Polizei, we contacted Bob Magee. A friend for longer than any of us might care to consider, his in-depth knowledge of this historical epoch proved invaluable. So much so, he even appears here as a character.

Thanks, guys.

And, a final note. In a film many years ago, the late Boris Karloff once made the distinction between horror and terror. He said he dealt in terror. And, so do "the werewolveSS."

JERRY and SHARON AHERN
Commerce, Georgia
1989

Of Historical Interest . . .

Toward the end of 1944, Reichsminister Goebbels made a radio speech. In it, he delineated the mission of an organization known as "Werewolf." The Werewolves were to allow themselves to be passed by as advancing Allied armies overran German occupied lands, even the Fatherland itself. They were then to strike within the newly occupied Allied territory, strike without mercy and "drown the enemy within a sea of blood."

There were actually three separate distinctions of Werewolf, as customarily considered. One was a group of pilots within the Luftwaffe who vowed to employ the Japanese kamikaze style of attack, crashing their aircraft into Allied targets at the cost of their own lives. But the other two groups were to operate on the ground. Goebbels and his fellows within the Nazi hierarchy wanted the German people to raise up in arms to defend their homeland, a spontaneous uprising which would, indeed, have precipitated a "sea of blood."

The second of these two groups were to be specially trained intelligence commandos, operating in much the same manner as Partisans in France and other occupied lands had fought against the Nazi occupation forces.

The SS trained these latter units.

As surely as Hitler sought to homogenize the Wermacht, Himmler sought, in the SS, to build that special esprit de corps of the elite volunteer unit. For this reason, he selected names for units that were rich in German cultural identification. The SS rank designations were more imposing-sounding, more involved. Badges used by the SS often incorporated cryptic symbology, none more infamous than that of the Third Panzer Division, the mandibulated skull and bones of the Totenkopf. This became the classic SS symbol found on banners and rings and patches, nearly as well known as — and perhaps more terrifying than — the SS lightning bolts and the twisted Nazi cross itself.

The cross is a symbol from the racial subconscious of man, as indeed are the werewolf, the vampire and other creatures of the night, steeped in legend as surely as the strains from Wagnerian opera to which the Nazis marched, and often steeped in terror. It is the ancient symbol known most often as the Swastika, the origin of the term — actually *svastika* — from the Sanskrit, meaning "It is well."

The right-hand facing cross marks the passage of the sun as it is seen in the northern hemisphere. The left-hand facing cross, however, stands for black magic and the death cult of Kali. Sanskrit was the written language of the Aryan peoples and embodies considerable and diverse literature. It was the Aryan — or "noble" — race from which Hitler claimed historic German descent. The idea of Aryan supremacy was not new, however, with the German dictator. During the nineteenth century there arose the term "Aryan race," as a human subgroup identified by speaking the Indo-European languages and being at the core of all of humanity's finest achievements. The Aryan race was, according to those who believed in its existence, superior in every respect to the Semitic peoples and those persons whose skin happened not to be white.

Not all persons who were "white," of course, were superior. Slavs, even though their skin was the appropriate color, for example, were to be enslaved.

Hitler saw the German people as the ultimate expression of Aryan purity. This notion was one of the pivotal points of *Mein Kampf*. To Hitler, racial inequality was a given.

And, Hitler, as recent films have pointed out to us with rather uncharacteristic accuracy, was very much the slave of superstition and what today would be called "crackpot" theories. Hans Horbiger, who believed that the planets were made of fire and ice and only the earth combined the two, could count among his devotees both der Führer and Heinrich Himmler. Hitler's beliefs in astrology and other

9

forms of mysticism posing as science are well documented. Hitler did indeed spend considerable time and effort, for example, in the search for the Holy Grail, as well as other artifacts of supposed mystical potency whose power could be used to his own advantage.

Clearly, the symbol of Nazism was a charm against bad karma, designed to ward off the sort of evil which, to more rational men, the Swastika itself represented.

The Werewolf concept, the precise origin of the name as it applied to the Nazi insurgency movement unclear, easily lends itself to speculation. A werewolf seems as innocuous as any man by day; but, by night — the inverted Swastika or *sauvastika* was itself a symbol of night as well as black magic — the man becomes the beast.

In the name of Aryan supremacy and for the glory of the Fatherland, otherwise innocuous men donned the symbols of the death's head and the runic lightning bolts and became the SS.

There may be no difference at all; both bore the mark of the beast.

Prologue

The blond spun away from Billy Hyde and Billy just lay there in the wet grass, the mists half obscuring him, his scream no louder than any of the others. Blood dripped from the blond's mouth.

Harry Milford fired out his rifle into the blond. Harry was the team demolitions man and, at least among the Americans, the worst shot in the outfit. But that still meant an expert rating with the Garand and the .45, too, or he never could have become a Ranger. At maybe ten feet, not even Harry could have missed the hulking blond.

The blond staggered, fell. Harry turned his M1 around, held it by the barrel with both hands, and swung the heavy wooden buttstock down to crush his head and finish the job.

The blond caught the rifle in midswing, ripping it away from Harry.

Harry stepped back and his face was white as death.

The blond was standing again, hunched over but no more so than any of the rest of them, as if the eight .30-06 ball rounds Harry'd fired into him were nothing.

Harry tried to draw his pistol.

The blond swiped at Harry's face and ripped away Harry's left cheek and tore out his left eyeball.

Harry's teeth sprayed out of his mouth, he stumbled, started to fall.

The blond reached out and grabbed Harry under the sternum on both sides of the rib cage, palms outward, then merely seemed to flex those massive shoulders. It was as if there were no effort to it at all.

And then Harry was all split open and the blond's mouth

disappeared for an instant inside Harry's chest. Harry screamed, but the scream choked off very quickly. The blond's head snapped back.

Harry's heart was in the blond's teeth, the heart still pumping blood for several seconds, the blood oozing out from the corner of the blond's mouth.

It was the thing about breaking his own sternum which made him remember Harry and brought the images back.

Evan Hardy supposed that, even without the old nightmares, he wouldn't have slept too terribly easily. Because "cabbage," as they euphemistically called Coronary Artery Bypass Grafting, although its success ratio was unbelievably high, was still a procedure that could result in fatality. Sometimes, the heart would not restart.

"Roll over and let the doctor see those sweet cheeks."

His tongue was coated with something the consistency of glue, and about the same taste. But it was his saliva. Nothing by mouth since midnight. When he drew his tongue back under his teeth—he actually had his own—he could scrape the film off and there were little ridges at the corners of his mouth where the stuff had dried.

"I'm saving myself for the right woman, Celestine," Hardy told the nurse. She was black, a little chubby, nearly as old as he was—which meant she would likely retire any day now—and brightened his spirits with her banter, something she had begun when she'd first entered his room yesterday afternoon to check his elevated blood pressure.

Hardy slid left in the bed so he could roll over to the right and his left arm wouldn't get in the way. He turned onto his stomach.

The chest pains had started almost two weeks ago. He'd tried assiduously to ignore them.

They not only stayed with him, but became worse.

"Oww!"

"You got such a tender backside, Mr. Hardy," Celestine sort of laughed.

The doctor—Hardy guessed the man was an anesthesiologist—told him, "The effect of this, Mr. Hardy, as you already know, will be to relax you. Kind of like tying on a pleasant

12

buzz. If you feel as though you have to urinate, ask for assistance. Don't try to get up, because this is a sort of cocktail—there's a muscle relaxant in it as well."

His tongue felt thicker than it had before and the dried saliva tasted even worse.

Hardy smiled. It would be so stupid if, after all he'd been through, he died like this.

Just him and Hugh MacTavish.

Out of all the rest. "There was this guy I knew years and years ago." He felt like singing. "Just a kid, then, but he's probably almost as old as I am now." For some reason, Hardy didn't think MacTavish, if he were still alive at all, would be having open heart surgery. Mac was— "He was a hell of a guy. We were both hell of a guys." You wouldn't say that. It was like saying mother-in-laws or son-of-a-bitches, because you didn't say that. "Mothers-in-law," he said very carefully. So, you'd say "hells of a guy?" Naw.

"What, Mr. Hardy?" Celestine asked. "You can roll over now."

He rolled over, watching out for his left arm again.

Celestine looked prettier than she had before. "Shouldn't drink cocktails on an empty stomach." Hardy laughed.

Celestine stroked his forehead. "You'll be fine, Mr. Hardy."

"I ever tell you about the first time I got really potsed?" He assumed he hadn't. And, come to think of it, that was the only time he'd gotten acutely drunk. "Me and Mac—Mac and I, excuse me— Anyway, we found all this wine in this barn? And, so, hell, it was the only thing to do because it was the only way to get to sleep because we figured they were maybe still after us and, us—and—whew—"

Time was distorted. On one level, he was perfectly aware of all of that, but it was somewhere deep inside his brain that he had that awareness and the place—wherever it was—was buried so deeply that it was impossible to do anything but observe, almost as a disinterested third party. This Evan Hardy was acting pretty stupid, talking about Mac and the barn and the wine and—

"How are you feeling, Mr. Hardy?"

"I'm OK—I'm okay. Yeah."

13

Was he really going to gain all that weight through fluid retention when they put him on the heart lung machine that they'd had to take his wedding ring? That didn't seem logical. And he laughed.

"What's so funny, Mr. Hardy?" It was the same voice, a doctor's voice?

"All right—look. The operation takes a few hours, right?"

"Usually, yes. But you won't be aware of the time." The doctor wore a gray skullcap and a mask and glasses and his eyes smiled behind the glasses.

"No, no, see—if I gained say, gosh, twenty pounds? Well, if the operation took a lot longer, gee whiz—I could blow up! Boom!"

"No. That's not something to worry about, Mr. Hardy."

"Easy for me to say."

"This stuff really hit him," a strange new voice said. "I betcha he's a hell of a guy at a party."

A new needle.

"Aww, that hurst—I mean, hurts—"

"It won't after a second."

His crotch itched where they'd shaved him.

". . . hell of a guy at a—. . . hell of a guy—. . . hell of a—"

"I—ahh." The outside part wanted to say something, but the inside part of his brain was content to let the flow pass . . .

He'd always liked fall best of all the seasons, and even though it was well along into spring, in these last days the coolness in the mornings and a smoky taste in the air at dusk made it seem like autumn. The smokiness may well have been his imagination, a remembrance of autumns past. Except for the weight of his rifle—he preferred the Garand to the Carbine or the Thompson—and that there was a hideously foul smell when he removed his boots to sleep, it was almost pleasant walking in these woods.

The companionship was pleasant, too: the Rangers of his own unit, some of them men he'd first trained with, but none of them strangers; the three Canadians and the dozen Brits,

14

Royal Commandos. One of the Brits, a lieutenant like he was, had been a junior instructor when the Rangers had gone through school with the Commandos. Of all of the guys in the outfit, Forrestal, now the commander of the British detachment, was the only one who was a prick.

Last year's leaves crunched beneath his boots.

He shifted the Garand's sling on his shoulder. The bank of dark clouds he'd been watching all afternoon well off to the east were starting to come in, giving the sky a gun-metal gray look and making the slanting sunlight seem brighter than it was. It would rain soon, and he'd always liked the rain, too. That was before he'd learned that in the Army when it rained and you were walking someplace, you kept walking. He'd seen pictures of British officers with umbrellas; Forrestal seemed the umbrella type.

"Excuse me, sir!"

Hardy pulled out of his thoughts and turned to face the voice. It belonged to Hugh MacTavish, youngest of the Brits and, Hardy suspected, the youngest of any of them, quite possibly too young for military service at all. "Yes, Corporal?"

"I was just wonderin,' sir, this Waffen SS unit we been hearin' about."

"Yeah?"

"Well, I mean, sir . . ." And MacTavish shrugged his massive shoulders. He was a tall, lanky kid, big-boned and strong but still not filled out into manhood. Already, under the beret he wore, the hairline was well back. High cheekbones, the cheeks themselves slightly sunken and, when he talked, drawing in to form something similar to large, quarter moon-shaped dimples, but too big for ordinary dimples and not quite in the right place. His brown eyes often gave the impression that he was laughing at something under the heavy dark brows, but there was no hint of that now. And, he was very quick-witted. Native intelligence and a lack of formal education were equally obvious in him.

"What Captain Erskine told us is all I know, Mac. This Kraut your people got talking told them there was a whole element of the First SS Panzer Division hiding out in these

15

mountains, lyin' low until we passed them by, with orders to hit our guys from behind."

"First SS Panzerdivision Liebstandarte Adolf Hitler, organized 1933. It was originally Hitler's personal guards regiment." Mac nodded. "They shouldn't be in Bavaria at all, they shouldn't — less, o' course, this 'ere's their bleedin' Alpine Redoubt they all been whisperin' 'bout."

"I don't buy that Alpine Redoubt crap. In another month or so, we'll all be in Berlin. Even Hitler, even given that he's a friggin' screwball, no way he could think he's suddenly going to turn the tide of the war." He changed the subject as he started digging for his cigarettes. "I've been meaning to ask you," Hardy began, shaking a Camel out of his pack for himself, offering one to Mac — Mac customarily refused — and then lighting it in the flame of his Zippo. "How come you know so much about the Nazis, Mac?"

"Well, sir, was always interested in learnin' things, I was, and always interested in joinin' His Majesty's forces. So I figured right off, I did, this Hitler bloke was gonna bloody well start 'isself a war and we'd bloody well be fightin' 'im. It only stood to reason, if you know what I mean, Lieutenant, regardless o' what Mr. Chamberlain was tellin' us. And a fella like meself should be learnin all 'e could 'bout the bloody Nazis, the better for fightin' 'em. Six years ago, I took myself down to the newspaper office and started lookin' through everythin' I could lay me 'ands on 'bout 'em."

"How old were you then, in 1939, Mac?"

"Old enough to read, I was, sir," and Mac winked.

Hardy laughed, felt himself grin. He started to say something, to pursue the age thing. But the rumble of thunder in the east took his attention.

"We're gonna be bloody well-drenched, we are."

Hardy agreed. They kept walking together, silently then.

The eastern sky was now all but entirely obscured and a wind was picking up.

Hardy flipped up the collar of his field jacket, hunching his shoulders a little. If he walked them just right, he could make his collar slip under the lip of his helmet and really keep the rain out.

16

And he smelled the rain now.

Throughout the late morning and the early afternoon they'd been steadily climbing through the mixed forest of pines and deciduous trees of every variety imaginable. If it had been the German people fighting to hold on to this part of their world, he could have understood that. It was beautiful.

Up ahead of Hardy and Mac, Captain Erskine and Forrestal had stopped; the other men were crowding around them.

Tactically, it was as bad to bunch up as it was to string out. So, whatever was drawing everyone's attention had to be something special. "Come on, Mac," and Hardy tucked the butt of the still-slung Garand against his hip and quickened his pace to double time. Mac matched Hardy stride for stride, holding back a little, it seemed. Mac was taller, longer limbed, younger. The German MP-40 submachine gun — all of the Brits carried captured German weapons instead of British or American arms — Mac carried at high port.

The ground rose abruptly and Evan Hardy slowed, then stopped, Mac overshooting him by a yard or so. There was the audible crunch of gravel slipping under their feet. "It's a castle!" Mac exclaimed, his voice almost cracking and for once betraying an age something close to real. A low whistle issued from Mac's lips.

Hardy stared.

Walls of gray stone, smooth-looking as a pretty woman's cheek, rose beneath the pale streaks of sunlight which had the force to pierce the gathering dark overcast. The plain at the farthest edge of which the structure was set glowed in the softly shimmering streaks of sun. Beyond the keep, stretching toward and lost beneath the cloud cover, were the blue waters of a vast lake. The castle's ramparts, turrets, and spires stabbed skyward, as if in some obscene gesture of defiance toward heaven. At the very instant Hardy thought this, chain lightning crackled out of the blue-black curtain and across the water and all the sounds of the forest seemed suddenly stilled. Evan Hardy felt a chill race along his spine . . .

There was a copse of skinny, old-looking pine trees, their years evidenced by their considerable height. All three offi-

17

cers and Sergeant Bickel, the senior noncom, threw down their gear there. Hardy lit a cigarette, Forrestal doing the same, taking his from the expensive-looking gold case he always carried.

Captain Erskine, his pipe odd-smelling because he burned cigarette tobacco in the bowl, crouched down over the map, exhaling the pipe smoke through his nostrils. The wind caught the smoke, began blowing stronger with an almost unnatural abruptness, the rain not yet started but inevitable, the smell of it mingling with the tobacco smoke, like a memory of sitting on the front porch on a Sunday afternoon in anticipation of a spring thunderstorm. Captain Erskine drew the big stag-handled Bowie knife which he always carried and all of them secretly coveted, then rested it across one corner of the map in order to keep the rectangle of printed silk from blowing away.

Forrestal drew his British commando dagger and set it down on the opposite corner of the map. There wasn't that much additional need for anything else to anchor it, the trees breaking much of the force of the wind.

Captain Erskine's knife was heavy enough, Forrestal's knife really superfluous. But Hardy snagged the one-piece Ek knife his dad had given to him from its sheath under his open field jacket anyway, adding it to a corner of the map. Sergeant Bickel just cleared his throat, as if suppressing a laugh, his already ruddy cheeks flushing a little more.

Captain Erskine said, "Now is the time to mention this. Our G-2 and your Intelligence boys, too, Forrestal, and the OSS all seem to think there's some damn secret base Himmler's set up in these mountains, a last redoubt where the top SS men and some of the party big shots are prepared to hold out. 'Cause they know these mountains very well, and they could keep fighting up here for months, maybe, like that. Hell, I don't know. That's what they tell me."

"I seriously doubt, sir, that even the SS with their inflated sense of theatrics would so openly take refuge in such a structure as this castle." Forrestal waved a hand limp-wristedly in its general direction.

There was a woodpecker — maybe more than one — in the

tree just above them, the tapping sound incessant, distracting.

Captain Erskine looked at Forrestal, nodded noncommittally and said, "Evan, whatchya think?" without looking at Hardy at all.

Hardy's attention was already where it belonged. He exhaled cigarette smoke, said, "Well, Captain, we've been walking all this way. Won't hurt to take a look at it. Maybe just a couple of us, then that way if this is some sort of Alpine Redoubt we won't wind up walking into something bigger than we can handle with a force of our size. I mean, we're on an Intelligence mission, more or less—or is that different, too?"

Captain Erskine shrugged his eyebrows, his green eyes smiling as he chewed down on his pipe. He said, "We are under orders to do what we can about grabbing any enemy prisoners as necessary. We need information. We don't have information. That's why we're here, and if kidnapping some SS superman gets us the stuff we need, then that's damned well what we do. Forrestal? Any further comments? Bickel?"

"None whatsoever, Captain."

"Not me, sir." Bickel nodded.

Captain Erskine—he was short and stocky-looking for a Ranger, and at West Point he'd been a boxing champion—stood up and stretched. Hardy and Forrestal stood, as well, Hardy getting a faceful of pine bough for his trouble, swatting it away. Sergeant Bickel—he was the oldest man in the outfit—was the last to his feet, and Hardy thought Bickel'd noticed the encounter with the pine tree, because it looked like the old man was suppressing still another laugh. Captain Erskine said, "We'll advance into that divide below, which puts us well out of view of the castle. Unless the Nazis smuggled some Kriegsmarine up here, we won't have to worry about an attack from the lake, either. So that only gives us the castle and two other directions to worry about with establishing a perimeter. Hardy . . ."

"Yes, sir."

"You can pick some guys and tonight get as close to that castle as you can and scout it. Pick 'em now and use 'em running interference for the main body, too."

19

"How about getting inside, sir? Tonight, I mean."

Captain Erskine's eyebrows shrugged again and he seemed to chew harder on his pipe. "Let me think on that, Evan."

"Yes, sir," Hardy nodded . . .

Portions of the forest had been planted as a natural barricade. That much was obvious. The spacing between the trees was too regular, more like a Christmas tree farm than a forest. But the trees were old for pines, maybe planted for some tactical purpose during the last war, or the one before that.

The men in the main body under Captain Erskine moved in a single file, but paired, each man protecting his buddy's back as they entered the defile. At one time the uneven, rocky cut was probably a streambed. Slowly, they advanced on the valley.

It was darker the deeper they moved into the cut because of the higher trees. And there was privet hedge growing in long, zigzagging fencelines, paralleling the treeline. Hardy's observations only reinforced his earlier notion. The trees and the privet hedge had been planted to break up a horse-mounted cavalry unit and trap men and horses.

Hardy looked away from the main body of the force and signaled to Mac, Billy, and the two Canadians. Silently they moved ahead, well in advance of the main body under Captain Erskine, but roughly paralleling its route, well back inside the treeline, the privet hedge on both sides of them now.

Thunder rumbled more loudly by the minute and the rain smell was so intense that with the wind blocked out here by the trees, the air was oppressive.

They kept moving—he lost track of exactly how long—but the main body was halfway down the defile, only the tallest spires of the castle were still visible above the trees against clouds that were now almost black.

It was Mac, on point, who signaled the halt with a raise of his left hand, his right hand fisted around the pistol grip of his submachine gun.

Hardy made a circular motion with his left hand and stabbed the index finger downward and everybody went flat

20

into the pine needles. Hardy held his breath, listening. He could hear an occasional disconnected whispered syllable, or was it the lapping of the water against the shores of the lake? He couldn't be sure. He looked toward Mac, the only one of them not prone, hugging the pine needles and rotted leaves. Mac crouched behind a tree, holding himself as erect as he could so the trunk of the pine would conceal him.

Hardy waited.

At the first sound of trouble, Captain Erskine and Sergeant Bickel would take one element and Forrestal the other and the main body would break for both sides of the defile, into the trees. Unless that first sign of trouble came much too quickly. It was Hardy's job to prevent that latter from happening.

Hardy studied Mac's face. The corners of the young man's mouth were turned down hard, the dimplelike things in his cheeks narrow trenches now, extending nearly from cheekbone to hard-set jaw.

Very slowly, Mac was moving his left hand outward so it would be in line with the trunk of the tree but behind him. He started flexing his fingers outward. Five. Ten. Fifteen. Twenty. Twenty-five. Thirty. Thirty-five. Forty. Forty-three. And he shook his hand right and left a little. Hardy interpreted that as meaning "more or less."

Hardy stared at Mac. He wanted more data.

Mac nodded. Then, drawing with his left index finger, he made the initials "SS" in the air.

Under his breath, Hardy hissed the word "Shit" into the pine needles.

Evan Hardy thumped the knuckles of his left hand hard against the forest floor. It made a sound like an acorn or a pinecone falling, but enough to get every one of the men with him to turn around and look at him.

He made hand and arm signals then that they should withdraw to the west.

There were silent nods. Slowly—laboriously so—the men started moving, crawling on knees and elbows like recruits in an infiltration course . . .

"At least forty-three of the bloody arseholes, Waffen SS, mixed field gray and that damn sissy-lookin' spring camouflage. One mortar I could see. Heavily armed with automatic weapons—damned sight better than you Yanks 'ave got, no offense, Lieutenant—and on both sides of the defile."

Hardy glanced at his watch. It had been nearly a full two minutes since Mac had spotted the SS and, as best Hardy could figure, in another three at the outside, the main body of the Allied Force under Captain Erskine would be walking right into the SS killing zone.

"Billy."

"Yes, sir?"

"Get the hell back to the captain. First you get there, make sure they know it's you and tell the captain everything. Don't let Forrestal sidetrack you."

"Amen to that, beggin' the lieutenant's pardon," Mac added.

Hardy ignored the cut on Forrestal. "Then get 'em up here. Or we're gonna be dead, Billy. Got it?"

"Yes, sir."

"Then why aren't you moving?"

Billy was up, moving in a fast, long-strided commando walk, his rifle in a tight-to-the-chest high port.

Hardy looked at the others, his voice a rasped whisper. "Forty-three versus us isn't so good, so we hit as hard as we can. Mac—you got Elbert and Groggins." Elbert and Groggins were the two Canadians, also armed with German MP-4O's. "You have the maneuver element. Work 'em down the defile so we can suck the SS into you. That'll give our guys the chance to hit from behind. We'll cover you with these." He slapped the receiver of his Garand and it rattled reassuringly.

"Yes, sir."

"We go now, gentlemen. Quiet until we get ready. Mac, you fire the first shots and we're on them."

"Yes, sir."

Hardy nodded.

They were moving . . .

The rain began falling, for about ten seconds like a pleasant, warm spray, and then hard, fast and cold as death.

Evan Hardy saw the muzzle flash a split second before he heard the report from MacTavish's submachine gun and, in the next instant, Hardy's finger flicked forward disengaging the Garand's trigger guard safety, then drew back against the trigger and the rifle bucked, slammed into his shoulder and his ears rang and one of the men of the 1st Panzerdivision Liebstandarte Adolph Hitler seemed to spring forward against the tree behind which he was in concealment.

The man had to be dead.

Gunfire was all around him now.

The first eight-round clip was expended, ejecting. From his belt, Hardy took another, the heel of his right hand against the rifle's operating rod handle as he inserted the next, letting the bolt fly forward.

Hardy snapped off another round, toward a tall figure in Field Gray, the man rallying a dozen of the SS into something like a wishbone formation in football, the men charging into the trees toward Mac and the two Canadians.

Hardy's shot missed.

The SS officer spun around so quickly as he threw himself to cover that his hat flew off and Hardy had a glimpse of a thick shock of blond hair, all but skinned away at the sides over his ears.

The rain was hammering down now

Hardy fired two more shots, peeling out massive-seeming chunks of tree bark but not striking his human target. There was a flash of movement and the SS officer was running, firing a pistol as he dodged back into the cover of a segment of privet hedge choking the trunks of a small stand of stilted pines.

"We're moving!" Hardy shouted, ramming a fresh clip down into the action of his rifle, his hands slicked by the falling rain and moving so fast that he nailed his thumb knuckle as the rifle's bolt flew forward, like some kid in basic training. His armpits sweated and he could feel his heart

23

pounding in his chest.

He jumped over a deadfall pine, caught his right ankle in a spot of privet hedge, extended his rifle to both arms' length, and took the fall in a roll through the new mud, coming up, the butt of the Garand tucking tight against his hip. Hardy fired point-blank into the chest of an SS man running toward him, a submachine gun firing in the man's hands.

The ground in front of Hardy took the force of the shots and a wave of rotting leaf material and dirty water splashed up into Hardy's face.

Hardy spat, rubbed his left sleeve across his eyes.

His helmet was gone and the rain was streaming down so heavily across his face that he had to squint his eyes against it just to see.

"Let's go!" Hardy shouted, half his men already past him, some of them engaging the enemy hand-to-hand.

Hardy saw the SS officer again, the blond. Hardy snapped the butt of his rifle to his shoulder and fired, but he was so out of breath and excited that his aim was bad and he missed. "Dammit!"

"Grenade!" It was one of the Canadians from off to his left nearer to the water's edge who shouted the word. Hardy threw himself right, hoping he was moving away from the blast. The concussion came and his ears rang with the explosion and there was a great cloud of the wet, rotted debris rising from the forest floor, then falling, filling the air around him as he looked up.

Hardy got to his feet, snapping off the rest of the rounds from his rifle into a knot of SS personnel trying to get a mortar working. He killed one of the men, his rifle empty now. He charged toward the mortar, no time to reload, throwing down his rifle as he pulled the .45 from the holster at his right hip.

Hardy snapped back the slide to chamber a round out of the magazine, stabbing the pistol ahead of him, firing almost point-blank into three of the still-standing Nazis. Two of them were hit. Hardy threw himself sideways into the third man, bowling him over to the ground.

The Nazi's right knee smashed up, catching Hardy above

the belt instead of below. The man was incredibly strong. As Hardy lurched forward, the wind going out of him, Hardy managed to backhand the man across the bridge of the nose with his left fist.

There was a howl of pain.

Hardy rolled off the man.

The Nazi was up, blood spurting from his nose, a pistol in his hand.

Hardy heard Mac's voice. *"Heil Hitler!"*

The Nazi's eyes flickered and his head snapped toward the voice.

There was Mac, flying toward the man, tackling him at the waist like a kid playing football instead of a fight to the death.

Mac and the Nazi went past Hardy in a blur.

Hardy started to his feet.

Another SS man—maybe one of the ones Hardy had only wounded with his pistol—was poised beside it, about to drop a round down the tube. Only half in focus through the rain and beyond the SS man was Captain Erskine, Bickel beside him and a dozen or so of the men with them. If the mortar were fired . . .

Hardy reached for his knife, the only weapon he had left, throwing himself at the German, driving the blade deep into flesh at the juncture of the neck and right shoulder. Evan Hardy fell with the SS man's body under him into the mud, pulling out the knife, driving it into the body again. And then he just sat there over the body as Captain Erskine and some of the men ran past. There was blood on his hands and it didn't seem to wash away with the rain . . .

He could close his eyes and then open them and see the blood there on his hands, but he'd washed his hands by the shore of the lake and there really wasn't any blood there at all. The fighting had ended. At last matched in numbers when Captain Erskine's men joined the battle, the SS Unit retreated through the woods, escaping into the castle.

The rain stopped, so suddenly it was startling. And the

sun returned for an hour or so and, by moonrise, the sky was clear. The moon, full and yellow-orange in tint, seemed enormous. The night was so bright that Evan Hardy could almost read the serial number on his pistol as he reassembled it, cleaned as best he could accomplish it of the mud.

Captain Erskine approached and Hardy started to stand up. "Rest easy, Evan."

"Thanks, sir."

"I'm recommending you for the Silver Star." Hardy didn't know what to say. Captain Erskine sat down beside him. "What you did at that mortar emplacement was really something. I don't ever wanna see you take a chance like that again."

"Me neither." Hardy smiled, holstering the pistol on his web belt.

Captain Erskine laughed. "You really feel up to this deal tonight?"

"Yes, sir. If they want to keep us out of that castle of theirs so badly, it's gotta be for a reason."

Captain Erskine cleared his throat, nodded. "First time you were ever in it that hot, isn't it, Evan?"

Hardy just looked at him for a moment, then nodded. "Scared the shit outta me. It wasn't like when we bailed out over France last June. It's different when—when it's, ahh—"

"When the guy's that close?"

"Yes, sir."

"I know. You feel like some fuckin' animal ripping apart another animal. But, maybe that's what war is anyway. Beats me. But never doubt yourself, Evan. I've seen some good men in this war, and too many of them went down. I put you right up there with the best of them." And Captain Erskine extended his right hand.

Hardy took it . . .

Captain Erskine briefed Hardy and his six-man team, Mac among them. Forrestal wasn't recommending Mac for a citation and Hardy intended to talk with Forrestal about that, one way or the other, after they got back. If they didn't get back, he figured Captain Erskine would make certain that the mother or wife or sweetheart of each man had some medal to remember him by. They sat well up along the lakeshore, the spires of the castle glowing in the moonlight far off beyond the trees. "Lieutenant Hardy will get you men over onto the other side of the castle, well away from it, then you'll move down toward the lake and approach along the shore." The sounds of the water here were almost peaceful and the moon across the water's surface made the water itself seem to glow with its own light from beneath rather than a reflection from above.

Erskine lit his pipe and resumed speaking. "The SS has something to hide with that castle And I'm betting what they're hiding is that there aren't that many men inside, not enough to hold us off. Consider the logic, gentlemen. If they'd had heavy-duty manpower, why attack us in the woods. If we passed the castle, we passed it. If we made to enter the castle, then hit us. And maybe they got something else to hide. Documents, Intelligence reports, God knows. And, if God's watchin' out for us, maybe you guys'll find out."

Those who smoked lit cigarettes. Captain Erskine puffed on his pipe. Mac sat right at the water's edge, just staring out.

And then, it was time to move out . . .

It didn't take much convincing for Hardy to agree to leave the Garand behind and take one of the half-dozen captured submachine guns instead. Inside the castle, if they were discovered by the SS, the fighting wouldn't be at long range, but up close and fast and dirty.

He'd forced himself to eat and then thrown it up, although the rations didn't taste any worse than usual. But now his stomach growled so loud he was almost certain some SS sentry would hear the sound. Once, Mac whispered, "They'll think it's a bloody frog, Lieutenant." Hardy counted off the noisiness of his empty stomach to adrenaline, or maybe that he was scared.

They were approaching the castle from the far side, moving along close beside the lakeshore now, as Captain Erskine had only suggested, not ordered, Hardy to do. Here, the lapping of the water might mask any telltale sounds of their approach. He hoped.

The walls of the castle, which had seemed beautiful in a strange way when there had been light, now seemed like solid, impenetrable blocks of blackness, as if segments had been sliced from night's darkest heart and thrown up before them as a barrier.

Or, a warning.

They kept moving slowly, guarding each others' backs, the feel of the German submachine gun becoming more familiar in Evan Hardy's hands. Besides the "liberated" German weapon, he carried a German pistol as well, not a Luger but the newer one called the P-38. It, too, along with a holster and spare magazine, was taken from the body of a dead SS man. Mac had given it to him, explaining, "It might be a good idea, Lieutenant, to have a pistol in the same caliber. We do that, o' course."

So, Hardy carried it, but he had the .45 he'd carried on his hip since before D-Day as well, because he trusted it more.

They discovered a small stream feeding into the lake and draining down, it seemed, from the castle walls themselves. Hardy theorized it might be some sort of sewer outlet, although there was no offending smell to indicate that it was. They followed along its banks, toward the rear face of the castle.

The stream disappeared as the ground rose, and Hardy and the others moved from a low crouch into a hard crawl on knees and elbows. In other times, the castle had clearly been surrounded by a moat, but the ditch which had once held water now was a spongy-floored tangle of vines and shrubs, reborn with the spring, the stream abruptly reappearing again. Hardy, Mac all but beside him, the other five men well to their rear, clambered down into the ditch, moving toward the sound of the stream. Hardy was not quite sure how they would get inside yet; but, if the stream was a sewer for the castle, wherever it exited they could enter. And, as the lake had done on their approach, the sound of the water muf-

28

fled any sounds of their movements.

Trailers of mist clung in the air at shoulder level. Only when they parted on an errant gust of wind was the black of the castle walls visible at all.

They kept moving.

At last, by following the stream, they reached the wall. The stone was damp, cold, and somehow almost obscene. Touching it was like touching a wound, or an open sore. Hardy rubbed his hand along his trouser leg.

In the moonlight, filtered through the mist here and imparting an aura of unreality, Mac looked younger still, and more than a little afraid.

Hardy only nodded, clapping the Brit on the shoulder; despite the difference in age and rank and background, he considered Mac a friend. And, Hardy remembered suddenly he hadn't thanked Mac for saving his life today. What did one say? "Hey, thanks, fella!" No, Hardy thought. He would think about how to say it. If they didn't survive the castle, something else he wouldn't have to worry about.

They moved along the wall, Hardy not touching it again, nor Mac touching it, either. Had Mac felt the same thing, Hardy wondered. In the enforced silence, there was no way to tell.

A few paces on and the stream intersected the wall. But the hopes Hardy had held of somehow utilizing the stream's exit from the castle as their entrance vanished. There were five pipes that he could readily see, the stream moving from one side of the wall to the other by means of these, the pipes set several inches apart, their diameters six inches at best.

Hardy stared at them.

The water flowed rapidly, powerfully.

He looked into Mac's face.

Mac cocked his eyebrows upward, as if they could penetrate the mists.

Hardy looked upward along the wall.

Climb.

Touch that thing.

He nodded . . .

29

By forming a vertical human chain, Mac at the base, they gained another eighteen feet on the wall, one man standing on the shoulders of another. Hines, one of the Canadians, was raised on a ranch near Calgary and was a fair hand with cowboy-style roping. Standing at the top of the chain, on the third try the improvised climbing-rope lasso loop attached itself to something.

And Hines started to climb, the next man below him belaying the rope for him, then climbing up after him as Hines disappeared over the wall.

In the next few seconds, although the time seemed an eternity, a second rope was dropped, near to the first, Mac already moving up this, after Blankie and the other man, Hardy starting up the second rope.

This was too easy . . .

As soon as they reached the top of the wall, the wind picked up. Gone the occasional gusts, replaced with a steady howling rush. On the coattails of the wind, the clouds, the darkness which these promised fraught with opportunity for Hardy and the others as they moved down from the wall. But then, why did the darkness make him shiver just at the thought of it?

From the wall—where were the guards?—all that could be seen were darker shadows in the blackness.

Hardy dispatched Hines to the corner where the wall up which they'd come met the north flanking wall, the Canadian cowboy also a good rifleman and possessed of exceptional night vision. For the same purpose, and because he possessed similar skills, Hardy stationed Eddy Broncovitch at the south wall. The second Canadian Ranger, Bain, Hardy posted at the center.

With Cabrini and Donnelson covering them, Hardy and Mac started down into the deeper darkness of the castle quadrangle. And, with the clouds returning the sky to full, impenetrable overcast, the wind abruptly died.

Hardy crouched at the base of the rope down which he'd

come, Mac beside him in the next instant.

There was a building, of course, the castle itself, the towers of which were visible beyond the walls, but the actual building was set at the exact center of the grounds, surrounded entirely by carefully spaced and, at least as far as Hardy could see, meticulously ordered row after row of pine trees, but each row at a right angle to the former row and at a right angle to the next.

Hardy tried to see Mac's face, but all he could see were shadows, no detail. So he fisted the rope, shook it violently and stepped back. Cabrini and Donnelson had the signal to descend and, as he belayed the rope, he could feel one of them starting down . . .

Wisely, he had kept them together.

The right-angle bends made with the tightly spaced rows of pines formed a maze and they were in it now, at what Hardy judged to be near the midpoint between the wall they'd scaled and the castle itself.

He knew why there were no guards on the walls. With a maze such as this, men could be stationed anywhere, in greater security and for greater effect.

As Hardy, Mac, Phil Cabrini, and Bertie Donnelson moved, each one covered the other, all of them except Cabrini with a captured submachine gun in one hand, a pistol in the other. Cabrini had both hands on a .45 caliber M-3 Greasegun.

Cabrini was on Bertie Donnelson, but it was Donnelson who shouted out, not Cabrini, all but obliterating the low growl which had started Hardy turning around a split second before.

"Crimminey!"

And there was a scream, not the kind of scream Hardy had ever heard from a man before, but clearly Cabrini's. "Jesus!" The growl was an ear-splitting roar now.

In the bad light it took a second too long to see Cabrini, and then Hardy could only see Cabrini's boots, disappearing at chest level into the row of pines at their left. "Let's go!"

31

Hardy ordered, Mac already starting to bull his way between the densely grown-together trees, Hardy after him in the next second.

But there was no more sign of Cabrini.

From behind them, on the other side of the trees through which they'd pushed, there came a shout, this time Bertie Donnelson. "Lieutenant! Mac!"

And then a scream, the same kind of ear-splitting roar but the pitch different.

Back through the trees, Hardy and Mac beside each other.

Hardy slipped and fell to one knee.

As his hand touched against the ground, his palm and the butt of his .45 were suddenly sticky.

"Stay back, Lieutenant," Mac hissed, striking a match, the hiss and smell of burning phosphorous as Hardy pulled back into the trees, the match snapping to the ground. The flame flickered for an instant and died, but Hardy saw what he'd put his hand into and his bowels started to loosen. He'd seen a man's insides before, on D-Day, when Corporal Tommy Wilson had thrown himself over a grenade to save his buddies.

Before the match died and Hardy blinked, he saw human entrails and a pool of blood.

"What the bloody hell—"

"Quiet, Mac," Hardy said, amazed at the sound of his own voice. It still sounded all right, firm. "On my signal, fire behind us, I'll fire ahead, right through the fuckin' trees, but save the handgun."

"Yes, sir."

"Now!" And Hardy, the blood-sticky pistol tucked into the front of his pistol belt, the German submachine gun in both sweating fists, opened fire, hosing the muzzle left to right and down and zigzagging up and back left again, hot brass cartridge casings pelting his face and throat, his ears ringing as Mac, behind him, did the same.

When the gunfire died, there was no sound for a second or two.

Then there was a sound. Mac changing magazines in his submachine gun. Hardy remembered to do the same.

"What—"

"I don't know," Hardy said, the fear in his stomach creeping up into his throat. "Strike another match and hold it this time."

"Right, sir." Scratch. Scratch again. Hardy blinked against the flame then, his night vision just returning, gone again. It didn't matter now. Alternating his gaze from the ground to the trees surrounding them and back to the ground, Hardy forced himself to look at what he'd seen a moment earlier. Sausagelike tubes—intestine—trailed from the puddled blood into the trees opposite them. "Jesus!" Mac whispered.

"Not Him," Hardy said, his voice choked-sounding now, talking hard. "Back-to-back through that row of trees. Something moves, fuckin' kill it."

"Right."

They moved, crouched, a gun in each hand, pushing through the trees, branches swatting at them, but Hardy at least not willing to move a firearm off-line long enough to protect his face The branch that struck him across the eyes was actually convenient. The tears had been coming a little already, and now he had an excuse. Phil Cabrini had been with him since D-Day. He'd never liked the guy, really. But Cabrini had a young wife and a kid. What would he tell her in the letter he'd write? "Dear Mrs. Cabrini—I regret to inform you that your husband disappeared during a mission against the enemy. I think he died bravely. I think he was disemboweled, because the other guy was." He licked his lips, realized that he was muttering the "Lord's Prayer" under his breath.

They were through the line of trees. Another match. A trickle of blood. "Keep going," Hardy ordered, and back-to-back with Hugh MacTavish, they crossed into the next row of pines.

"Aww, Jesus," Mac gasped.

Hardy looked behind him toward the sound of Mac's voice.

Hanging in the trees he saw what used to be Donnelson. Half Donnelson's face was missing, the throat ripped out so badly that the head hung limply over the right shoulder. And

Donnelson was split from crotch to breastbone, things hanging out of him.

"Bloody Nazi bastards!" Mac shouted, firing his submachine gun and his pistol into the trees, branches and pine needles spraying around them, Hardy squinting his eyes against the debris, firing both weapons as well.

"Mac! Mac!"

Mac's gunfire ceased. Hardy had an empty pistol and a half-empty submachine gun. He changed magazines in both as he spoke. "We've gotta get back to the wall. The other guys are going to think we bumped into a damn division."

"Where's Cabrini?"

"I don't know. He's dead, though, got to be."

"Lieutenant—"

"I don't know what happened, but we'll hit this place hard and find Cabrini's body and bury Donnelson. Come on!" Hardy started toward the wall, or at least he hoped it was the wall. The trees were so high and the darkness so intense that he wasn't certain anymore whether or not he'd been turned around. He didn't tell that to Mac.

There was the growling noise again, and he thought he heard the sound of running feet behind them, but Mac would have said something. Perhaps, unless it was imagination totally, the movement was to one side of them, then the other.

And then he froze, Mac bumping into him.

There was a howl, long and loud, raising gooseflesh on his arms and thighs.

It came from ahead of them.

"What the bloody hell was that?"

"A dog or something . . ." As a boy and a young man, he'd always hunted with his father or his friends, and sometimes they'd hunt with dogs. And the dogs would howl sometimes, bay at the moon or merely yelp their discontent. But he'd never heard a dog make a sound like this.

The howl came again, louder now, and then another joined it, and another after that. The howls continued; as one died another beginning, not just from ahead of them, but all around them now.

Hardy started to run, shouting to Mac, "Stick together!"

Gunfire, from the direction of the wall, he realized. It had to be. Hardy quickened his pace.

The maze took another twist and as he turned into it, there was a blur of movement and Mac shouted, "Look out, Evan!" Hardy threw himself left, the right sleeve of his jacket torn away. Gunfire from behind him, Mac shouting, "You bloody motherfucker!" More gunfire. Mac hurtled past him, almost cartwheeling. Hardy stabbed his submachine gun toward the trees and fired, surprised at himself that he kept to neat, three- and four-round bursts, even more surprised that his hand was still at the end of his arm. "To your right!" Mac shouted.

Hardy fell left and fired out the submachine gun before he looked.

"God Almighty!" Taller than a man, broader, lurching toward him, a hulking blackness with long fangs so brilliantly white they seemed luminescent. The shape seemed to hesitate, to stumble.

Mac was on his knees beside Hardy, firing his submachine gun. He emptied it. Mac was up, running toward whatever it was, the captured German weapon smashing against the black shape's head. An arm, but it was the size of a tree limb, swiped outward and Mac flew back.

Hardy edged back, changing to the last full magazine for his submachine gun.

The thing took Mac's weapon, raised it high above its head, and twisted the gun like a piece of string, hurtling it into the night.

Mac edged back, shouting, "Run for it, Lieutenant!"

"Nuts!" Hardy let the submachine gun fall to his side on its sling. He punched his pistol toward the black shape. "Try a .45 for size, cocksucker!" The pistol bucked in Hardy's hand again and again, the thing howling now, but not like the other sounds still all around them, but as if in pain. It staggered, it fell back. "Now, Mac! The wall! Come on!"

Hardy started to run, looking back once that Mac wasn't staying behind to be a hero; Mac was running, too, sprinting past Hardy now, both men reaching a wall of trees where the maze took a twist, punching through it, falling, dragging themselves to their feet, running.

They forced their way through more of the trees and suddenly they were before the wall. On the parapets, as Hardy looked up, there were two more of the great black shapes, one of them holding a man at arm's length, shaking the man as if the man were weightless, then its other arm reaching out, a scream from the man it held, the scream dying. Hardy put his last fresh magazine in the .45 and fired upward toward the thing. The bullet, if it hit, seemed to have no effect.

Mac was scaling the rope, a submachine gun slung across his back, Hardy vaguely wondering where the weapon had come from.

He stumbled over a body, one of his men, unrecognizable, and he lurched forward, vomit welling up in his throat. He knew where Mac had found the extra gun. "Try this, you unholy bastard!" Mac cursed from above.

Hardy clawed the rope, the second black shape moving along the top of the wall, on two feet but somehow unlike a man. Mac rode the back of the other one, the one Hardy had shot at, a knife in Mac's hand.

As the second thing reached out for Mac, Hardy, just barely to the top of the wall, fired the .45, upward, into the thing's rear end, hoping to hit the anal opening.

There was a sound then like nothing he'd ever heard. The thing wheeled, charged toward him, and, as Hardy fired his last shot, the hulking black shape flew over him. There was a smell to the thing, more disgusting than anything he'd ever smelled.

Hardy hung there on the rope, staring down into the blackness, seeing the thing writhe below him. And then Hardy stuffed his pistol, its slide still locked open, into his belt. Both hands to the rope, he hauled himself up again, Mac thrown to the walkway surface, the creature or thing or whatever it was to which Mac had clung pawing at its throat, a knife buried there to the hilt. Hardy got to his knees on the walkway and grabbed for the submachine gun hanging on its sling at his side. He fired a burst, then another and another, the thing falling forward, but not like a man, the knees bending wrong, wailing in pain.

"Come on! Leave the knife!" Hardy reached for the rope leading back down into the overgrown ditch which had once been the moat.

"Look out!" It was Mac.

Hardy stepped back. Still in midair — it had to have leaped up from the ground — was another of the things, maybe the one he'd shot with his .45. But that had to be impossible. Hardy stabbed the submachine gun toward it and fired, long bursts, the thing's line of movement changing suddenly, the bullets driving it down, its body crashing onto the walkway with such force that the boards beneath Hardy's feet shook.

But in the blink of an eye it sprang to its feet.

And Mac was there, Mac's submachine gun spraying into its face and upper torso. The thing reeled, howled, stumbled, fell back.

"Mac!" And Hardy grabbed onto the rope again, vaulted to the top of the battlement, and flipped over, climbing down hand-over-hand, Mac just above him.

A dozen feet from the bottom now, and at the height of the wall, Hardy saw another of them grabbing for the rope. Hardy shouted, "Flat against the wall, Mac!" and fired out his submachine gun toward the thing. It fell back from sight. Hardy let go of the rope or lost it — he didn't know — and half-jumped, half-fell, hitting the ground hard, but going into a roll.

He looked up, Mac halfway down the wall. The thing or another of them was back, hauling up on the rope, lifting Mac like a marionette, the rope going into its mouth. Mac swung there. Hardy fired the liberated P-38 he'd brought along, either missing or the rounds having no effect.

The rope snapped as Mac jumped.

Hardy dragged himself up, his right knee hurting, maybe twisted. Mac was on hands and knees, shouting, "You can't kill the bleedin' things!"

"Can you move?"

Mac nodded, coughed.

"Then move!" Hardy shouted.

And Mac was up, running beside him. They clambered

37

down into the ditch, Hardy reaching to his belt, finding first one, then the second, then the third of the three grenades clipped there. "Take one of your grenades and be ready," Hardy ordered as they waded into the densest tangles of vine and brush. Hardy tore a grenade from his belt, freeing the cotter pin as he did it, holding the grenade tight to keep the spoon from popping away and starting the fuse. Hardy sank to his knees in the brush, Mac falling down beside him. "Be ready. When they come for us, we use these and then we run for the lake. They won't be able to find us in the lake, because they smell us." It was what one of his instructors in Officers' Candidacy School had once labeled a "confidence-building lie," something said as if there could be no other possible option, with enough conviction to it that the men under you would believe it.

Mac rolled over onto his back, looking up at Hardy, breathing hard. "You mean they look like bloody big dogs to you, too."

"You're a city boy, Mac. They're like wolves, but they're not. But they sniff us out—I hope."

"Wolves." Mac was up to his knees, a grenade in his right hand, his submachine gun in the left. "Wolves? That big?"

"Like wolves. I don't know. All I could see was they were big. They howl like wolves. I heard a wolfpack once in—" He never finished it, a howl from by the wall, then another and another. Hardy thought he could hear the thumping of feet on the ground. "Like wolves."

The brush between them and the wall crackled, snapped, seemed to be almost alive. "Be ready to run. See you in the water, Mac."

"Right, sir."

Hardy hauled his right arm back, shouted to Mac, "Now!" and threw, then turned on his heel and ran.

The explosions came almost simultaneously.

But Evan Hardy didn't look back.

If the grenades worked, there was a chance. If they didn't, all he would see was something huge snapping its fangs in the last instant before he died or wished that he had died. Mac was beside him. Hardy's right knee hurt. There wasn't time

38

to worry about that, though.

They ran beside the streambed, the lake ahead of them. Was the sound he heard the padding of animal feet behind him, or his own heart beating?

Running.

"I see it, Evan! I see the water!"

Hardy could hear the water.

And he could hear the thumping.

It wasn't his heart.

He felt something, like breath, only it was the smell again, the same as when he'd shot one of the things and it had fallen over the wall into the castle grounds, passing within inches of him.

He tried to run faster, his right knee locking up.

Hardy could see that Mac was holding himself back, to keep abreast of him. "Run! For that water! Now, dammit!"

He could barely see Mac's face in the darkness but knew that Mac turned, stared at him for an instant.

Hardy tried to run faster.

The thumping sounds were louder, the smell stronger.

He thought he felt breath on his neck.

Hardy tried to run faster.

Something touched at his left hand.

He tried to draw his hand away.

His hand wouldn't move.

"Run, Mac!"

Hardy tried pulling away.

There was a loud popping sound and his shoulder felt like it was on fire, and numbing pain seized him, hammered into his body between the shoulder blades and Hardy could feel every muscle in his body wrenching, every part of his body except his left arm. His feet no longer touched the ground at all. He was twisted around.

There was a face.

It wasn't human at all, except the eyes, the whites around them making the dark centers look like holes in the night.

The smell.

The low growl.

"Jesus!" Hardy slammed against the ground, his left arm

still attached to his body — he knew that much — but only aware of its presence because he crashed down on it.

Hardy looked up.

One of the things leaned over him. Were they arms reaching for him? They were too big, too long, and what moved to his throat weren't hands, but they were, though.

Hardy tried to reach for his knife.

The submachine gun was lost.

The thing touched him and Hardy wet his pants and screamed, but he had the knife. Holding it like a saber, he snapped his right arm up in a broad arc and the blade gouged into the thing's left eye and Hardy's right hand was suddenly wet. There was a howl, and Hardy's ears rang with it.

"Try this, you bleedin' motherfucker!"

Mac's voice.

A blur as something black — Mac's submachine gun? — swung across Hardy's field of vision, impacting the thing in the face.

Hardy tried to stand. The pain caught him when he didn't think it would and the blackness around him engulfed him . . .

They came out of the water. Mac half carried him. Hardy shivered uncontrollably. His left arm was still part of his body but didn't feel like it was there anymore. Hardy could see it though, when he looked down.

There had been general gunfire for more than fifteen minutes now, and the howls only louder and more of them.

The sun was rising, mists lingering over the ground there in the defile by the shores of the lake where Captain Erskine had made their camp.

The things that had stalked Hardy and Hugh MacTavish in the darkness were everywhere in the defile now. There were more of them than Hardy had the soul to count.

Forrestal had one of the German submachine guns in each hand, firing at three of them as they closed around him, the creatures falling back, dragging themselves to their feet, moving inexorably closer.

Both submachine guns stopped firing at once.

Forrestal threw them down as the creatures encircled him, Forrestal's hand moving to his tunic. For a moment, Evan Hardy thought the man had gone insane and was reaching for his cigarette case.

But Forrestal's hand reappeared instead with a gun, some kind of small semiautomatic pistol Hardy had never seen Forrestal use before. Forrestal aimed the weapon at the nearest of the three beasts and fired point blank. Tufts of fur flew from the thing's face and what might be its forehead. The other two creatures closed on Forrestal and each of them grabbed for him and their mouths opened and as they fell on Forrestal, Forrestal screamed.

There was a machine gun on a mount at the edge of the treeline, one of the German weapons confiscated after the previous day's fight with the SS. Captain Erskine had ordered it set up for perimeter defense.

Most of the body parts of one of the Canadians lay slumped over it, oozing gore.

Mac eased Hardy to the ground, then kicked at the entrails to clear them from the weapon.

Hardy felt vomit rising in his throat as he reached toward the severed right hip and leg of the dead man and took the pistol from the bloodstained holster. Hardy caught the rear sight of the handgun—it was a High Power 9mm—against his soaked trouser leg and was able to friction the slide in the fabric enough to work it back, then pulled the gun free to let the slide slam forward and chamber a round.

Mac swung the machine gun around, then opened fire.

Hardy caught a glimpse of Captain Erskine, a carbine in one hand but inverted like a club, the captain's big Bowie knife in the other. One of the things came at him. It was different from the others. The fur which completely covered the bodies of the others was various shades from black through light brown. But this one of them, its fur was blond.

Mac opened fire, cutting into a concentration of the creatures fighting hand-to-hand with a half dozen of the men, the men thrown into the air, torn limb from limb. As the ma-

41

chine gun bullets struck the things, they would stumble, some of them fall, but then rise again, as if they couldn't be killed, were incapable of dying.

Hardy steadied the dead Canadian's pistol across his left knee, his injured right leg outstretched, his left arm limp and useless. He fired, knowing he struck the blond. There was a howl sounding like rage and the blond looked back.

And Hardy saw it fully for the first time.

Evan hunched forward. It stood well over six feet on its hind legs, the legs jointed like those of an animal, the knees at the rear. There was a short, wide brush of tail. There was something like a waist, where the enormous upper torso came in at the hip joints.

The back was as broad as the body of a gorilla, and where the front legs or arms joined the trunk, there weren't really shoulders but rippling knots of muscle, the blond fur which covered the entire body — matted now with blood and mud — thinner here.

The neck was long and enormously thick, the head seeming to grow out of it without any clear division where one body part stopped and the other began. There were long, canine-looking ears, pointed, alternately drooping or pricking up. A long, sloping forehead flowed without angle into the muzzle. This was enormously wide, fanged, the fangs dripping saliva and gore. The muzzle tapered in a blunted nose, nostrils flared as though the creature sniffed something on the air. The eyes. The creature's eyes were blue.

Hardy fired again, saw a tuft of hair fly, knowing he'd hit it. The thing swatted at the wound like a man might swat at an insect. And Captain Erskine attacked then, the Bowie knife in both hands, hacking toward the creature's neck, but the thing seeming somehow to sense this, catching the captain's arms and with a mighty flex of its upper body ripping the arms from their sockets.

Captain Erskine fell down dead.

Hardy fired.

Mac's machine gun was firing again.

Billy Hyde ran up toward the blond, but the blond's left arm or foreleg swiped at Billy, the blond's claws tearing away the left side of Billy's face.

The blond bent over Captain Erskine's armless body and sunk its teeth into the captain's throat. Hardy shouted, "Come and get me, you bastard! Come and get me!" Hardy fired, knowing he was striking the creature, but knowing, too, that his bullets had little if any effect.

Billy Hyde grabbed at the blond's left hind appendage. The blond dropped Captain Erskine's body, turned and growled, then bent down and snapped and Billy's hand was gone.

The blond spun away from Billy Hyde and Billy just lay there in the wet grass, the mists half obscuring him, his scream no louder than any of the others. Blood dripped from the blond's mouth.

Harry Milford fired out his rifle into the blond. Harry was the team demolitions man and, at least among the Americans, the worst shot in the outfit. But that still meant an expert rating with the Garand and the .45, too, or he never could have become a Ranger. At maybe ten feet, not even Harry could have missed the hulking blond.

The blond staggered, fell. Harry turned his M1 around, held it by the barrel with both hands, and swung the heavy wooden buttstock down to crush the blond's head and finish the job.

The blond caught the rifle in midswing, ripping it away from Harry.

Harry stepped back and his face was white as death.

The blond was standing again, hunched over but no more so than any of the rest of them, as if the eight .30-06 ball rounds Harry'd fired into the blond were nothing.

Harry tried to draw his pistol.

The blond swiped at Harry's face and ripped away Harry's left cheek and tore out Harry's left eyeball.

Harry's teeth sprayed out of his mouth. Harry stumbled, started to fall.

The blond reached out and grabbed Harry under the sternum on both sides of the rib cage, palms outward, then merely seemed to flex its massive upper body. It was as if there was no effort to it at all.

And then Harry was all split open and the blond's mouth disappeared for an instant inside Harry's chest. Harry screamed, but the scream choked off very quickly. The blond's head snapped back.

Harry's heart was in the blond's teeth, Harry's heart still pumping blood for several seconds and the blood oozing out as drool from the corner of the blond's mouth.

Mac shouted, "I'm out of ammunition for this thing!"

Evan Hardy turned and looked at him, but he could still see Harry Milford's heart dripping blood from the blond's mouth. Evan Hardy looked back at the field of battle.

And he started to laugh.

This wasn't real; it was a nightmare. "You're in my nightmare, Mac! Ha!"

The blond threw Harry Milford's body to the ground, discarding it like a child tossing away a broken doll.

The blond howled.

The other creatures were through fighting. They feasted on the dead now, hulking over them, tearing flesh from severed arms and legs as the mists rolled in great waves over the ground.

There was an isolated human scream.

The blond howled again and the others came to him, some waiting hunched forward, only standing on their hind legs, others on all fours chewing on human limbs.

One of the creatures came beside the blond and sat on its haunches at the blond's feet, a human head clasped easily in its jaws, as calmly as a family pet might patiently hold a fetched ball waiting for the approval of its master.

And the blond broke into a run, on all fours, toward Evan Hardy and Hugh MacTavish.

"One hell of a nightmare." Hardy laughed.

"My arse," Mac rasped, and Hardy felt himself being hauled to his feet.

He remembered suddenly realizing he was freezing cold from the previous dousing in the water, and Mac was carrying him into the lake again.

As he closed his eyes, he heard the thumping of feet and the howls began again . . .

They were in shallow water, reeds growing up around them. Evan Hardy still held the dead Canadian's pistol and he shivered uncontrollably.

This wasn't a dream.

Growling, jaws snapping.

Mac's left arm was around him.

As the growling came closer, Mac's hand covered Hardy's mouth and Hardy wanted to tell Mac that it was okay because he knew better than to cry out. And the blackness of unconsciousness came again. And, this was a dream now. He saw the blond, fangs dripping blood and drool, bending over him, to tear out his throat; and, as he looked into the blond's ice-blue eyes, the thing's face began to transform and there was the face of the SS officer with the blond hair.

Hardy opened his eyes, Mac's hand over his mouth. Mac was pulling him under the water.

Chapter One:

The Nightmare Resumes

She tossed her head back involuntarily as the water crashed around her, and smiled at herself for letting it startle her. Richard would have told her, "Your locks will freeze, getting a car wash in weather like this." But Richard wasn't here. Richard was sexy and attentive and loving and made her feel good and each time he was away she missed him that much more than the last time. But the car — a Mercedes — had been a present from her father when she was awarded her Ph.D., and she didn't want Evan Hardy seeing it, let alone riding in it, covered with salt stains and mud.

The yellow light came on, and she knew that was the wax starting. Richard always told her that wax jobs in automatic car washes were just a waste of money, but she thought that any wax job was better than none and made the gun-metal gray look shinier.

Gun-metal gray was not exactly her color preference, either, but you didn't tell your father, "Daddy, it was sweet of you to give me this expensive car, but could you exchange it for something like white or yellow, maybe?" She'd grown up with girls who would have done just that, but maybe they didn't feel about their fathers the way she felt about her father.

The green light came on and she put the transmission into drive, starting forward out of the tracks. If she'd bought the car herself, which would have been impossible because she could never have afforded it on a first-year assistant professor's salary, she would have somehow gotten a manual transmission. But, as it turned out, the automatic transmission was all to the good, because Richard was terrible with a stick.

Traffic. Everywhere. Even worse than it had been all week with the homecoming crowd, at first dribbling in, now filling the streets and restaurants around Highcliffe in a torrent. "Shit," she said under her breath, tightening her hands on the Mercedes's steering wheel and diving in.

Snow was starting to fall again, and that would only make the traffic worse.

It was only a short distance to the station, something that under normal circumstances would have taken her under three minutes, but during Highcliffe's most severe annual attack of football fever it was five minutes before she was able to turn onto Railroad Avenue and just see the old terminal in the distance.

Aside from some of the Fine Arts Building, the Arthur Highcliffe History Library, and the chapel, all on campus, Highcliffe Station was not only one of the town's oldest structures but also the most imposing. It was from that brief period in American architecture when form and function seemed at once at loggerheads and yet in harmony, when magnificence still didn't cost too much.

Two vans in front of her blocked both lanes and she missed a green light and had to sit, waiting. She turned on the radio. ". . . taking caller number nine. If you can do any Highcliffe cheer, you win a free tailgate party pack for tomorrow's homecoming game against Sutton. And, speaking of Sutton, we don't want any more Sutton sickos calling us up with Sutton cheers, huh. So, give us a call at —"

Dannie Hardy turned off the radio. She was sick to death of the homecoming game.

The light was already green, but the intersection was jammed with an open convertible full of Sutton fans and a limousine with Highcliffe flags plastered all over it, and neither would give way to the other.

She looked in her mirrors and confirmed that there weren't any cops around, then made a quick right into the exit driveway for the McDonald's. She got an angry horn from an Audi (probably one of those schmucks from Sutton, she

48

laughed) and made it past the drivethru and to the exit leading onto Roosevelt Avenue. She made a fast left and kept driving, the traffic lighter here. As she passed the heroically posed statue in the small square at the center of the intersection, she shot the granite figure a wave under her breath, saying, "Thanks, Teddy!"

At the intersection with University Way, she made a left, cutting across to the far right-hand side of the street to a chorus of angry horns but making a sharp right into the service drive for Highcliffe Station. It was illegal to enter unless making a pickup or delivery, but she hoped she wouldn't get caught. Highcliffe didn't have that many policemen and they would already be stretched thin with the homecoming crowds.

The tricky part lay ahead, driving the wrong way for the distance of a half block or so to get into the terminal parking lot. It was one wide, single lane, and if an actual service vehicle came her way, she'd have to back up into the service lot again, no room to turn around.

Nothing in view, she gunned the Mercedes, wishing again for a manual transmission. The snow was heavier now and her wiper blades weren't doing the best job in the world of keeping up with it.

She started braking about two-thirds of the way along the drive, her heart sinking. The station's solitary parking lot was entirely filled as best she could tell, and even though there were spaces along the curb fronting the station in the yellow zone, there was a uniformed police officer writing out tickets.

"Damn!"

She hooked toward the yellow zone curb, slowing, stopping parallel to a slot amply large enough to accommodate the Mercedes. The ball of her index finger depressed the button powering down the front passenger window. The police officer started toward her.

It was Bill Walenski, a student in one of the two European Civilization classes she taught nights. He was tall, broadshouldered, looked like he should have been resting up for tomorrow's football game, but, from a biographical form she'd had each student fill out, she seemed to remember he'd run track instead. The way his pretty dark eyes sparkled, he always looked like he was happy, which right now was very irritating.

"Dr. Hardy! Hi!"

"Hi, Bill. Look, Bill, my father's coming in on the train . . ." She glanced at the watch on her wrist. It barely kept time anymore; but she anticipated that Richard would take care of that problem with the Christmas present he'd been hinting about getting for her every time they passed Filsom's Jewelry out at Lake Point Mall. She'd just wound it though, so she thought it was close to accurate. "He'll be here in three minutes. Can I park, please?"

Bill Walenski rested his right hand on his holstered gun, looked at her, then up and down the street. "I can't let ya park, Dr. Hardy."

Her heart sank. "I, ahh . . . I understand, Bill. It's your job and everything—"

"Look. You can't park, but you can leave the motor running. I'll keep an eye on it for you. That okay?"

"Yeah . . . yeah, that's just terrific, Bill."

"You got it."

She twisted around in the seat, her coat falling off her shoulders as she started reversing into the spot. And Dannie Hardy made a mental note to add ten points to Bill Walenski's next test score . . .

The click of her bootheels sounded impossibly loud to her as she ran across the stone floor of the terminal building, jockeying her purse as she got her arms into her coat, trying to capture the triangle of silk print that was draped over the coat as it started to slip away.

The platform area was just ahead and she stopped, glancing up at the incongruous-looking electronic arrivals/departures display on the television screens. Her father's train was bang on time and just in.

She stopped, caught her breath.

More slowly now, she walked toward the platforms, no in-

50

tention of passing under the security arch because she resented the whole idea of innocent, normal people having to be snooped on because a handful of lunatics liked hijacking public conveyances or, worse yet, blowing them up.

She stopped again and stood beside a marble wall. It seemed to radiate cold and she drew herself more deeply into her coat.

There was no sign of her father coming along the platform yet so Dannie opened her purse, took out her compact, and checked her hair and lipstick. Her hair was a little windblown, but her father had never liked women looking overly fragile. She caught a stray curl and put it off her forehead, then looked along the platform again before searching for her lipstick.

As she finished with her lips and looked over the mirror along the platform, she saw him. And, she almost dropped her lipstick.

If Evan Hardy wasn't the handsomest man in the world, she would be enormously surprised. He was almost seventy, but despite his age and the quadruple bypass surgery he'd had two months ago—it had scared the shit out of her—he was gorgeous. Fashionably long hair but pure white, wavy to the point of almost being curly. His blue eyes—he'd never needed glasses for anything but reading—sparkled, visible even at a distance. His face was lean, but not skinny, not bony, just perfect. And he carried himself better than any man she knew even half his age.

His left hand was thrust inside his overcoat pocket, out of sight as it always was in public. But, the effect was stylish in a Douglas Fairbanks, Jr.-ish sort of way. She suddenly pictured her father dashing about with a gleaming sword in his hand, a rakish grin on his face as he vaulted railings and barricades, mercilessly taunting his heavily armed enemies while he soared from a swinging chandelier, just out of their murderous reach. Cutaway shot to the beautiful girl, hands clasped together prayerlike against her breast, her eyes tearglistening, her heart his.

Dannie Hardy bit at her lower lip and almost giggled.

As her father noticed her and waved, the corners of his

51

long, wide mouth curled upward in a wry smile, which always made his mustache look crooked.

She'd heard or read something about Cary Grant once, that the actor with the legendary good looks had once employed a man to tug his tie out of skew a bit before he'd make a public appearance, just so he wouldn't look perfect. The mustache had the same effect for Evan Hardy, but only when he smiled. Otherwise, he looked hopelessly perfect.

"Daddy!"

Her fashionable but useless silk scarf started slipping again and she caught it, then in the next instant Evan Hardy was there, taking her into his arm. "Baby, how are you? You look fantastic. Wow!"

She kissed him, just let him hold her, realized she was listening for the rhythm of his breathing. He hugged her so hard that her own breathing was becoming problematical and she pushed gently against his solid chest with both open palms. "God, it's great to see you! How was the trip for you. I mean—" There, she'd started to ask about his health.

He looked down at her and smiled. "You're a lot more worried about my heart than the doctor is, young lady. And I'm fine. Haven't felt this good since I was thirty, for God's sake. Everything's healed, even the damn gouges they put into my legs. I walk a lot, I run a little, I swim every chance I get, watch what I eat for cholesterol. I dropped fifteen pounds." And he tugged at his jacket front to show her. "I don't even drink as much as I used to and the doctor said I didn't have to worry about that. And I don't even miss smoking—not much anyway," he concluded, laughing. "So. Satisfied?"

"Aww, Daddy!" And she threw her arms around his neck and just held him tightly . . .

Harp music.

The Highcliffe House was the one place in Highcliffe where the homecoming game crowd generally never came. High prices, long, leisurely meals, the flower-bedecked atmosphere of a manicured garden perpetually in spring—and

52

the music. A woman in floor-length black evening dress playing classical music on the harp and talk of runningbacks and pass interceptions and who was going to pound who into the stadium turf didn't seem to mix.

"So . . ." her father began. "How's Richard?"

"Ohh, he's great. But he won't be back until after the game tomorrow. There's some paranoid schizophrenic at Aigner Hospital down in the city who caught his eye, fits in with the new book Richard's working on about paranoid delusion."

"Sounds fascinating; I can hardly wait for the movie."

She looked away, beyond the gently dancing water spouts, through one of the white painted cross-hatched trellises where red and yellow roses climbed. Her father didn't exactly like Richard.

"His last book did very well, I understand," Evan Hardy said, she guessed by way of small apology. If anyone would know, he would, because he'd been one of the top men in New York publishing before his retirement, and was still occasionally involved with his old house. "Pop psych isn't easy to make palatable, but Richard seems to do that very nicely. I even read it." He smiled.

"Hmm." She nodded, halfway through a sip of wine. As she touched her napkin to her lips, she tried to interpret her father's meaning. She decided she should add, "Really, Richard's one of the top clinical psychologists in the whole country, Daddy. But he feels that 'pop psych,' like you call it, is the best way to educate the average man and woman about psychology. It's such a mystery to most people. He's really dedicated."

"I know he is, baby."

"But with Richard away, you've got me all to yourself," she said brightly, trying to get off the subject of Richard completely now.

"I love you very much," he told her, then started to resume the attack on his crab salad. But instead, he set down his fork. He looked across the table at her. "All I want for you is the best; and if Richard loves you and you love him, that's good enough for me." And Evan Hardy reached his good hand out to her, squeezing *her* hand, then drawing back,

53

picking up his fork again.

She'd seen his left hand for the briefest instant as the waiter seated them at their table for two by the fountain near the exact center of Highcliffe House's main dining room, the best spot. Evan Hardy's hand looked unnaturally pale, and half closed as it always was except when he'd sit with a rubber ball or a grip exerciser and work it, which he rarely did while anyone else was around. But the hand never worked. As a little girl, she'd always hoped that someday it would return to normal. After years of hoping, she learned he only exercised it to keep the blood flowing properly, that there wasn't any hope. Now the hand was below sight level but not in his pocket because the left side of his suit wasn't pulled down. All he'd ever told her about his hand and his half-lifeless left arm was that he'd injured it in the war when he and Mac had been the only survivors in the battle with an SS unit in the spring of 1945.

He never talked about the war to any great degree, except that he talked about Mac a lot, in recent years with advancing age describing Mac as though, somehow Peter Pan-like, Mac had never aged, was always a kid and always would be.

She'd never met Mac, and her father and Mac had lost touch years ago. She wondered if the man was still even alive? World War Two, although sometimes it had to seem like yesterday to the men who fought it, was more or less a half century removed for most people. As an historian, not just as a daughter, she'd often wanted to ask her father about the war in greater detail but never had.

"So, any luck trying to hunt down your pal Mac like you said you were going to do?"

"No."

"Haven't tried yet or just no luck, Daddy?"

"A little of both," he said, "This crab's excellent. Like a little bit?" He offered a forkful to her. Richard would have curled up and died. But she took her father's fork and tasted the crab. What Richard didn't know wouldn't hurt him. "See?"

"It is good!"

"What's on for tonight, Dannie?"

"I thought we'd spend the evening at home, relax, get a good night's sleep—"

Evan Hardy smiled at her. "Going to check my blood pressure and give me some warm milk before we settle in, are you?"

"No! I just thought we could have a few drinks, take it easy, you know. I'm not worried about your heart, all right?"

"Right. And Highcliffe and Sutton don't really care who wins the homecoming game tomorrow, because it's all just for fun." He cocked an eyebrow at her and lowered his voice. "I am not planning on dying anytime in the near future, young woman. When I am, you'll be the first to know Okay? I'm fine."

"All right."

"Besides, if I died right now, and my head just toppled over into my salad, just think of all the people who'd be upset with me for doing something so socially objectionable in here."

She looked at her father and at some of the other people around them—women dripping furs and diamonds, men with Gucci loafers, a Rolex or Patek-Philippe on every wrist. And then, Dannie Hardy started to laugh . . .

Evan Hardy poured himself a generous double Cutty Sark and thought sincerely about water for at least a second and a half as he turned the tap quickly on, then off again. Sometimes in a bar or restaurant or at the club, he'd order it as whiskey and then quickly correct himself. All the Brits he'd hung out with for all those interminable weeks in England while the rains kept coming and the rumors were born and died until, at last, D-Day, they had profoundly influenced his drinking habits. Even the thought of ice in Scotch whiskey made him shiver.

He found himself thinking about Mac, again; however, the only spiritous beverages he'd ever shared with Hugh Mac-Tavish were the wine they'd found hidden under the false floor in that barn when they'd been on the run from the SS and bad wartime champagne at his—Hardy's—wedding. Mac had been best man. For some reason, that homemade red wine and the watery champagne were the best-tasting drinks he'd ever consumed.

He hadn't been able to get Mac out of his mind for more than a day or so since the nightmares had started returning just before his bypass surgery. Dannie had asked when they'd dined if, as he'd said he planned to, he was going to track down Mac. And he knew why he kept putting it off. What if Mac were dead, and he—Evan Hardy—were the only one left?

"Daddy?" His daughter's voice interrupted his thoughts.

He looked around and saw her, and for a moment it was as if the years had never passed and it was that cold-water flat in suburban London all over again and he was looking at his wife instead of his daughter. Dannie stood beside the couch, pretty in a loose-fitting blouse that looked like a high-fashion white T-shirt with long sleeves, the neck so large that it hung off her left shoulder. A khaki skirt that looked full enough to be a tent, started somewhere below the voluminous T-shirt thing, ending just at the tops of her bare feet. Her mother would never have been barefoot. Their little apartment was just too cold for that.

In Dannie's hands, pressed against her abdomen, was her photo album, the one with all the pictures of her mother that he hadn't kept for himself and all the photos of him during the war, except for the few special ones that he'd always kept in his office, now kept at home. There were the other photos, of course, and memorabilia: his old school yearbooks, his own parents' marriage license, a lock of Dannie's hair, his medals, the .45 he'd liberated when he was honorably medically discharged. Things like that.

Even as a tiny girl, Dannie had always had her mother's grace; and as she sat down, he was reminded of her mother again, their slightest body movements and facial expressions uncannily identical, and all the more strange since Dannie and her mother had never met. His wife had died in the instant his daughter was born. He'd sometimes wondered if there was, miraculously, something like a transference of their spirits. There was an all-but-indefinable specialness about them, the pure ease of real comfort with oneself.

56

Evan Hardy resigned himself to the album again. For his daughter, it was learning and relearning. For him, it was only remembering . . .

"Now, who's that again? Captain Erskine?"

"Right," Hardy told her. "I hate to say this, because I'll start you off on this heart attack routine again, but I've got some boxes of pictures and some other stuff stored in the attic at the summer place. You ever go through all that after I'm gone—"

"Don't talk like that," Danny chastised, running her fingers of her left hand back through her past-shoulder-length auburn hair. She looked like her mother when she touched her hair that way, but she *always* reminded him of her.

"I'm not talking 'like that,' Dannie. I'm just saying, you can always tell Captain Erskine by that big knife of his. And he's chunky, sort of."

"Chunky and a big knife, right. Now, that's not Mac."

"No," Hardy told her patiently. "That's Lieutenant Forrestal. He died very bravely." Even if Forrestal was a prick, Hardy reflected.

"So, then he was a lieutenant just like you were?"

"Yeah. I was a first lieutenant. He was a lieutenant in the British Army. So that was like a first lieutenant."

"Which one's better?"

Hardy felt himself starting to laugh. "They're the same, baby." She turned the page of the album and, if seeing his dead friends—and Forrestal too—,had torn at his heart, this nearly made his heart stop. "Hearts."

"What?" She leaned forward, staring at him unbelievably earnestly.

"No . . . nothing." He stared at the photograph of Danielle. Tall for a woman, in those days at least, she stood about five foot seven. Her hair looked darker than Dannie's, but it was a black and white photograph, and in reality they both had auburn hair, both had green eyes, high cheekbones, full mouths.

"Mom was pretty."

"Your mother looked just like you, *was* just like you. Your voices even sound alike. I think that's why I kept sending you to Berlitz, to learn French, and then always took you on vacation to places where you could practice. Especially when you were older; because just hearing you brought her back to me."

She hugged her arms around his right arm and kissed him softly on the cheek, then rested her head against his shoulder.

Hardy started to tell her about her mother for the ten thousandth or ten millionth time, maybe just a little because of the Scotch; but, he knew she liked him to tell the story. She.

Evan Hardy exhaled. "When we got out of there, the Germans were right behind us. We hid everyplace we could find. But, after Mac and I finally reached our lines and debriefed and everything, they sent Mac for R&R in Paris."

"Rest and recuperation?"

"Good girl. And they sent me to England because of this damn arm. And that's where I met your mother. God, was she beautiful—just like you, baby. And about the same age you are now. She was a nurse. She got out of France when the damn Vichy decided kissing Nazi ass was the best move, and she volunteered for helping with the men who were in the English hospitals. In those days, they were mostly Brits, the really serious cases coming in from North Africa and the Aegean and God knows where.

"She drew me for a patient," Hardy concluded.

"I was telling Richard about you and Mom," Dannie almost whispered. "He, ahh—"

"What, baby?"

"He, ahh . . . Richard said it's quite normal for a man to think he's in love with his nurse."

Hardy looked at his daughter. "And what'd you tell Richard?"

Dannie smiled a little. "I told him you two were really in love."

Hardy hugged Dannie tight to him, then, wanting to say to her, "Your Richard's an anal retentive yuppie son of a bitch," but not saying it, he contented himself with telling

58

her, "Thanks, baby." She flipped the page again. He laughed, staring at the photograph and pronouncing himself "the world's skinniest grad student."

"The world's cutest," Dannie said, smiling.

Hardy shook his head, looking back at the photograph. Just back from England with a new wife and no job and a crippled arm, he had every reason to be skinny, working full-time on his master's, working full-time at Ledermann's, Danielle working full-time as well and still trying to polish her English. But they were happy days.

"Why are you smiling?" Dannie asked him, touching the tip of a pink manicured fingernail to his face in the photo.

"Well, you're always supposed to smile in a photograph, right? And anyway, it was a chance to stand still for a minute."

Dannie laughed.

On the page opposite, he was sitting at his paperwork-mounded desk at Ledermann's. A candid photo, he wasn't smiling, just working. But at Ledermann's he learned the publishing business, or at least he'd thought he had. There was, it turned out, a big difference between a small firm which produced on average six scholarly works for limited distribution each year and a New York mass market publisher.

Publishing, for junior editors at least, was always a game of musical chairs, and he was on his third New York publishing house by the time Danielle became pregnant. He stayed with them longer than he really wanted to because of the insurance coverage, the only way to pay for the baby without going to the poorhouse. And then, after the death of his wife and the birth of his daughter, he'd been afraid to seek a different job. How would he support his infant daughter if he couldn't find one?

So he stayed with that house for eight years, and when he left he got a new title: he was officially an editor.

By the time Dannie was nine, he moved again, this time higher up the ladder. When she was eleven, they bought the summer place. By the time she was fifteen, he was a corporate vice president and ran two of his own lines.

He'd gauged his life by her life. When the heart trouble had begun to seriously surface—he put off the shortness of breath and the occasional discomfort for more than a year—he was deathly afraid for the third time in his life.

The first time, he'd feared that those things would kill him and kill Mac the way they'd killed everyone else in the outfit. The next time he experienced that kind of fear was when his wife died. This last time, he became terrified that he'd join his wife in death before Dannie was finished with her Ph.D., before she was married, before she gave him a grandchild.

But now, since the surgery, it seemed that he gauged his life not by his daughter's age and his accomplishments but by what happened before the bypass surgery and what happened after it.

Survival bred a self-centeredness he didn't quite like and tried to resist.

"What are you thinking about?"

He looked away from the photograph of him standing beside the first author he'd actually gotten onto the lists, an old man with a marvelous gift for wordsmithing and body odor so strong that whenever they met, Hardy insisted it be out-of-doors. "I was pondering the meaning of life," he told her, then let go of her shoulders and picked up his glass of whiskey.

"And at what conclusion did you arrive?"

" 'A wet bird never flies at night . . .' " Hardy announced.

"Gee whiz, can I write that down?"

Hardy shrugged his good shoulder and sipped at his drink. "I bet you'd rather write that down later and hear what I've got to say."

"What?" Dannie edged forward, just looking at him.

"I was going to save it and tell you when Richard came back, but I think you shouldn't have to wait."

"What, Daddy?" She looked half worried, half eager.

"Your doctoral dissertation's going to be published by Rutledge and Sons, if you want them to."

"My . . . but—"

"I didn't use any of my connections. In fact, when I got it submitted, I even had it retyped so nobody'd make the con-

60

nection between us because of the same last name. They don't typically pay the best advances, but their royalty schedule isn't bad and they do pretty well with big non-fiction titles. I can recommend a really good agent, if you're interested."

"Interested?" And she threw her arms around his neck and shrieked like a teenager . . .

Sutton College's number forty-two, Phil Smith, faded back for the pass as Highcliffe's defensive team split. Just as Smith was about to go down, he made the throw.

She couldn't believe her eyes. "Intercept the damn ball, somebody!" Dannie Hardy shouted.

But number fifteen for Sutton, Tom White, the intended receiver, had the football, jumping for the midair catch, twisting in midair like basketball players sometimes could, then running.

Highcliffe's Reggie Greenwood dove for him. "He can't even remember what year the War of 1812 started. Gee!" Greenwood missed, Sutton's Tom White out of danger now, running, the Sutton fans on the opposite side of the stadium screaming their lungs out.

Touchdown, just as the clock ran out for the second quarter, the Sutton band striking up Sutton's fight song.

She looked at her father. "Well?"

"What can I say? Sutton's got some good players."

The score was tied and Sutton was on a roll. "Dammit."

"You're such a big football fan now?"

She tried gesturing with her mittened hands. "Well . . . I have some of those guys in class, and—"

"Right. But what do you care more about, right now I mean? That they pass the ball or they pass history?"

She felt her cheeks flush, and she made her right hand into a fist and mockingly beat her breast with it. "Mea culpa, mea culpa, mea magna culpa."

"I, kiddo, am going to answer nature's call. Want me to buy you another hot dog?"

He had to say "another." "No, thanks, Daddy." And he gave

61

her a smile and started out of the bleachers.

She stood up, catching up the blanket wrapped around her so it wouldn't drag on the concrete. Her hind end was stiff and cold and she rearranged the stadium cushion she'd sat on, trying to fluff up the foam rubber.

The grandstands on both sides were filled, the biggest turnout she'd ever seen for a college game considering stadium size. The last homecoming game she'd attended, a year ago, had huge attendance as well, but not like this. She opened her coat for an instant to gather her skirt around her; it was past mid-calf length and well below the tops of her boots. Lined and of heavy wool tweed, with the heavy stockings she wore and the coat reaching almost to her ankles, she was still cold. She thought again about the previous game. She sat down, tucking the blanket around her. Her father had been having chest pains before and after the game, although he never mentioned it.

And the thought of his death had terrified her.

Although it sounded trite even to think about, Evan Hardy had been both father and mother to her. And, in a very chaste and properly daughterly way, she had been both daughter and wife to him. He told her his troubles, asked her advice. By the time she was eleven, she was in charge of the grocery shopping. By the time she was thirteen, she was paying the household bills; he'd put her name on one of the checking accounts, never bothering to tell the bank she wasn't legally old enough to sign her name.

She'd cooked for him, cleaned for him, cried with him when they would visit her mother's grave.

She loved him . . .

"Dammit."

A pipe had burst from the cold, an angry-looking middle-aged man was mumbling, walking away from the closed men's-room door.

Hardy stopped and considered the situation. He'd been at soccer games in Europe where fans pissed through a rolled-up newspaper onto the ground beneath the bleachers, but there were three problems with that: he didn't have a newspaper, there was no gap between the seats and steps (all cement), and his daughter would be seated right beside him. Hardy pulled his fedora lower over his eyes and started round to the Sutton side of the stadium, hoping the men's room in enemy territory was in running order. He thought of the line about "any port in a storm." Who knows, he almost mused aloud, but this was why the Highcliffe boys were having a hard time of it on the field, because they couldn't go. The image of an entire team of football players trying to hold their knees together was more than a little amusing.

The crowd was building up in the ground-floor concession area, mostly men who'd either gotten caught in conversation or had decided late that they were hungry. He could smell the popcorn, but the butter on it had too much cholesterol and there would be too much salt anyway. Being old sucked, Evan Hardy decided.

He turned the corner, a solitary yellow line midway between the north and south ends of the stadium indicating that the border was about to be crossed.

He'd jumped into enemy territory before.

And, suddenly, he thought about D-Day, which was better than thinking about the other thing, better by far. Off into the slipstream of night, hooked up to a static line with your buddies floating anonymously through the air around you. And you knew that some of them wouldn't make it, that a chute wouldn't open in time or a neck would be broken on impact. Or worse, what if the enemy were waiting below and opened fire while you were helpless, unable to defend yourself?

For him, that had always been the worst part: not his own mortality, but the potential for loss among his men. Captain Erskine, when once Hardy had shared this with the man over a drink, had said, "That's what makes you a good officer, Evan." Evan Hardy had never been quite sure about that. If he'd been that good, couldn't there have been some way of getting his men out of the castle grounds that night, couldn't he and Mac have saved some of the others when dawn came and the beasts attacked? Saved some of the others instead of just saving themselves?

Hardy had discussed his feelings, in sufficiently general terms of course, with one of his authors, a renowned psychiatrist. He'd admitted to the men that sometimes he felt guilty for still living while all his friends but one had died. No real answer had been forthcoming, so Hardy had continued on as he always had, trying to find his own answer and never finding it.

He turned the next corner, deep inside enemy territory now, deep in thought as well. The colors of his clothes were neutral enough not to indicate that he was a Highcliffe man, and it had been too cold to wear a damned school tie.

Hardy kept moving.

There seemed to be an equal number of fans in the concession area here, too. Odd, the Sutton people seemed as human as he was, interested in consuming hot dogs and overcooked hamburgers and bad coffee or hot chocolate from a mix.

As he snaked his way through the crowd near one of the concession stands, he saw the men's room.

There was no out-of-order sign on it.

Hardy quickened his pace, the desire to urinate even greater now than it had been.

He noticed the ladies' bathroom (there was a line stretching from the entrance door) and he was grateful for his more convenient male plumbing.

Hardy walked into the men's room, got in line behind a man at the nearest urinal, and waited. The man, black, almost Hardy's age, stepped aside, murmured something about cold weather. Hardy nodded, went up, unzipped, and did what he had to do. He took the exit door out and was into the concession stand crowds again.

Hardy looked to his right. There was another tunnel, on the near side of the stadium, which would get him back to his seat faster and allow him to avoid concession stand crowds on both the Sutton and Highcliffe sides.

He turned right. There were very few people here as he walked on, and after only a moment it was deserted enough that he could hear his heels scuffing on the cold cement floor.

This way went past the visiting team locker room area, and he could hear some laughter up ahead, saw a man in a Sutton team jacket heading down into the little tunnel. They had every right to be happy, having played brilliantly so far.

He was even with the locker room tunnel now, a solitary Highcliffe police officer stationed there. Hardy turned toward the policeman, trying to think of some pleasntry.

But Hardy looked past the policeman and only stared, mouth half open.

Hardy took a step back. "No." Chills ran along his spine and his stomach went queasy and he moved still farther away from the tunnel entrance.

The policeman took a step forward, asking, "Are you all right, sir?"

Hardy was aware of the policeman's question, but he couldn't make his mouth work to form a reply.

Halfway down the length of the tunnel beyond where the policeman was, two men stood, animatedly engaged in conversation. One of the men was short and stocky, a stocking cap on his head in the Sutton school colors of black and white.

It was the other man, though—

"Sir?" The policeman was talking again.

Hardy shook his head, stammered, "I'm . . . ahh . . . I just remembered something." He gave the policeman a nod and started walking back the way he'd come.

The man standing in conversation with the stocking-capped fellow was tall, well built, looking somewhere in his middle or late thirties.

The man had a shock of blond hair, very close-cropped at the sides but full on top.

As Evan Hardy walked—so quickly his breathing was becoming labored—he told himself, "It can't be."

Chapter Two:

The Man Who Couldn't Be

He'd seemed out of breath. Dannie told herself it was because he'd had to walk back quickly to avoid missing the start of the third quarter.

He'd looked pale. She didn't believe his offhand remark about worrying about them getting the Mercedes out of the parking lot in one piece with the huge crowds.

When Sutton trounced Highcliffe, all he'd said under his breath was, "Dammit," and not his usual string of immediately afterward recanted epithets.

And he drank from his glass of Scotch very quickly once they were seated at Larrigan's.

Evan Hardy had hardly spoken a word since rejoining her after the half.

On the drive over, he'd been just as silent. They'd parked two blocks away, almost fought their way to Larrigan's door, and then still had to wait ten minutes despite their table reservation.

The waitress was a Political Science major named Debbie, cute-looking in her faded denim miniskirt. But the instant Debbie had said, "Hi, Dr. Hardy. What can I get you guys?" her father had said, "My daughter'll have a Michelob. I'll have a double Cutty, no water, no ice. We'll order food later."

Dannie hadn't even wanted a beer, more interested in something warmer.

She said nothing. The drinks arrived after a few silent minutes and her father said, "Come back later, will you?"

By the time he was half-finished with his drink, Dannie finally spoke. "What's going on?"

"I don't understand."

"That's my line, Daddy. You've been silent as the grave—"

He laughed when she said that.

"What's wrong, Daddy?"

"Nothing's wrong, Dannie. I was cold, that's all." And he forced a smile as he sipped more slowly this time at his Scotch.

"You've been acting strangely since you came back after the half. What—"

He cut her off. "Worried about a heart attack or something. Well, forget it. I'm fine, see? Now leave it alone."

She leaned back in her chair, her hands drawing back into her lap.

There was a lot of noise here, the jukebox playing sixties oldies just at the barely audible and most irritable level. Every table was filled with postgame quarterbacks, each man trying to talk over the other while the women with them sat with bored-looking faces or chattered and giggled as they sipped their drinks. The overall effect was something akin to what an asylum must sound like, she thought. Larrigan's was Highcliffe's place, but there was even a substantial Sutton contingent here. If the average age of the crowd had been ten or fifteen years younger, there would have been all the makings for a brawl or even a riot.

On rare occasions before, she'd experienced moods like this in her father. The cause was always some tremendous worry or another. And she knew better than to press for the source. Instead, she sipped at her unwanted beer . . .

The meal came and went, Larrigan's trademark ribs which he'd always enjoyed. Somehow, they didn't taste quite the same with the dieter's sauce instead of the Special Secret Sauce, which wouldn't have been good for him.

And Evan Hardy promised himself two things the next time he took Dannie to Larrigan's: the hell with his diet, he'd take the good sauce, and he'd try to be better company for his daughter the next time, too.

Either the whiskey or reason—Hardy wasn't quite sure which—relaxed him. The whiskey was good and, reviewing the facts, he'd convinced himself that the blond-haired man standing in the tunnel leading to the Sutton locker room and the commanding officer of the SS unit almost five decades ago could not possibly be the same man. Maybe a grandson. That was possible, unless senility was creeping up on him totally. At that chilling prospect, his earlier worries were replaced.

"I'm sorry I've been a grouch."

"Feeling better, are we?" Dannie smiled back overly sweetly.

Hardy pasted a smile on his face. "Fine. So kick me."

"I would, but I can't reach my feet that far under the table. You want to tell me what was bothering you, or should I just shut up?"

Hardy looked down at his drink. "I, ahh . . . just thought I saw somebody. I've been having a lot of restless nights, jittery nerves. That's all."

"Who did you think you'd seen?"

"Somebody that it would have been impossible to see." *There, idiot,* he railed at himself. *Now she'll probably think you thought you saw her mother!* He'd never told her mother, never told anyone. After he and Mac had finally reached friendly lines, they'd "sanitized" the story, mentioning nothing about the beasts which attacked them, never daring to even say to each other that somehow the SS unit and the beasts were one and the same.

The blond.

Hardy shivered.

"Daddy? What's wrong?"

"No. Nothing's wrong." He forced a smile again. "I'm fine. I've got the prettiest and smartest daughter in the world and I've got my health back. I'm fine."

Dannie was starting to say something in reply, but the waitress in the little miniskirt returned, interrupting. "Dr. Hardy? There's a phone call for you from Dr. Pearsall."

"Richard?"

Hardy supplied, "He would have guessed we'd come here after the game."

Dannie looked at him. "I wonder if he's all right?"

Evan Hardy smiled indulgently. For all her competence, her remark was incredibly dense. "Why not take the phone call and find out, baby?"

Dannie laughed, threw down her napkin, then followed the waitress toward the front of the restaurant, looking over her shoulder once and smiling back at him.

He wished for a cigarette. He'd lied when he implied he missed them only a little.

Hardy's eyes drifted across the room in the direction of the entrance toward which Dannie had disappeared in the wake of the pretty young waitress.

As he started to look down to his drink, he saw a shock of blond hair. His eyes riveted to it.

Tall, athletic-looking, mid-thirties or so on close inspection. The haircut was exactly the same as he remembered it from 1945.

It was the man from the tunnel outside the Sutton locker room, a jacket on his back that made him look like one of the coaching staff, perhaps, a pretty girl on his arm who clung to him as if she were afraid he'd float away.

Evan Hardy handled it better. It had to be the alcohol in his system.

He told himself he was watching the man casually, but he knew he was watching him intently.

As the blond and his girlfriend and a half-dozen other

men and women, all very athletic-looking, all of about the same ages, crossed the room, the hostess leading them through the maze of pushed-out chairs and pulled-together tables, the blond turned his head.

Evan Hardy reached for his whiskey, almost knocked over the glass.

The eyes.

Hardy realized he was standing up only as he did it, that he was walking across the room, hands balled into shaking fists.

"You!" All the background noise he'd become immune to was suddenly there and immediately gone.

The blond turned and looked right at him.

They were no more than six feet apart.

The eyes.

They were the same.

Blue.

Like the beast with the blond fur that had torn Harry Milford's heart from his chest and stood there staring as the heart still beat between its blood-drooling jaws.

"Billy Hyde. Harry Milford. Captain Erskine."

The blond started to turn away, laughing, the eyes as blue as polished crystal.

Hardy shouted. "You!"

The blond turned back and looked at him.

"Before, I was telling myself that it was impossible. But it is you. More than forty years. But it's you and you haven't changed. I wanted to lie to myself and tell myself all of it never happened, but I knew it had. And you're here, no different." At the corner of his right eye, Hardy was marginally aware of his daughter having reentered the room. His voice trembled. "I used to pray that someday I'd wake up and find out it was all a damn nightmare. But it isn't. It never was." And he looked at the other three men; they formed a wedge around the blond as if he were somehow their leader. "Are they like you? How do you do

70

it? Does changing into those fucking things keep you young? Huh?"

The blond stared, the eyes unflinching.

"Daddy!" Dannie's voice. Hardy ignored her.

The blond his voice as smooth as good Scotch whiskey, said, "Old man, I think you have mistaken me for someone else."

"What are you? Besides a fucking Nazi?"

One of the other three spoke, but Hardy never moved his eyes. "Look, Gramps, you're drunk."

"Kiss my ass," Hardy snapped. And he said to the blond, "What do they call you? I mean, when you're like that? What are you?"

The blond started to turn away.

Evan Hardy took a step, saw one of the three blockers move to get between him and the blond. And Hardy's old Ranger training clicked into place. If he'd had a usable left hand, he could have stopped him. Instead, reaching cross body, he could only slow him up, striking with the full force of his open palm against the man's chest, knocking him back.

The blond was trying to get away and Hardy threw himself against the man, the force of his body driving the blond slightly off balance, it felt, Hardy's right hand inverted, clamping over the blond's throat to crush the larynx.

And then there were hands on him. A woman screamed. He was dragged back, the blond shoving at him. Hardy tried to take a swing, but by now his right arm was numbing, somebody's powerful grip on his shoulder.

"Daddy!" It was Dannie, pushing through to him, shoving at one of the blond's three friends. "Leave him alone! Can't you see he's old!"

Evan Hardy sank back, crashing into a chair, hands and arms pressing him down.

Somebody was saying, "We should call the police."

But the blond shouted, "Too much to drink and a sore loser to boot. Let's get the hell out of here. All these Highcliffe losers are starting to smell!"

Men in Highcliffe maroon-and-gold sweaters started for the blond and his three male friends, waitresses trying to pull them back.

The blond was near the door and then, in a sea of heads, Hardy lost sight of him.

And Dannie was kneeling there, looking up into Hardy's face. "Daddy? Who was that man?"

Evan Hardy swallowed hard. She'd been right, his daughter had. He was old.

He looked at Dannie and felt his voice starting to tighten, to crack, tears welling up in his eyes, disgust in his heart. "He's somebody who never gets old, damn him."

Chapter Three:

Truth or Dare

Richard hadn't let himself in with his key to her apartment; although her father had to know she and Richard lived together half the time, she appreciated Richard's good intentions nonetheless.

Her father was drinking more coffee than Scotch and she figured that was a good sign.

As she fetched Richard his unasked-for but customary Rum Collins, Dannie Hardy looked across the kitchen counter into the living room where the two men in the world about whom she cared most deeply sat in total silence, eyeing each other. She had known from the first that her father didn't like Richard because Richard was a know-it-all (like charges repelling?) and that Richard disliked her father because he detested publishers as a breed; Evan Hardy was one of the best known and best liked in the business and, although retired, still wielded power when he wished.

And, she realized, there was also a factor of jealousy at work. It flattered her, in a very feminine yet morally uncomfortable way; and she continually tried to dispel it. Her feelings for Richard were in no way compromised by her love for her father, nor was her love for her father at all diminished by caring for Richard

Richard could never be as good-looking. At thirty-four (which her father had told her more than once was too old for her), Richard was shorter by a head than Evan Hardy, and balding, too. She didn't mind baldness in men, but

73

Richard's hair was neither there nor gone, just sort of in between. What remained of it was a washed-out-looking brown with some strands of gray.

On the other hand, it would be impossible to find a man as good-looking as her father.

Richard's doctoral dissertation had focused on obsessive-compulsive behavior in sports training, the eventual results his appointment to a special presidential committee on fitness and his becoming a devotee of physical training in his own life. He looked like a much compacted Superman, without the cute spit curl.

She had a drink for herself as well, the Cabernet Sauvignon she'd wanted earlier that evening when the game was over and she'd been mildly freezing.

After getting her father home and sitting him down with some coffee, she'd grabbed a hot shower, soaked under the steaming water for a long time, then dried her hair and dressed in blue jeans and a sweat shirt. She'd started to pour a glass of wine. But then Richard had arrived.

"Hell with it," Dannie Hardy said under her breath now, and took a sip as she walked across the room to join them.

"Why don't we talk about this?" Richard suggested as she sat beside him on the couch, but roughly equidistant between both men. Her father sat in the chair at a right angle to the end of the couch, his shoeless feet propped on the edge of the coffee table.

Her father looked at Richard, then at her, then shrugged his shoulders. "You've got a right to an explanation, baby. Maybe Richard's got a point."

Dannie Hardy wondered for a moment if she'd really shaken her head in disbelief or just thought she had; but she could not honestly believe her ears. What her father just said was as uncharacteristic of him as spitting on the carpet.

"That's a good idea," Richard said, smiling, nodding, slipping into his professional shrink's voice.

She cleared her throat. "Daddy had an encounter today with a man at Larrigan's and they almost got into—"

"I had a fight and I was too many sheets to the wind and too damned old to win. And too out of practice. Call a spade a spade, baby."

"Someone you knew, Evan?" Richard queried.

"A long time ago, I think. If this were a book or movie, my next line'd be, 'At least I thought I knew him.' But there's no doubt in my mind. And, that's what scares the hell out of me. Either I'm going nuts or something exists in this world which shouldn't by any reason exist at all."

Richard leaned forward beside her, almost over her, obviously intrigued. "Explain that last, if you would, Evan.

"All right. I don't know how much Dannie's ever told you about my wartime experiences, Richard."

"I know you were quite heroic, sir."

Her father laughed, but not happily. And he reached to the table, not for his cup of coffee but for his full glass of Scotch. He took a long swallow and stared into the glass as he began again to talk. "Not heroic, at least not that last time. I was wounded during a battle with a group of SS, a unit that shouldn't have been anywhere near where we found them. They were holding up in an old castle — just like the castles on the Rhine that you see in the coffee table books, beautiful, but it was on a lake. I became friends with a young Scot in the Royal Commandos, just a kid, really, too young to be legally enlisted I think. His name was Hugh MacTavish.

"The man I saw today," Evan Hardy whispered, then drank from the glass of Scotch, "was a man Hugh Mac-Tavish and I saw in 1945. Only he hadn't changed at all."

Richard didn't say a word.

Her father took another sip of his drink, then looked at her and smiled. "You two guys go out and bring back some good old-fashioned junk food, like a pizza or hamburgers."

"But your heart, sir," Richard said.

Dannie just listened.

"I'm really good about avoiding cholesterol and I don't think a pizza — and that's what I want — I don't think a

75

pizza would hurt. One of the ones with everything on it, except black olives and anchovies. You guys go get it and I'll do some thinking, and over the pizza I'll tell you the rest."

"I can go, Evan, and—"

"I don't need a baby-sitter, I'm not falling-down drunk and my heart's just fine. Probably as healthy as yours dismissing the age factor, Richard. Now you guys do that, have a drink or something while you wait. I'll be here. I've got a phone call I want to try."

"Mac?" Dannie asked him, smiling at him.

He smiled back. "Yes."

She stood up, saying, "Richard—let's try Dino's."

Richard just stood up, saying nothing. She leaned over her father and kissed him on the cheek . . .

Evan Hardy gave the overseas operator the country code and was connected with London directory assistance. He asked for "Hugh MacTavish. No, I don't know an address, Operator." He left his calling card out on the counter beside the kitchen wall phone.

When the operator came back, she gave him the sad news that there were more Hugh MacTavishes listed than she could possibly give out over the telephone, unless this were a police emergency. He started to complain, realized it wasn't the operator's fault, then remembered something.

As best man, Mac had signed the wedding license as witness. "Thank you, Operator." He hung up and went over to the coffee table where the photo album was still out from the previous evening of dusting off memories. He opened it to the very front. Dannie, God bless her sentimentality. Under plastic, the creases in it still evident, was a photocopy of her parents' marriage license. Either the print was smaller than he remembered or his eyes were finally going bad.

It was a two-bedroom apartment and Dannie used the second bedroom as an office, all sorts of books and related paraphernalia for her history research there. After two minutes or so of rummaging, he found what he was looking for: a magnifying glass.

Almost running now, Hardy returned to the living room, dropped to one knee beside the coffee table, and moved the magnifying glass back and forth trying to bring Mac's signature into focus.

And he had it.

There was a middle initial: "A."

He leaned back against the couch and sat on his haunches. Angus? No. And he remembered. It was Aaron.

Hardy stood up, went to the kitchen counter, realized he was still holding the magnifying glass and set it down, dialing for the overseas operator again. He gave the country code, got directory assistance. "Yes, Operator. London or suburban London. MacTavish, first name Hugh. The middle name is Aaron. It might be listed as Hugh A. MacTavish. I'll hold."

His hand shook as he picked up the pen and held it poised over the notepad.

Hardy had no way of knowing on any rational basis whether or not Mac were still alive, but knew in his heart that he must be. What if he didn't live in London but rather in Manchester or had returned to his native Scotland and lived near Edinburgh or someplace?

The operator read him a number, the only Hugh A. MacTavish in the listings. "Thank you, thank you very much."

Hardy looked at his watch. It had to be before dawn in England. He got the overseas operator back and gave his calling card number and placed the call anyway. Mac would understand.

The phone rang and rang and—"Mac?"

"Who's this?"

"Mac, it's me, Evan Hardy." The voice sounded a little young.

"Evan what?"

"Evan Hardy."

"Is this some bloody awful joke? You know what time it is?"

"Is this Hugh MacTavish?" Hardy heard the faltering sound in his own voice, the shakiness.

"Yes."

"Hugh Aaron MacTavish?"

"Me middle name's Anthony. Who is this?"

Hardy told himself he could have been wrong about remembering what the middle initial stood for. "Did you fight in World War II?"

"Sure. I was the youngest bloke in the bleedin' RAF, I was. I was five. Who—"

"I'm sorry to have bothered you, sir. I was looking for a friend. Good night." Hardy hung up the phone, leaned his head into his hands as the pen fell from his fingers. He wanted to cry . . .

Only Richard was eating the pizza, thoughtfully, of course, as he did everything.

She watched her father. She wanted to cry.

"It was the wrong MacTavish. Maybe he's dead. He stayed in the Army, I know, got into a lot of that hush-hush British stuff. The last time I tried getting hold of him, I couldn't find him. That was to tell him my wife died."

Richard sipped at his water. "That's a long time ago, Evan. A quarter of a century ago."

Her father nodded his head in silence.

He cleared his throat.

He spoke. "If we could find Mac, somehow get him a picture of this man. He has to be on the Sutton coaching staff."

"The man you saw at Larrigan's," Richard supplied.

"I saw him earlier at the game, during halftime."

"So who was the man at Larrigan's that you—"

Sometimes she wanted to hit Richard. "Daddy saw the

78

man twice, Richard! Once at the game and then again at Larrigan's." Dannie looked at her father. "And that's why you looked upset, and you were so quiet when you got back to your seat, Daddy."

Evan Hardy nodded, staring at his empty hands.

Richard sipped at his water again. Still holding the glass, he said, "As a scientist, I have to tell myself nothing, no matter how improbable, is completely out of the realm of the possible. I think we can all agree that for a man to be unchanged in more or less fifty years is extremely unlikely, emotions aside. But to erase any doubt, I've got some friends at Sutton."

Her father started to say something.

Richard smiled indulgently but sincerely. "If this guy is a member of the coaching staff, and should you be right, that he's the commander of the SS unit that you encountered in 1945, it would be patently dangerous to alert him." Was Richard humoring her father? Obviously, yes, but not in a patronizing way, she realized. He really was just trying to prove that this was impossible. "I can get yearbooks and we can not only get this man's photo, his current photo, but we can check into his past a little, see what he looked like say twenty years ago, in college or even high school. It will take a little digging, but I like playing detective."

She turned toward Richard and threw her arms around his neck and kissed him hard on the mouth.

"What's that for?" Richard asked her.

"Because you're nice."

And she heard her father, his voice sounding lighter, more at ease, more confident. "Let's check those photos, play detective as you say, Richard. I know you're humoring me, but maybe I'm humoring me, too." She looked at him, took her arms from around Richard, holding his right hand in her left, reaching out for her father, touching his knee. "If the photos prove we have an anomaly, then we go from there. If not, if it's just a coincidence in how the man looks, at least it'll shut me up and let me sleep at night."

"Ohh, Daddy," and she let go of Richard's hand and dropped to her knees beside her father and just hugged him.

Chapter Four:

In The Middle of The Night

He enjoyed the cold weather, long an ascriber to the philosophy that one could always put on more than one could take off. Sunshine was much better enjoyed wrapped in a cool breeze.

And he walked a lot. Leaving his apartment each morning for a good hour or more, while swathed in a heavy quilted ski jacket and a knit watch cap, he would explore the midtown streets, smell the smells of food cooking, listen to the myriad accents of the pedestrians surrounding him, look for minute differences in the familiar shop windows.

And, each evening, he would do the same.

Although it was illegal to do so, for his evening walks he carried a small handgun he'd owned for years and shot occasionally on the backlot of the summer place by the ocean where, even if it might be illegal, no one cared. He liked the city, but wasn't naive enough to think that everyone in the city liked him back.

With conscious effort, Evan Hardy relegated his experiences two weeks earlier in Highcliffe to dispassionate research. It had been very difficult for him to return to the free-lance editing of that sweepingly dull historical saga he'd agreed to handle for his old house, but he'd done it, completed it, and told Herschel Goldberg that he didn't want another project until sometime after Christmas, that he was working on something of his own that required all his attention.

Herschel had squirmed, that it might be the memoirs

81

Evan Hardy often (jokingly) threatened to write.

But, rather than his memoirs, each morning after his walk he would sit and read. About werebeasts.

Much of the "literature" in the field was, at the least, amusing. There were stories, told as though they were in deadly earnest, about everything from werepanthers to werefrogs — and, of course, werewolves.

And he read all that he could about the SS.

Midday was lunch, his biggest meal of the day and the one to which he was most devoted. Whether alone or with a friend, at home or the home of someone else or in a restaurant, he banished the research from his mind and would either enjoy conversation, observing the people around him or merely read an adventure novel or a western — never horror, because that would be too close to the other thing.

After lunch, he would devote an hour to analysis of his readings, notetaking where appropriate, and backchecking, trying to find any supporting evidence for the more promising avenues he uncovered.

This was grueling work, and often disappointing, not that he expected more.

By six each evening, he would close shop. A play, a movie, dinner with friends, or just a good book to read or a fine old film on the VCR in store for him.

But first, his evening walk.

Cast off the casual clothes of the day, into his warm things again and grab the keys, the wallet, the money clip and, lastly, the little gun. It was a five-shot stainless-steel Smith & Wesson .38 Special and tucked nicely into his pocket.

Tonight, because he'd worked very hard at his research, he promised himself total couch-potatoing to the nth degree. From his shelves filled with video recordings, he had already made the selections. A Three Stooges short, the one where they became involved with helping a rocket scientist and his pretty daughter, then an Arnold Schwarzenegger adventure film and, before retiring, a half-hour western drama with the late Richard Boone.

He'd had a chicken breast thawing for the microwave all afternoon and a can of ball potatoes and a can of string beans ready to be opened.

Evan Hardy closed his apartment door behind him and went out.

At six-fifteen it was very dark, darker than usual tonight, it seemed, because the overcast which had rolled in during his morning walk was still much in evidence.

And it was very cold, a biting wind making him hunch his neck down deeper into the upraised collar of his jacket, tug down the sides of his watch cap to better cover his ears.

He allowed himself, in these evening walks, to consider his research.

What was unfolding for him, more through his looking back into everything he could get his hands on concerning the SS in particular and the Nazis in general, was that the German high command had wished to promote in the German people during those closing days of the war a spirit of resistance. And the formalized units, oddly enough lumped together under the name Werewolf, were merely to be a spear head, leadership for this hoped-for spontaneous uprising of Teutonic resistance.

Such never happened, of course, but some of the Werewolf units did indeed pull off an amazing bit here and there of what would today be labeled terrorism, while most of the personnel involved sooner or later realized their cause was hopeless and quietly slipped away.

The Nazis, and the SS in particular, had a fascination with superstition, used it . . . but why the name Werewolf?

Was it inspired by something other than folkloric metaphor?

It was on this question that gradually Evan Hardy was realizing he must focus his research.

Hardy stopped walking, realizing he had already reached his halfway point. He turned the corner at the park and started his return route around the Plaza Hotel, watching and half laughing at smart-looking women and lounge-lizardly men, all of them seeming half frozen in evening wear as they rushed from cabs and limos past ruddy-cheeked ear-muffed doormen toward the glittering lobby.

He listened to his heels click over a metal freight elevator as he walked on round the corner.

Dannie had called him this afternoon and, amid her less-than-subtle questions concerning his health (he'd rarely felt better), she'd allowed that yes, indeed, Richard had secured a Sutton yearbook. Had she looked for the blond? Not yet, but even if it were the same man, that would prove nothing except that Sutton employed boors as football coaches.

In the end, she promised to bring the yearbook — Richard still had it — when she and Richard came down to visit him over the weekend.

Evan Hardy laughed at himself. He was getting to like Richard, and that was worrisome. Nine years older than Dannie, and sometimes such an unremitting stiff. But a decent guy despite it all.

She could do considerably worse, Hardy told himself. As he thought of it, her happiness had become the consuming passion of his life. His love for her and for her mother before her and his friendship for Mac, these were his finest moments.

He heard a noise as he stepped down off the curb to cross the alley and he looked to his right toward the sound. There was something familiar about the sound.

As he looked and something shoved at him from behind, threw him onto the alley pavement, Evan Hardy remembered what the sound reminded him of.

Hardy reached for his revolver even though he knew from experience that, even if he got his hand to it, ordinary bullets were useless.

Chapter Five:

Dead

It wasn't that Richard was some sort of spectacular lover, but for that matter, she'd had too few lovers in the days since she'd let Pete Mitchellson make it with her after the senior prom to make any sort of authoritative comparison.

She stared up at the ceiling, missing Richard, and prowess having nothing to do with it. He'd flown off with Dr. Crawford, the head of his department, to a meeting in Albany. She looked at the bedside clock, wondering why she couldn't get back to sleep.

It was almost five in the morning. Richard would be back by now, sound asleep. Or was he awake, remembering past lovers by way of comparing her, as she was with him?

After Pete, she'd felt as if she'd sinned.

They weren't engaged, weren't even going steady.

But it was a romantic evening and Pete had always been one of the handsomest boys in school and it was a night to feel grown up.

After Pete, she'd remained repentantly near-virginal until she was a sophomore here at Highcliffe. But that fall, her resolve vanished in the blue eyes of Ted Morrison, a senior, star of the football team (was that why ever afterward she'd thought football was a little silly?) and with a body like nothing she'd ever seen before or since, not to mention touched.

It wasn't once and never again, either. They'd make love three or four times each week, sometimes twice in the same day, but never just before a game because Ted was superstitious about that, thought he'd lose his edge because love was

85

soft and he needed to be hard.

Needing to be hard never seemed to be a problem for him.

By the time summer came, two things happened: She missed her period and was terrified that the pill wasn't working and she was pregnant; she realized that above Ted's neck there was an empty gourd.

When, in a roundabout way, she explored Ted's feelings concerning her should she become pregnant, she found he had no feelings at all.

The missed period was probably because she'd been practicing especially hard for a tennis match and had a heavy case of nerves over final exams. Whatever the cause, no baby. And she told Ted she wished him the best of luck in the world and told him how much she'd enjoyed all the pleasant times they'd had together — all of which was true — but, because her father had always emphasized that she should conduct herself as a lady, she neglected to tell Ted that he was a self-centered asshole.

And then, Richard.

She met Richard in her senior year when she took a course from him that she'd avoided taking when she was a sophomore and avoided again as a junior. She was the oldest person in the class, next to Richard

She didn't actually talk to him again, aside from smiling and saying hello as they'd pass on campus, until she was researching her master's thesis. Their library times coincided, at least so she'd thought. He told her later, and she was very flattered, that he'd always remembered her as the prettiest girl he'd ever seen, and as being so very bright. That first time in the library had, indeed, been sheer happenstance. His apartment had just been painted and he'd needed a quiet place where he could not only work on his lecture notes but also breathe. After that, he frequented the library regularly while he summoned up the nerve to ask her out. That had really flattered her.

And, with Richard, she knew it was all true.

Love, in the grand passion sense she'd always known existed between her father and her mother, didn't seem to be in the cards for her. But Richard was a wonderful man.

86

"Nuts," she said to the ceiling, sat up in bed, and looked at the clock again. She'd always despised even the smell of warm milk, but maybe the rare cigarette and playing channel tag on the television set for a little while would help.

She leaned toward the nightstand and turned on the lamp.

Dannie pushed down the covers and put her legs over the side of the bed, her feet searching for the fuzzy slippers Richard had given her last Christmas, finding them. She stood up, her gown falling to her ankles. Her robe, a nice, sensible heavy woolen one, pink-and-blue plaid, lay across the foot of the bed except when Richard shared the bed with her. She slipped into the robe, belted it around her waist, and started from the bedroom.

Her cigarettes were, predictably, hard to find. Richard detested smoking, her father had just quit smoking and she'd never smoked more than a pack of cigarettes in a week, her usual consumption about a carton's worth a year.

Dannie found the pack. It was nearly full. Owning a lighter would have been stupid so now she had to search for matches in the kitchen drawers. She found a half-empty book. Now an ashtray. That was easier to find.

She went into the living room, just a worklight over the kitchen counter on and a faint yellowish glow from the bedside lamp diffused through the open bedroom doorway. She picked up the remote that controlled the television and VCR and curled up on the couch.

Lucy and Ricky were at it again.

So were Ralph and Ed, but in a different way, of course.

Barbara Stanwyck and her television sons and daughter were in trouble.

She settled for the news.

The woman reading the news looked as tired as Dannie Hardy felt.

Dannie lit a cigarette from the pack, inhaling as deeply as she could. The cigarettes were unfiltered, her reasoning that since she smoked so rarely she might as well enjoy herself. She'd smoked Camels but switched to Pall Malls because they were longer and she'd felt a little butch buying the short cigarettes.

Her nightgown was twisted a little and she stood up, rearranged her clothing, and plopped back into the couch.

She was proud of Richard, helping out her father in what Richard obviously considered silliness at best and paranoid delusion at the worst. Would the yearbook from Sutton College satisfy her father, or would they be forced to find out more about this blond-haired man on Sutton's coaching staff?

She should have asked her father more about the war he fought. Maybe then, she would be better able to understand what drove him so.

The news switched to a health feature, graphic stuff about open heart surgery, and that scared her to death because it made her remember how she'd almost lost her father.

She switched channels. God, was Barbara Stanwyck good-looking, despite her age.

She fantasized her father and—

The telephone rang.

It startled her and she just looked at it for a moment.

"Richard?" Dannie asked no one aloud.

She pressed a button on the remote and the television set shut off. She walked quickly toward the kitchen, the nearest telephone.

She caught up the receiver in her left hand on the third ring.

"Hello?"

A man's voice, unfamiliar, a little gruff-sounding. She was about to hang up, but he identified himself as a New York City policeman and she dropped the telephone receiver . . .

It was cold, even wearing her longest and warmest winter coat, even with Richard's arm folded around her.

A policeman, short, a little pot-bellied, very tired-looking behind his dark-rimmed glasses and a youngish black man wearing a gray lab coat (or was it just dingy white?) stood beside the bank of cabinet doors, all of them closed.

The policeman, the same man who'd called, said, "There doesn't seem to be any evidence of foul play." His voice didn't sound quite so gruff now.

She looked at Richard. It was the first time she'd ever seen Richard fully dressed and unshaven at the same time, and he looked odd. There was a lot of gray in his beard, too. "Maybe it isn't Daddy?"

Richard just held her more tightly.

She looked away from him, at the little door the young black man was opening. She'd called her father's apartment first, before calling Richard. No answer. She called Richard. He called the building management where her father lived. Mr. Hardy had not returned from his customary evening walk.

A slab—she remembered from television and movies and mystery novels that a slab was what they called it—was rolled out. There was a body on it, covered by a sheet.

"I can identify him, Dannie," Richard said beside her, holding her.

She shivered, stared down at her tennis-shoed feet. Her shoes were wet from stepping in New York City slush and she flexed her knees, swallowed. "No," Dannie Hardy said, trying to smile.

The policeman cleared his throat.

The black attendant drew back the portion of the sheet covering the head.

"Daddy!"

Richard said something she didn't understand. She closed her eyes . . .

Dannie Hardy sat on the edge of the hotel-room bed, a blanket wrapped around her, wearing nothing but her panties underneath.

If she'd looked out the window and craned her neck to the left, she might be able to see her father's apartment. But she sat there on the edge of the bed, unmoving.

There was going to be an autopsy, the policeman—his name was Sergeant Rucker—had told her. But he'd said again, there was no indication of foul play. Pending the autopsy results, they were putting Evan Hardy's death down to a heart attack. It looked as if he'd been running, or doing something strenuous, because his clothes showed signs that he had perspired heavily, partially frozen when he was found two blocks from his apartment, about a block from where she sat.

She heard the door into the small suite Richard had rented open and close. "It's me, honey."

She said nothing.

Richard entered the bedroom, a large but rather thin book with a shiney black binding under his arm. He was still wearing his overcoat. "I think this is a mistake right now, Dannie," Richard said.

She said nothing.

"I think we ought to wait, at least until the police have finished their investigation."

She spoke. "What investigation? If he died of a heart attack, that'll be the end of it."

Richard didn't answer for a moment, then said, "Maybe it should be, honey."

She looked at him.

Richard shrugged out of his coat and dropped it down on the chair beside the bedroom door. He walked over to her, handed her the book. "Page nineteen.

One arm out of the blanket, the blanket in her lap, she opened the Sutton College yearbook. The blanket fell from her shoulders and she was only faintly conscious of being topless. But Richard had seen, touched, kissed almost every inch of her flesh anyway.

She recognized the blond from Larrigan's. He was very handsome, albeit his hair was very short on the sides, disproportionately so to the healthy shock on the top of his head. "William Paul Stein, Ph.D. He's a history professor, Richard. Isn't that odd?"

"Yes. It's an odd coincidence. Look, ahh—"

"He's an assistant coach for football, wrestling, and track."

"I read it, Dannie."

"He's good-looking."

"I guess he is."

"He killed my father."

90

"Dannie, you don't—"

She drew her legs up under her Indian-fashion and co-cooned the blanket around her again, the Sutton College yearbook in her lap.

She stared at the face of Dr. William Paul Stein. Maybe no one else knew, but she knew . . .

". . . in the sure and certain hope of the resurrection . . ."

Dannie Hardy, beneath her black veil, Richard beside her as he had been and promised her he would always be, wasn't sure of anything anymore.

Where had the mercy of God been?

Evan Hardy was dead and his killer was alive.

The autopsy had shown that her father had died of massive cardiac arrest. There was evidence to suggest that he had been in the midst of some tremendous exertion. There was a slight bruise on his left forearm.

With Richard helping her, not really because she'd wanted him to, but because it would have hurt him to shut him out, she'd searched her father's apartment. The books on Nazis, the books on things she'd always considered the subject of horror movies and nothing more, the notes he'd taken in his broad, neat hand.

When the police arrived after a passerby—a sweet little man named Oscar Grotten who was a janitor—found him, her father's Rolex wristwatch, his wallet containing identification and two crisp hundred-dollar bills, his money clip with sixty-three dollars, his keys, everything had been where it should have been, except her father's life, which was gone from him.

Everything, except one thing.

The police made no mention of it, so she had not.

Instead, with Richard helping but not knowing the true object of her search, she'd gone through her father's apartment from one end to the other, looking everywhere.

It was all very good, her father, the survivor of extensive coronary bypass surgery, found dead of cardiac arrest. All of his valuables untouched. Natural causes, not even an inexpli-

91

cable street mugging to arouse suspicion.

But, evidently to allay suspicion, one critical article was taken. She'd argued with her father about his habit of carrying his gun on his nighttime walks, asking him what would happen if he were discovered and arrested. He'd countered by saying that option was preferable to being killed by a mugger or being afraid to walk the streets of a city supported by one's own tax money.

But there was no sign of his gun.

She moved her veil back from her face and, Richard at her elbow, navigated the bumpy graveside carpet in her heels. She looked down into her father's grave.

She didn't say it aloud, because Richard already seemed worried about her hold on reality.

So, Dannie Hardy said it inside herself. "If he did it, I'll prove it and he'll pay, Daddy."

She started crying again, just letting the tears come, her body aching with them. It had been snowing all morning and was bitterly cold and she shivered. After a moment, she let Richard lead her away.

Chapter Six:

Sorting Things Out

Instead of canceling the appointment her father had made for her a week before his death, now a week after his death she elected to keep it. Driving down from Highcliffe the previous afternoon for the reading of her father's will, she spent the night in Evan Hardy's apartment.

She was close to being rich, inheriting more money from her father than she'd ever thought he'd possessed during his lifetime. With the exception of a quarter million dollars left to Highcliffe's American literature department, she was her father's sole financial heir. Many of his papers were bequeathed to Highcliffe, while their actual disposition was left to her discretion. She could keep whatever she wanted.

She'd called Richard, told him about the will, told him that she was just fine and not to worry, then ordered a pizza and sat up half the night going over her father's books and Xeroxed copies of magazine articles and his meticulous notes on Nazis and werebeings for the hundredth time, hoping that somehow reviewing them here where he'd lived and worked these last years might add some new insight. It did not. Yet she came away from her all-night blitz even surer that these notes were not the manifestation of a demented mind but rather careful research that was, above all, quite rational.

There was still the matter of her father's gun, which she'd wished she had while spending the night alone in the apartment. But a fireplace poker had to do. She'd called to Mrs. Kitchener, the woman who managed the summer house property for them, saw to it that no windows were broken, that the heat was turned on and off as required, kept the grounds cleared in the summertime. Mrs. Kitchener searched the house as Dannie directed, finding no gun.

In the morning, she just pulled on sweats and a heavy coat and scarf and gloves, then went walking, following her father's route on the night he died. She knew the route, had walked it with him often enough over the years. There was nothing to arouse her suspicions, nor to allay those she already harbored.

Back to the apartment, wedging a chair under the doorknob again because she hadn't thought to have the locks changed. The telephone rang as she started to undress, and she stood there talking for five minutes with one leg of her sweat pants on and her arms hugged over her bare breasts. But it was only the building manager, very solicitous, very curious, wondering if she intended to keep the apartment or was interested in selling. She said she intended to keep it for the time being and hung up, then went into the master bath to shower.

She could explain away everything, almost, except her father's missing gun. But if her father were the victim of some terrible conspiracy, by whom? The Nazi connection was self-evident from their conversation following what had happened at Larrigan's after the homecoming game. Her father genuinely believed that somehow this blond-haired man had never aged, was the same man who'd led an SS unit during World War II.

But why this sudden passion for werewolves and creatures like them?

She'd made the connection between the Nazis and the

Werewolf resistance program during the closing days of the war, and perhaps that was it. Modern European history wasn't her major field of interest; however she'd read a great deal about World War II simply because it had involved her father But her father's notes actually dwelt on werewolves, the kind Lon Chaney, Jr., had played in all those movies she'd sat up late on Saturday nights to watch with her girlfriends on their television sets because her father would never take her to horror movies, or even let her watch them at home.

Out of the shower, dried, her hair still damp, she shuffled through the things she'd hung in the spare bedroom closet, settling on the best dress she'd packed. Her father had always told her that to do her best she should look her best. When other girls would show up for a college exam in faded jeans and little or no makeup, even one girl she remembered who'd come with her hair in curlers, she had always dressed her best—except for the makeup. Always lipstick, a little eye makeup sometimes, maybe a dab of powder, but she'd never fancied herself with cheeks so artificially blushed that one appeared to have a high fever.

The gray sheath dress, her good pearls, her good watch, heels, and her mink coat—a college graduation present—she cabbed it to Park Avenue South and the offices of Goldblatt, Morgenstern and O'Brien, Literary Consultants.

She gave her name to a receptionist and sat because that seemed more proper, idling through a copy of *Publishers Weekly*, not really caring what the words said or the pictures were trying to sell.

A tall man, skinny, balding, but a warm smile in his eyes came up and stood before her. He was somewhere in his sixties. "I still thought you might change your mind at the last minute and put this off. I'm glad you didn't. I'm Abe Goldblatt, Miss Hardy. But it's Dr.

Hardy, isn't it?"

"I remember you from my father's funeral, Mr. Goldblatt." She tugged off her right glove and offered her hand. He took it.

"I could have made myself free for lunch. For a man my age to be seen with a pretty young woman like you, well, it's good for the ego."

"Maybe next time," she told him, smiling.

"Come on into my office. Would you like some coffee?"

"Not really, but thank you."

They moved along a long corridor, the walls covered with some sort of textured fabric like burlap; elaborately framed, enlarged book covers hung everywhere. She recognized most of the titles and authors, either from her own reading or from glances at the best-seller lists over the years.

There was an outer office, a smiling-faced secretary in her midtwenties at a desktop computer. "Don't let us be disturbed, Marge."

"Yes, Mr. Goldblatt," the woman answered.

Abe Goldblatt held the inner office door for her, then closed it behind him. She surveyed the office. It was quite large, almost the size of the living room of her father's apartment, a bank of windows on the far wall, a desk just before them, the desk cluttered with what looked like manuscripts and stacks of file folders.

"Please sit down, Dr. Hardy."

He held a chair for her just opposite the desk. It was big, leather, padded, comfortable, and she sank back into it, not knowing how to begin.

Fortunately for her, Abe Goldblatt began instead. He sat on the corner of his desk nearest her, hands in his lap almost like a woman would do. "The book deal just requires a signature, as soon as we get the contract. You don't know me from Adam's housecat, so you might

96

want to arrange to have a lawyer review the documents."

"You were my father's friend. There's no need to examine the contracts."

"Thank you, but I'd still advise a lawyer."

"If you want."

"I liked your dad a lot, Dr. Hardy."

"Dannie."

Abe Goldblatt nodded. "He was just about the nicest guy I ever met in this business or anywhere else. It was a sin, him dying like that."

"Yes. The donation you made to the Heart Fund in his memory was very thoughtful."

"I liked him more than that. It was the only thing I could think of at the time. I mean, I'm a guy who sells books, not a real-estate man. Maybe if I was in real estate, I could have found someplace to build a statue to him. He's a lot of good memories. You ever need anything, just pick up a telephone, Dr. Hardy—Dannie."

She licked her lips. Her lipstick was all but gone. "Do you have a connection in London?"

Abe Goldblatt looked startled, looked away from her then, and stood up. He apparently wanted to talk more about her father. As he walked toward the windows looking down on Park Avenue South, he said, "I'm already working on foreign rights, but—"

"No. That's all in your hands. I just need help to do something."

He turned around, smiled, evidently happier now. He said nothing.

"Then you do have a London connection?"

"Beulah Thornberry. She's an old friend of your father, for that matter. Why?"

"Sort of as a last favor for my father, then. I remember a nice note from a Mrs. Thornberry after my father's death. Was that her?"

"Probably, yes. In fact, I'm certain of that."

She nodded to herself. "Then would this Mrs. Thornberry be able to engage the services of a private detective for me?"

Abe Goldblatt left the windows, leaned forward with his hands on the desktop. "A private detective? For heaven's sake, why?"

"My father had one very dear friend from World War II—"

"Wait a minute . . . ah—Mac?"

Her breath caught in her throat and she leaned forward in her chair, almost standing up. "Do you—"

"Do I know him? No. But I almost feel like I do. Your dad always talked about Mac. In fact, just a couple of days before—"

"Before he died," she said for him.

Abe Goldblatt nodded. "Yes. We had lunch. We'd usually get together once a month or so for lunch, just the two of us. Evan was talking about you a little, asked about the book deal, of course, and he mentioned your young man—"

"Richard."

"Yeah. He said he was really getting to like him."

She smiled.

"And then he started talking about how he was going to nail down some information on a project of his and, once he had it, fly to London to look for Mac."

"Did he say—"

Abe Goldblatt shook his head. "He said he'd tried finding him but never could. I figured a trip to England wouldn't hurt your dad, or I would've suggested a private detective or something. But a trip would have been good. He looked kind of down in the dumps about something, but not sick or anything. Was he . . . ah—"

"Worried about something? I think so. It had to do with finding Mac in a roundabout way. Do you think this Mrs. Thornberry could hire a detective to find

98

Mac?"

"You write down— Better yet, I'll get my secretary in here. Give her everything you can remember about Mac. And I'll do the same. If I know Beulah Thornberry, she won't need a private detective."

Chapter Seven:

Confrontation

The Sutton campus wasn't unknown to her. She'd attended a dance there once as an undergraduate, and several times during graduate school and, since, had attended various professional functions, AAUP meetings and the like.

And, as she pulled the Mercedes into a visitor slot beside the History building, Sutton Hall, she was still wracking her brain to remember if she'd actually met William Paul Stein. She had to have, of course, but he could have been a fleeting introduction at a cocktail party or a face in a lecture hall.

Her own department chairman, Thaddeus Welles, knew him. "Stein? Very good. His period interest is modern Europe. One of the best Nazi men there is."

"Nazi?"

Dr. Welles laughed that laugh of his that made him sound like Hopalong Cassidy dressed up as Santa Claus. "He's not a Nazi, Dannie, for goodness' sake. No, I mean he's one of the top authorities on the period. Several times, if memory serves, some of the film companies have sought him out for those rare moments when authenticity was required."

"I suppose he collects the stuff?" After all, she collected from the Civil War period, buttons, belt buckles, miniballs, documents, but only the affordable things.

"No. I asked him that once. He hates the Nazis, told me. Always got the impression he'd rather hang dirty socks behind his desk than a damned Nazi flag. A lot of things must pass through his hands for authentication. He does that, too, I understand, but evidently he never holds on to it."

"I see."

"Bit of a womanizer, I understand." Dr. Welles smiled then.

She assured him she'd be careful.

And she had every intention of being careful, but not of Stein's supposed skirt chasing. She locked the car, put her bag over her shoulder, and started up the steps from the parking lot to the building entrance.

Sutton was as new, really, as Highcliffe was old. The old Sutton College of fifty years ago had all but bankrupted. New financing not only saved it from collapse, but also allowed it to expand. Fifty years ago, from what she'd read of Highcliffe's history, Sutton's greatest claim to fame was a race rowing squad or team (she wasn't sure just what a group of men in their underwear paddling a long, skinny canoe at high speeds should properly be called). But, in the fifties, their football team, once great among the smaller colleges, came back, attracting some of the better high school athletes. Much the same could be said of all Sutton's athletic teams.

But Sutton was not devoted only to the jockstrap.

Sutton scholars ranked high in the job market and more and more each year, Sutton attracted some of the finest men and women for its freshman class.

Sutton Hall, as an older building, was in the minority, but vastly more charming than the steel, concrete, and glass edifices which otherwise dotted the campus. She let herself in, to the musty, dry smell of forced air heating, immediately letting her coat fall open.

Her bootheels clicked on stone floors polished smooth

101

by nearly a century of use.

Dr. Stein's office was on the second floor, and she took the stairs, touching lightly at the railing with her gloved hand. What would the man be like?

She reached the second floor, searching for Stein's office.

It held a commanding position at the far end of the hall. She walked the length of the hall, stopped before the door, and knocked.

"Come in!"

The voice, the same as at Larrigan's, but of course it should be. He wouldn't have one voice for partying and one voice for professoring. When she'd heard it on the telephone when she'd called for the appointment, she'd almost hung up.

It was a solid voice, a rich voice, musical—and without even the slightest trace of accent.

She put her right hand on the knob. She still wore her gloves and didn't plan to remove them. She turned the knob and stepped inside.

The man sitting behind the desk . . . it was unmistakably Stein, from his yearbook picture, from her recollections of him—admittedly vague—at Larrigan's.

He stood up.

He was taller and more athletically built than she remembered, in a white shirt with the sleeves rolled up past his elbows, a sleeveless dark-blue V-neck sweater, a blue knit tie knotted neatly at his chin.

He had a pleasant smile as he extended his hand. "Since you're not one of my students, you must be Dr. Hardy. I'll confess, I'm a bit mystified by your phone call." He extended his hand. Oh, how she wanted to refuse it, but she took advantage of her woman's prerogative and left her glove on as she let him touch briefly at her fingertips. "Sit down, please."

Dannie sank into the wooden captain style teacher's

chair he gestured toward.

Stein sat down. "As I said, I was a bit mystified by your phone call. But a colleague I mentioned it to recalled reading in the *Highcliffe Journal* about the death of your father. There was a photograph. I remembered the encounter at Larrigan's after the homecoming game. And I felt horrible. I was a little drunk. That's my only defense for such rudeness. You see," and he smiled, his voice rising and dropping along the scale as he continued, "I'm very loyal to our sports program and I was so elated that we'd won. It was such a close game. My high spirits got the best of me. That's a poor apology, Dr. Hardy, but the truth. I can only pray that my conduct in no way contributed to your father's heart attack."

"Liar." She hadn't wanted to say it that way. Well, she really had, but had told herself she shouldn't.

He looked positively aghast. "What? What did you say?"

She licked her lips, her voice shaky-sounding as she reiterated. "I called you a liar."

"But—"

"My father knew you. He recognized you. And you couldn't afford that, could you?"

"Miss—I mean, Dr. Hardy. Really!"

"He recognized your face from 1945. I don't know how, but I know my father. He wasn't crazy just because he was old. If he said he knew you—and he did say that—then he knew you. As an SS officer."

Stein's face went ashen. "You, ahh . . . Why did you come here? To confront me, as it were? Look at me! For God's sake, look at me! Could I even have been alive in World War II? I'm thirty-six years old."

She had no answer for that, but if she pushed hard enough she might be able to provoke him into showing his hand. And Richard and everyone else knew where she'd gone—or, at least, Richard would know, because

103

she'd left him a note. If this Stein tried to . . . And her hands started to shake. What was she doing.

But Stein began to speak again. "Look . . . , ahh — was it this that caused your father's death?"

"You know damn well it was."

Stein's eyes — they were china blue, almost too bright — began to move and he stood up with such energy that for a split second she thought he was about to strike her. "Dr. Hardy. You're pushing me."

"What are you going to do? Kill me, too?" She was suddenly very afraid that he would.

He licked his lips. He shook his head. "No. You don't understand. I'll tell you something. And there's no way I can keep you from doing it, but please don't take it from this room."

She wanted to say she didn't understand what he was talking about, but she said nothing.

"I suppose this unfortunate incident has forced me to tell a truth I've been carefully avoiding for many years." He sat down again, made a tent of his fingers, leaned his forehead against them, and audibly sighed.

She was amazed, and now very afraid. He was going to admit that he was . . . But how could he admit that he was the same man her father thought he was, because that was impossible. Dannie Hardy wanted to get up and leave. She sat where she was.

"I suppose, aside from being a little drunk, just maybe I'm a little paranoid, was then when your late father confronted me. I've been avoiding coming to grips with this for so long. It's . . . ahh — you mentioned the SS. Hitler's SS. The crimes they committed!" He shook his head, his face a mask of disgust. "My father, Dr. Hardy, my father had a brother. Everyone in my family has always said I look to be his spitting image. My father and mother fled Germany early in 1939, afraid of Nazism, loathing what Hitler had already done, realizing the horrors that were still to come."

She didn't understand. She said nothing.

Stein paused, lit a cigarette, exhaled smoke through his nostrils. God, she wanted a cigarette, too, but her cigarettes were at home. "My father's brother—I really can't bring myself to think of him as my uncle. He was to become an SS-Standartenfuhrer. That's a full colonel in the SS. In the 1st SS Panzerdivision Liebstandarte Adolf Hitler. It was the first SS Division ever raised, in 1933, originally Hitler's own personal guard.

"My—my uncle, God help me—he was one of these, an officer. If your father," Stein said, looking at her hard, the cigarette burning down in his fingertips so close to his skin that she was certain he had to feel pain, "thought he recognized me, then I'm afraid the man he recognized was my father's brother. He took his own life, my father's brother, just before the 1st SS Panzerdivision capitulated in 1945. His orderly, a Sergeant Schmidt, was able to smuggle out his watch and ring. When my father died, I inherited these things. I still have them. They are in a safety deposit box. When I look at the ring, I wonder how many helpless people died to make it. So. You know something I never even told to any woman I've slept with, Doctor. If your father fought a man with my face in 1945, it wasn't me. But I bear the guilt just as if it were."

She looked down at her hands, folded in her lap, palms upward, one inside the other.

"There are so many Jews in the American university system, and in publishing, of course. If this became known, my career would be destroyed. I've made it part of my life's work to help the Jews, to try in my own small way to make restitution for the crimes against humanity my father's brother was guilty of. It's in your hands now. But I had to tell you, so you wouldn't think any the less of your father. Do you understand, Dr.

105

Hardy?"

"I hear you," Dannie Hardy barely whispered.

"Then?"

"I don't want to ruin anybody." She got up and walked out of his office, holding back the tears until she was outside, in the corridor.

Chapter Eight:

Decisions

"This is becoming an obsession with you, honey."

"No. It isn't."

"Yes. It is." He got up and sat on the side of the bed. Men looked funny naked.

Dannie sat up behind him and pressed her breasts to his back, her fingertips touching at his shoulders "I only want to talk with Mac."

"You don't even know that Mac is alive, do you? It's been how many weeks since you saw your agent and trotted off to see William Stein?"

It wasn't a question, but she answered it anyway. "Two weeks."

"Eighteen days," Richard corrected.

She kissed his neck. "What am I supposed to do?"

"Maybe think about your own life, all right? Or, maybe even think about me."

"That's mean, Richard. That's damn mean."

"You should know." He stood up and walked off toward the bathroom.

She balled up the sheet in her fists, staring after him, blinking as he turned on the bathroom light. She could hear him urinating, and as he flushed the toilet, he started talking again. "After all, what Stein told you makes perfect sense, a damned sight more sense than somebody who'd have to be eighty or better looking in his midthirties. Why not let the thing rest, Dannie?" He came out of the bathroom, stood beside the door, just looked at her. "If this Mr. MacTavish is still alive, Dannie, what's to say he'll remember Stein's face? We're talking forty-five years or so? And if MacTavish does remember and you give him the same explanation Stein gave you, he'll probably accept Stein's explanation. So Stein acted like a boor in Larrigan's. But he said he was a little drunk and he was exhilarated over Sutton's big win. And the man bared his soul to you about his family shame, for God's sake."

"It could have been a lie. And even if it weren't, what about Daddy's death, Richard?"

Richard stared down at his bare feet. "Your father had a history of a bad heart—"

"Bypass surgery. You know how common that is?"

"You know how old he was when he had it?"

She looked away, wanted a cigarette but knew it would infuriate Richard and she wasn't quite ready for that, not just yet anyway. "Daddy's gun."

"What?"

"Daddy's gun. A revolver."

"Your father owned a handgun? My God! I didn't think he was that sort."

That did it. She stood up, pulling the sheet off the bed after her, wrapping it around her to cover her breasts, dragging the rest of it behind her as she started for the kitchen.

"Dannie?"

"I'm getting a cigarette."

"That's wonderful. Pollute your own lungs and mine, too. Just wonderful."

She found the half-empty pack, this time a book of matches slid under the cellophane. "To hell with an ashtray," she said under her breath, lighting up, inhaling, shaking out the match and tossing it into the sink where it made a soft, hissing sound for an instant. Richard was wrapping up in his bathrobe as he came after her, stopping just on the other side of the kitchen counter. "Well?"

"Does that make you feel better? To harm your lungs?"

"I'm not harming my lungs—not very much."

108

"Those things are as addictive as heroin or cocaine."

"Bullshit. Bullshit, Richard!"

"If they find MacTavish tomorrow, are you just going to abandon your classes and leave for England. Don't you have a responsibility to your students, to Highcliffe, to yourself? With midyear finals coming up, would your father have wanted you to go running off chasing something that doesn't exist?"

"No."

"And jeopardizing the future he worked so hard for you to have?"

"No."

"Your father was a fine man, Dannie. But you have to face the facts. He may have been suffering from a paranoid delusion about this—"

She inhaled, deliberately doing it as deeply as she could. She watched the smoke as she exhaled it while she spoke. "Are you going to write about him in your new book, Richard?"

"That's dirty."

"Are you?"

"Dammit, of course I'm not. I love you."

She turned away. The thing about Richard was that he did love her, and he did make sense. And that last part was so damned annoying . . .

Snow was falling so softly that it masked every other noise and she thought that if someone were to whisper a block away, she'd hear it. There was a soft crunching noise beneath her boots as she walked toward her office, only a heavy Welsh nursing shawl wrapped around her, her purse slung from her shoulder, her briefcase in her hand.

A snowflake landed on her eyelash and she blinked it away.

Her last class finished, in a very real way, Dannie Hardy was looking forward to spending three weeks with

109

Richard, skiing and doing other things together.

When Abe Goldblatt had called to see if she'd signed the contracts yet — she had and they were already en route back to him — she'd asked if he'd heard from Beulah Thornberry. He had, on two fronts. First, there was a solid interest from one of Great Britain's most prestigious publishing houses in her book. But she'd had no luck locating Hugh MacTavish

It was basically the same report on lack of success in finding the right Hugh MacTavish she'd gotten when Abe had called two weeks before that and when she'd called Abe Goldblatt ten days or so before that.

But Abe assured her that Beulah Thornberry wasn't about to give up.

As she started up the steps toward her office, Dannie Hardy decided that she had given up. In the ensuing weeks since her blowup with Richard, she'd thought about Richard's arguments more and more and, more and more, they made greater sense than ever. Her father wouldn't want her doing this. She knew that now, or told herself she did.

Through the old double doors and into the hall, she shrugged out of her shawl and shook the loose snow from the wool, then wiped her boots on the mat.

Her first few steps across the black- and white-checkerboard-patterned tiles were cautious ones, her boots still a little slippery, and she held to the handrail when she took the steps.

On the second floor, she looked all the way down the corridor toward Dr. Dzikowski's office. He was a nice, very intelligent older man who specialized in the early Renaissance. But the position of his office in relation to the other offices on the second floor — at the far end of the corridor — exactly corresponded to that of William Stein's office on the Sutton campus.

She was getting paranoid.

She turned the other way in the corridor, fishing her keys out of the pocket of her skirt and letting herself into her office.

The telephone was ringing.

She picked up the receiver. "This is Dr. Hardy. You just caught me."

On the other end of the line—and it was a terrible connection—was a woman's voice that she didn't recognize, but the woman gave her name.

Dannie Hardy stared across her desk and through the window into the still-falling snow. At last she said into the receiver. "Yes, Mrs. Thornberry. I am still interested in seeing Hugh MacTavish."

Chapter Nine:

Mac, At Last

The taxi driver closed the door for them and suddenly Dannie Hardy felt more committed — or trapped — than she had since telling Richard she was going to London. He was furious, but drove her to the airport anyway. He'd bought her new skis as a pre-Christmas present. And now, what was he supposed to do with them? And this MacTavish fellow . . . Who could know what sort of man he'd become in forty-five years? There had to be some reason why he was so hard to find. Perhaps he'd been in prison. Or what if he still were? She'd told Richard that if Hugh MacTavish were on death row — did England even have a death row — she was certain Beulah Thornberry would have mentioned it.

"So, my dear, you'll never know just how terribly difficult it was. Your Hugh MacTavish is now Brigadier Hugh MacTavish. Retired, of course," and Beulah Thornberry lowered her voice, evidently so the taxi driver wouldn't hear her, "late of the Special Air Service."

"The Air Force? I thought he'd been in the Army," Dannie Hardy said.

Beulah Thornberry's clothing rustled every time she moved and there was a perfectly ridiculous feather mounted on the even more ridiculous looking hat that covered her very obviously dyed too-black hair. Her overly red lips pulled together into something like a kiss, the powdered whitish flesh around her mouth puckering up as old women's mouths sometimes did. "Shh," she admonished. And she leaned closer to Dannie, her perfume pleasant but mildly overpowering with the windows rolled up against the cold. "Special Air Service, my dear. Commandos. Clandestine military operations for Her Majesty's government and all that. The Brigadier was their training director. And, from what I hear, it's not at all uncommon for him to get called away for some hush-hush operation or another, even now. My dear, you just wouldn't believe how many favors I had to call in to get that much! He lives on a modest little estate, I understand. I rang him up and spoke with him, of course. Perfectly beautiful-sounding man. He'd had no idea that your father had passed away, of course. Something about no newspapers where he'd been. More of that hush-hush sort of thing, I suspect. But who knows with these johnnies? At any event, he'd like you to come round for tea tomorrow."

"How far away does he live?" Dannie asked her.

"Not much of a drive, really. We're a small island, you know," she laughed. "He gave me directions."

A Brigadier, even in the British Army, was some kind of general, she knew . . .

After sleeping like a dead person, she'd gone for a run to shake off the cobwebs, reading somewhere that the more sunshine one absorbed the more easily one's body adjusted to changes in time zones. But there was no sunshine, only light snow.

By the time she'd showered and dressed and breakfasted, the snow had turned to rain, and the snow of the previous day which had greeted her on the ground at Heathrow Airport where Beulah Thornberry had met her was reduced to isolated patches of gray slush.

But on both sides of the country road over which she drove the hired Jaguar now, snow remained in huge, pockmarked mounds in the fields and woods, clung tenuously in the trees, occasionally a slick patch on the roadway here and there that she'd steer out of successfully, then drive on.

She climbed for better than an hour into slightly higher

113

country, the villages getting a little farther apart each time, the woods less violated-looking, the snow encroaching upon the road surface even more.

The rain had stopped and the overcast seemed to be reaching down to cover her. She drove more quickly but not so quickly she didn't feel she could handle it if she encountered another icy patch. In a smallish village that looked like something out of a BBC series on Public Television, she stopped to double check her understanding of the directions. The man at the service station knew Brigadier Hugh MacTavish "right enough, miss. Them direction's good as any, too, they are. And how's our petrol today?"

She'd filled up, not that she really needed to, but the man had been pleasant. With a cup of hot tea from a machine at the service station to fortify her, she drove on, looking for the smallish sign the directions told her to watch for. And she saw it, the word "PRIVATE" printed neatly on it, woodburned she thought as she took the turn and passed it.

She was on a single lane now, what in some parts of America would be called a ranch road, dirt and gravel rather than pavement, rutted deeply on either side, so deeply she had to steer very carefully because she was afraid to damage the Jaguar's undercarriage.

The road wound and twisted and climbed, the woods on either side very deep now. She looked at her watch. It was a little after one and, according to Beulah Thornberry, she was to arrive at whatever time suited her in the afternoon, then stay for tea.

Dannie didn't want to plan that far in advance. She might bolt after five minutes with the man, or spend the afternoon learning things about her father during the war. Or just . . . She didn't know what.

As the road almost hairpinned to the right, simultaneously leveling out, she had her first glimpse of the house. And it seemed wonderfully out of place, yet warm, almost inviting. It was a massive, two story log home and reminded her of the ranch house Lorne Green had shared

114

with his three television sons on *Bonanza* . . .

The housekeeper, sixtyish, plump, gray-haired and, Dannie bet, the person who belonged to the near antique little Hillman Minx parked in the gravel drive near the side of the house, was named Mrs. O'Shea. When first Mrs. O'Shea had answered the door, Dannie'd thought the woman was Hugh MacTavish's wife.

But the housekeeper dispelled any thought of that immediately. "The Brigadier is expecting you, miss. He left instructions that you might wish to go through some things he'd left out for you in his study. When I came in this morning, the Brigadier was just leaving he was and he wanted me to make certain you were comfortable. My name is Mrs. O'Shea. How do you do?" And she made a little curtsy with her plain white apron.

"It's very nice to meet you. Tell me, do you live far from here, Mrs. O'Shea?" Dannie inquired as the older woman helped her off with her coat.

"Down in the village, miss. It isn't far really, though. This is a lovely coat." And she ran her hand through the fur.

"Oh, thank you. That's a narrow little road."

"Yes, miss, it is that, but I drive it up and I drive it down I do, three times each week to look after the Brigadier's needs."

"I see." Dannie picked up her purse, the older woman putting Dannie's coat away in a closet. The house, on the inside, looked more like she'd expected a British officer's home to look, at least in decor. Granted, there was a large, balconylike thing at the far rear of the house, stairs connecting it to the first floor where she stood, but the walls were tastefully papered and the few furnishings in the hall and those in the living room open to her right were at once masculine and antique. There were no stuffed dead animals on the wall, no pelts strewn over the floor, and that was a good sign. The floors were hardwood, polished until they

115

gleamed darkly, small Oriental rugs (they looked genuine) dotted here and there. Elegant if not opulent, she thought.

"This way, miss, please," and Mrs. O'Shea crossed the entry hall to the left, toward two large sliding doors. As she pushed them apart, she said, "The Brigadier's study, miss."

Mrs. O'Shea stepped aside, as if not wishing to interfere with the full effect. And this room matched the original impression she'd had from the house's exterior. Log walls, and hung almost everywhere on them, it seemed, photographs of men in cowboy garb, some of them quite recognizable from television reruns and old B movies, some of them obscure, and intermingled with the framed photos (she noticed a few of them were signed) were cowboy lariats and Indian stoneheaded warclubs and even a bullwhip. There were two cases on the far wall and between them something that looked like an extra thick hitching post with an elaborately carved saddle resting on it.

In the case nearest the front of the house was displayed an array of knives, many of these wickedly curving Bowies and long, daggerlike Arkansas Toothpicks, both of these types recognizable to her from her studies of the Civil War. And some of the knives were obviously American Indian, or clever reproductions. In the second case flanking the saddle rack toward the rear of the house were guns. She was mildly shocked because she'd always noticed in newspaper articles and magazines that the British had very restrictive laws concerning firearms ownership, something her father occasionally had railed over. But these weren't modern arms, after all, but from the period of American westward expansion. A few long guns—a brass-framed Henry lever action, a Winchester, although she hadn't a clue as to which model, a double-barreled shotgun with exposed hammers—and a sizable number of handguns. Some few of these she could identify, again from her intimacy with the Civil War period: a Colt 1851 Navy revolver, an 1860 Army, a Dragoon (maybe a Third Model, but again she wasn't sure) and several cowboy six-guns, Colt Single Action Army models as first made in 1873.

116

Dannie supposed something was in order for her to say, so she said it. "The Brigadier seems quite the afficionado of the American West."

"Ohh, that he is, miss. A regular buckeroo." She laughed.

"Great," Dannie said under her breath. She started into the room, heard Mrs. O'Shea clear her throat and stopped, turning around. "Yes?"

"I have a sick neighbor I promised to look in on, miss. What I was meaning to ask, if it wouldn't be a bother, was once the Brigadier has returned, would it be too much bother . . ." The woman knotted her hands once in her apron. "The tea, I mean."

"You were wondering if I'd pour? Certainly."

Mrs. O'Shea smiled. "Ohh, thank you, miss." And she curtsied her little curtsy again. "Can I get you any refreshments, miss?"

"No, thank you. I'll wait for the Brigadier if that's all right."

"Ohh, certainly, miss. The things the Brigadier left for you to look at are right here, miss." And she walked halfway toward the piano near the windows. It was a grand piano, out of character with the room completely, and very ornate. And Dannie hadn't even noticed it before. On the bench were several scrapbooks.

"I can find my way with them, Mrs. O'Shea, thank you."

"Very good, miss," and Mrs. O'Shea did her little curtsy and left the room, then drew the doors closed behind her.

Dannie breathed.

She turned, slowly, a full three hundred sixty degrees, surveying the room in greater detail. "Buckaroo, indeed," she said to herself. On the back wall were holsters, saddle scabbards, more photos, a pair of leather-wrapped steer-horns and a long, multitiered rack. Hanging on pegs from the rack were cowboy hats. It almost looked as if he'd found a Stetson catalogue and ordered one of everything, black, tan, gray, a massive white ten-gallon style, even one in cavalry blue with an officer's yellow-gold hatcord.

She found herself walking over to the wall, staring at the hats in closer detail. She took one off the wall and examined it for head size. A man's seven and five-eighths. She hung this one up and took down another, careful to have replaced the first one exactly as she'd found it. This one was the same size. He had a big head or had found a fire sale.

Shaking her head, she thrust her hands into her pockets and walked back toward the piano bench. Three looseleaf scrapbooks, similar to the one she was so fond of, but each of them quite a bit thinner than her one thick one.

She took the books into her arms and walked toward the couch. It was leather, of course, and she sat in the corner farthest from the doors, nearest the window, curling her legs up under her skirt.

She opened the first book.

Clippings of her father. She flipped through, and page after page was filled with articles from the New York papers and *PW*, covering almost every event of Evan Hardy's career. There was even a copy of her birth announcement.

She set the first book on the floor beside her. The floor here was polished wood, like the outer hall, a few Indian pattern woven rugs here and there. She opened the second book. Photos that she had seen before, of her mother and father at their wedding and afterward, at the reception.

Her father had pointed out Mac in these, a tall, ganglylimbed boy with heavy eyebrows and a silly grin and hands and feet which looked too big for his body, sort of like a puppy that would grow up into an Irish Wolfhound or Great Dane.

She put aside the second book, opened the third.

These were photos as well, some few of which she had seen, most of them new to her.

When she saw her father, handsome in his Army officer's uniform, she wanted to cry.

But most of the photos were candids, snapshots. Her father and Mac and a bunch of other men—she recognized Forrestal and Erskine and some of the others—in full battle gear, bristling with weapons and silly grins as they stood around, sat around, ate, smoked. There was a picture of her father standing beside a doorway and, on the wall beside the door, she recognized the classic World War II Betty Grable swimsuit photo, her, by today's standard's, modestly bared back and long legs, the cute smile as she looked over her right shoulder at the camera.

Dannie bit her lower lip.

And there was one other photo at the very end of the book. Her father with his left arm bandaged and slung and Mac with a look in his young eyes that was telling the cameraman to do something obscene. Her father and Mac were in battle gear but tattered, dirty-looking.

She closed the book.

She ran her right index finger under her nose and sniffed, then set the book down. "Damn," she muttered.

Dannie stood up, hands back into her pockets, swinging her legs a little as she walked, assigning herself the task of examining every cowboy photo on the far wall.

They were in no chronological order. Hoot Gibson. Tom Mix. Bob Steele. One she didn't recognize. Another. The Masked Man, mask and all. Jay Silverheels. Dan Blocker. Don "Red" Barry. John Wayne, of course, but in the early days of his career when he was very young. Richard Boone, mustached, black-hatted, and menacing. Ward Bond. Another one she didn't recognize.

Her father was big on cowboys.

She wondered, had Mac gotten the bug from her father, or vice versa?

On the back wall, where the hats were, she identified more of the photos. Roy and Dale and Trigger. Gene.

And Dannie Hardy stopped in front of the hatrack.

The big gray ten-gallon hat fascinated her somehow. She took it off the rack.

She held it in her hands.

She looked toward the doorway.

She shrugged her shoulders.

She tried it on and it sank over her ears.

There was a soft, scraping sound and, from the doorway, she heard the most beautiful man's voice she'd ever heard, baritone, warm, gentle, commanding. "That's very becoming on you."

She turned her head faster than the hat followed her. It was Mac.

Chapter Ten:

The Man Behind The Legend

He was tall, lean, muscular, fit-as-anything-looking despite his age which wasn't obvious except that she knew
how old he had to be. He was bald as a cueball on top, his
head large—the seven and five-eighths?—and there was a
close-cropped, healthy-looking fringe of gray, and he wore
close-cropped sideburns almost down to his earlobes, his
ears large but not too big. Clean-shaven, the dark-brown
heavy eyebrows totally animated his face, moving as he
talked, his brown eyes sparkling.

He was the handsomest man she'd ever seen—except for
her father, of course.

He wore one of those commando sweaters she'd seen in
movies and sometimes on the backs of her college class-
mates, and later her students. It was dark olive drab with
cloth patches on the shoulders and elbows, all of the same
color.

He stood easily, leaning against the doorway, left arm
outstretched, a smile on his face. He was well over six feet
tall.

Dannie Hardy took off the ten-gallon hat and hung it
on the peg. She stared at the hat, rather than staring at
him. "You caught me."

"There's a penalty for trying on my cowboy hats, you
know."

"What?"

"You have to agree to stay for dinner, not just tea."

"Maybe."

"Do you like tea?"

"Sometimes, but your Mrs. O'Shea has it ready, I think."

"Well then, I suppose we have to have it."

"Yes. You're, ahh—"

"Brigadier Hugh Aaron MacTavish, at your service, madame."

His voice was incredible. She imagined he'd bowed a little, but she didn't take her eyes off the hat.

"Brigadier, ahh—"

"It's not Brigadier 'ahh,' my dear girl, it's Brigadier MacTavish. But there's another rule here."

"Yes?"

"The daughter of the best friend I ever had must call me Mac. Understood?"

"Yes."

"Let me look at you." And, suddenly she realized he was standing almost immediately beside her. There was a nice, almost unnoticeable smell to him, a little tobaccoish, a little of the wool of his sweater, the leather of his shoes. She turned around and looked straight at him and realized she was staring square at the center of his chest. She turned her chin up and looked at his face. He looked down at her and smiled easily. "You're beautiful. And you look just like your mother, which accounts for your being beautiful. Your father was a hell of a guy, but he wasn't beautiful. Your mother, on the other hand, was magnificent. So are you."

She breathed. "Thank you." She realized she was also blushing. What was it with this man?

There was a knock at the door. Mac turned toward it and she dodged left a little and looked past him. It was Mrs. O'Shea with an impossibly heavy-looking silver tray in her hands. "The young lady, sir, she said that she would pour."

Mac turned toward her, looked down at her again. "Is this true?"

Yes."

"Well, then, that solves our problem, doesn't it?"

She felt herself starting to laugh . . .

Her cheeks still felt hot, not just warm. The tea sat in its pot, the cups half filled with Myers's dark rum. She took a bite of her fruitcake.

"I know it's terrible, but do you mind if I smoke?" There was a hint of the Scot in his speech, but he was otherwise accentless. Perhaps from all his travels.

"No. I smoke sometimes myself."

"Then, a cigarette?"

"Not just now, thank you."

Mac stood up, towering over her again as she perched there on the edge of the couch beside the low table where the tea things were set. He walked across the room to the bar—wooden, carved, very ornate-looking, even though it wasn't very long—and went around behind it, taking up a smallish wooden box in his hands. "Are you sure?"

"Yes, thank you."

He took a cigarette from the box, tapped it a few times against the box lid, and walked around the bar toward her. "I'm afraid I have a passion for your American cigarettes." He smiled, standing over her again, taking a lighter from his pocket and firing the cigarette. It was a lighter like her father had always used, a windproof Zippo.

She nibbled at her fruitcake, looking down at the plate, past it, her feet disappeared beneath the hem of her skirt.

"I'd heard about Evan's death just a few hours before your agent Mrs. Thornberry called me. You see, I take some American publications. I'd gotten back the previous night and—"

"Why does a British general read *Publishers Weekly?*"

"A Brigadier. You're confusing rank in your American Army with rank in ours. And, anyway, I'm retired."

"Why do you read it?" She looked up at him as he exhaled smoke through his nostrils in long, thin gray streams.

"A means of keeping up on your father, but I'd daresay

123

you've guessed that already."

"If you kept up—"

"Then why didn't I contact him when you were born? And when your mother died? Or ever? That's a very long, complex story, and in the end there's no good answer for it other than it seemed like the best thing at the time. And why did you search high and low for me, Dr. Hardy."

"Dannie."

"Ahh, yes, after your mother. Dannie. Why?"

The tone of his voice had changed and she suddenly didn't really know if she knew why, or certainly how to explain it. "My father thought very highly of you. He spoke of you often. In fact, he'd spoken about a great deal in the weeks before he was . . . before his death."

"One of the great regrets of my life is that I could not be reached when your mother died, didn't even know until long after your mother was buried and you were baptized. After that, I didn't try to contact your father. Because I couldn't tell him why I wasn't there when he needed me in his grief and wished to give me the ultimate honor of one friend to another, to be your godfather. Truth. Now, it's your turn."

"Where were you?"

He smiled, almost sardonically. "In a far distant land," he said, flicking ashes from the tip of his cigarette into the palm of his hand, "fighting for queen and country, to make the world safe for democracy—or, in our case, creeping socialism—and doing 'what a man's gotta do.' Sort of." He jerked a thumb toward the hatrack. "I couldn't tell him where, couldn't even have told him that much. And I couldn't lie, and I couldn't stand not to tell him something I knew he had both the integrity and wisdom not to misuse. So I never contacted him. Now. You."

"My father—"

"You started to say something before, before you said he had died, that he was . . . What?"

"I—"

"Then why did you come here?"

She looked down at the napkin on her lap, shook her head, the hotness in her cheeks gone, coldness creeping around her. "I don't —"

"Evan Hardy's daughter does something, but she doesn't know why? I can't truly believe that."

"Dammit!" She looked up at him. The cigarette was nearly burnt out. Would he stub it out into his palm, too?

He just looked at her. "Tell me."

She bit her lower lip, nodded her head.

He walked back toward the bar, apparently found an ashtray and extinguished his cigarette. He moved with the grace of a natural athlete, seemingly without any effort. Her father's stories about him as a young man hadn't done him justice, but she thought that if a woman had told her about Mac, somehow the stories would have been closer to the reality of the man. He leaned with his back against the bar, both hands resting on it easily.

She cleared her throat. "My father always spoke about you."

He smiled. "We caused quite a stir, your dad and I. When I was best man at his wedding, my being an enlisted man, him being an officer. Well, that just wasn't done, you know."

"How did you become a general?"

"A Brigadier. They would never have made me a Major General."

"Why?"

He just shook his head. Then, "I remained in the Army. My first promotions came along, I suppose, because I was dumb enough to let people shoot at me and lucky enough not to get hit too often. I had the chance to move over into . . . Well, I assume you know."

"Mrs. Thornberry said something about the Special Air Force?"

Mac laughed, rich and resonant and real. "My dear girl, there are some pubs near some certain military installations where a slip of the tongue such as that could earn you a black eye if you were a man. Special Air Service,

125

more commonly called just the SAS. A rare opportunity surfaced and I became an officer. So here I am, more or less retired."

"Maybe Daddy was murdered."

The corners of Mac's mouth turned down and there were deep depressions in his cheeks, more like canyons than dimples. "A street crime? I know New York City is infamous for that sort of thing. But—"

"But what?"

He shrugged his broad shoulders, thrust one hand into his pocket, and seemed to study his feet for a second. "Your father was the toughest, bravest man I've ever known, in the war or since. I'd hate to think some street thug—"

"No. I think maybe . . . he was deliberately murdered."

"Is that why you came to see me? So I could somehow help you to find his murderer? I'm not a detective, but I do have some friends—"

"No. I mean, yes."

"Death is never easy on the ones left behind, sudden death least of all. And one never becomes used to it. Sometimes, the shock can—"

"Cloud the judgement?"

"Yes."

"My father had quadruple bypass surgery not that long ago. You wouldn't have read about it in the publications you get."

"I didn't know."

She looked at her lap, took the linen napkin in her hands and twisted it. "But he was fully recovered. He watched his diet, walked a lot, swam when he could, did some running. It was like he was a new man. He even quit smoking cigarettes."

Mac just watched her.

"And then I get a call at five in the morning and he's been found dead on the street."

"But it was a heart attack; that's what the papers recounted."

"That's what it was, but there was something wrong. He was so covered in perspiration that his clothes were freezing up when this janitor found him. And his watch, his money, everything was just where it should be. Except for one thing."

"And what was that?"

She pointed to the cabinet on the far side of the rack with the saddle. "One of those."

He turned his head slowly, looked at the cabinet, then turned back and looked at her. "There could be a number of explanations for that, even down to a police officer taking it when the body was recovered."

"I know that." She reached down to her purse, set it in her lap, opened it, took out the legal-sized manila envelope she carried in it. When she looked up, Mac had left the bar and stood over her. His face was expressionless, his brows knit. "I want you to look at some things."

"All right." He sat down near her on the couch. She opened the envelope and played her trump card first, handing him the page razor-bladed out of the Sutton College yearbook, with Dr. William Paul Stein's photograph circled in red grease pencil. He took the page, seemed to study it, his face impassive.

She cleared her throat. "Do you recognize that man?"

"Should I?"

Her heart sank. Her mouth was suddenly dry and she reached for the teacup with the rum in it and drained half the contents. Her voice was trembling now. "My father bumped into him at a football game. And my father was shaken. That same day, we saw him at a restaurant after the game. They got into a row, Daddy and this Dr. Stein. Daddy was behaving almost irrationally. He was saying things about the man being a beast or something. And—" She knew it. Dammit. She was feeling like she was about to cry.

Mac evidently caught that, but he struck her from the first as being a man who was experienced with women. "And you think this man had something to do with your

127

father's death?"

"Yes."

"I had no idea Evan had raised a spy." She looked at him and he was staring right at her. There was no humor in his eyes and the muscles in the skin around them seemed tensed. "And did your father never tell you the real story of what happened in 1945, Dannie?"

"The real story?" It was a stagey response, but the best she could muster. "All I know is that Daddy thought this man, this Dr. Stein, was the same man who'd led the SS unit you and Daddy had that battle with where all the other men in your unit were killed. But that's—"

"Impossible?" His eyebrows rose as he said it and he just looked at her.

"Well, yes, I mean. I even went to talk with this Dr. Stein."

"And, what did he tell you?" There was a look of disapproval in his eyes, but he said nothing to indicate those feelings.

She inhaled, exhaled. "He told me that his uncle was an officer in the SS during the war, and that his parents fled Germany in 1939. He told me that everyone from his family always thought he bore an uncanny resemblance to his father's brother."

"That's a very plausible story, very neat and logical, Dannie."

"I know that. That's what Richard says."

"And who's Richard?" Mac asked her, his voice soft, easy to listen to.

"My, ahh . . ." Her *what?* Fiancé? They'd never really spoken seriously about marriage. Boyfriend? Wasn't she a little old for that? "My lover."

"Ohh. And what else did . . . Richard is it? What else did he say?"

"That all of this was impossible. That I was becoming obsessed. That my father wouldn't have wanted me becoming involved."

Mac looked down at his hands, his eyes smiling, his

128

hands enormous- seeming but gentle-seeming as well. "And what do you think your father would have wanted you to do?"

"I . . ."

He just looked at her.

She tried beginning again. "I don't know. If it was a real heart attack, then I should get on with my life."

"I understand you're a college professor. History, is it?"

"Yes, but I'm really only an assistant professor."

"And what if your father's death was not an accident?"

"What — ?"

"Hypothetically, of course. You were telling me what you thought your father would wish for you to do."

"Well then," she said, looking at Mac, "I guess he'd . . . I know he'd want me to go after the truth."

"You're half right. On one level, he'd indeed have wanted you to pursue the truth. But not at the cost of your own life."

She said, "Can I have that cigarette now?"

"Of course." He started to get up.

"No. I have my own." He lit it for her with his lighter and, as she replaced the pack in her purse, he got up anyway and brought her back an ashtray. As she exhaled smoke, she said, "So what really happened, Brigadier?"

"Mac."

"Mac."

He took up his teacup and raised it in a toast. "To Evan Hardy, and may he forgive me telling you this."

Telling her what? But she raised her teacup, let him clink his against hers, then swallowed down the remainder of its contents, her throat and stomach warm and the flushed feeling returning to her cheeks.

"You must understand, Dannie, that neither your father nor I actually lied about what transpired." He stood up, still talking as he went to the windows off to her left, her eyes following him. It seemed as though he was looking for something out in the driveway. "Going to this Dr. Stein may indeed have been the proper thing to do; but if your father was right, it may have been a tactical error nonetheless."

"Tactical error?" Dannie repeated.

"Yes. What else is in that envelope of yours?"

"More information on Dr. Stein, his official biography and things like that."

"Does it say he was born in Germany around 1910 or so?"

She leaned back, the warm feeling in her cheeks gone, a cold feeling rising from the pit of her stomach and goosebumps moving along her thighs. She drew her knees more tightly together under her skirt. "No. It doesn't say that. He was born in Ohio, and thirty-five years ago."

"Ahh, well then."

"Why was talking to him a tactical error?"

"I said it might have been, that's all. Anything else in that envelope?"

"I have Xeroxed copies of my father's notes. He was working on something before he . . . I have copies."

He came back from the windows, said, "Let me see what you have," took the envelope from her, and started back toward the bar. "Another drink?"

"Yes."

"I'll bring the bottle," he offered. He was reading through the things she'd put in the envelope, reaching the Xeroxed copies of her father's notes at last. She watched his face as he set down the bottle, then sat on the couch beside her. She looked away, watched the burning tip of her cigarette. When he got to the werebeing stuff—she shivered.

"And is Richard reliable?" Mac asked, looking up from her father's notes, setting the packet down on the little table.

"What do you mean?"

"He's a trustworthy sort, that sort of thing?"

"Of course!"

"That's good to hear. Because if your father was right, you could be risking your life, just as he risked his—and lost it."

"Risking my—"

"Hadn't you thought about that? If this Dr. Stein was responsible for the death of your father, ruling out ordinary meanness, it was because your father's knowledge of him posed a threat to him. And, if you pursue matters, you could pose a similar threat."

She bit her lower lip.

He refilled their teacups.

She took a healthy sip of the rum. "You read your father's notes. What do you think, Dannie?"

"I don't know what to think." She stubbed out her cigarette.

"What did you think about the business with werewolves?"

She wished she hadn't extinguished the cigarette. She had no answer to his question, had tried to avoid thinking about it.

"You see, werewolves are exactly what they were."

"What?"

"What really happened," Hugh MacTavish said, standing, walking toward the saddle, turning around and leaning against it, legs crossing. "As I said, we didn't actually lie in our respective reports. We encountered a strong force of SS personnel from the First Panzerdivision Liebstandarte Adolf Hitler. They were apparently under the command of a Standartenführer with bright blond hair and very blue eyes."

She was sipping at her rum and she nearly choked.

"I take it the good Dr. Stein has such eyes and hair?"

"Yes."

"Interesting, but not damning in itself. There was a battle. They lay in wait for the main body of our unit while your father, myself, and a few others went ahead, discovering the trap and springing one of our own. Captain Erskine, the American who was our commander, intended to nominate your father for the Silver Star for his bravery. It should have been your Congressional Medal of honor, instead. But, that never happened.

"Because, that night," Mac continued, starting to pace the room back and forth before the two weapons cases, "your father led a detail of volunteers into the castle into which we were sure the SS Unit had withdrawn. The Gerrys were waiting for us, but not in any way we could possibly have expected."

"I know about that part. There was an ambush and you two escaped, but—"

Mac shook his head, looking at her, then continuing his pacing. "A trap, yes, but not, I'm sure, what you think. Inside the walls of the castle there was a building, set at the exact center, the actual castle. But surrounding this structure was a maze. The maze was a very simple affair, but effective. Its walls were evergreen trees, planted very close together, incredibly dense.

"While within this maze, trying to reach our objective," Mac went on, "one by one we were attacked. I won't go into the details, but the men were dismembered, and brutally so. There were growls, and there was a strange howling. Your father and I tried to get back to the wall. Creatures were there. Not men, at least not in the usual sense, but creatures. They were tall, enormously powerful, covered with coarse hair and they had the feral smell of an animal.

"Your father and I were the only two who made it out of the castle grounds alive," he told her, leaning against the bar now, not looking at her. "But they pursued us. That's how your father's left arm became injured. One of the beasts was right behind us, grabbed at your father. I'd like to say I killed it, but I think I only slowed it up. We made it into the lake, your father's arm damaged beyond repair as it turned out. It was nearly daylight and, by the time we reached the shore near our camp in a defile well away from the castle walls, it was coming on dawn.

"What we saw," he said, turning around abruptly, "was the stuff nightmares are made of, Dannie. Werewolves. They fought as a unit—"

132

"You mean the Nazi units that were left behind to harass—"

"No. Come with me." He beckoned to her with his eyes and she stood up, followed him to the double sliding doors, then across the hallway and through the little living room she'd seen before and to a room on the far side of the living room. There was another set of double doors. He slid these open and reached around inside and flicked on a light switch. It was a library, windows at the front and on the far wall and the rear wall, the room running a third the width and the entire length of the house.

Mac walked to a dictionary stand.

On it was an older, leather-bound Merriam-Webster unabridged. "Look it up."

"What?"

"Look it up. Now."

There was something hard, almost dangerous in his eyes. She turned to the dictionary. She found the word, on page 2904. She read the entry, then looked up at Mac. He gestured toward a bookcase dominating the side wall. "Half the books in there have reference to the same thing, Dannie."

"This is—"

"Crazy? Exactly what the Allied command would have said. Can't you see Monty or Ike getting something like that across his desk? 'Werewolves attack Allied Commando Force.' But that is exactly what happened. The creatures were winning. Your father and I tried to turn the tide. But you couldn't shoot the things and kill them, because bullets only seemed to knock them down for a few seconds and then they were back on their feet, killing again. Their leader was unlike the others. The fur covering the bodies of all the others was dark, brown or black, every shade imaginable, some with streaks of gray. This one's coat was blond. And it had blue eyes, Dannie. Piercing blue, bright like a China plate. Did Dr. Stein have eyes that color?"

"Stop it! I don't want to hear it!" She started to walk away from the dictionary stand but felt his hands on her upper arms, spinning her around. His face was inches from hers now. "I won't listen!"

"Yes, you will!"

She closed her eyes.

She wanted to close her ears.

"Your father and I fought until the ammunition ran out and the rest of our comrades were dead. Then we ran, ran for our lives. It wasn't cowardice. It took me a long time to come to grips with that. We couldn't have stopped them with any weapons we had and all of our unit was dead. So we ran. And the damned things chased us. We went back into the water, and some of them swam after us. We made it to shore again, hid throughout the day, up in trees and buried under piles of rotting leaves, anything to hide our scent. Because that's how they followed after us, sniffing at the air, at the ground, a pack of them, and always the blond was there, their leader, keeping them on our trail.

"But we made it out alive."

She opened her eyes. "The barn where you two drank all that wine," Dannie began.

"We hid there on the third day. It was our first chance to rest. I stole a chicken, killed it, and we ate it raw."

Her stomach heaved and she tried to turn away.

"We were starving, Dannie. You've never had to starve. Pray to God you never do."

She just looked at him. Her hands were going numb, he was grasping her so tightly by the arms.

"When we reached our lines," Mac almost whispered, "we realized that if we told what really happened, we'd both be out of the war for good, locked up somewhere in insane asylums. So we deleted one part—about the were-wolves."

She closed her eyes, her breathing shallow, her stomach churning, her words even, low. "They are a figment of the imagination. They are—"

Mac shook her and she opened her eyes. "They are real, girl. I tried telling myself that, too. And I know your father tried doing the same. But, in the final analysis, it

134

doesn't do any good to lie to anybody, least of all yourself.

"It was years after the war." And he let go of her arms so suddenly she almost fell to her knees. But he'd walked away, was pacing again, and she just stood there trembling, afraid to remain with him, more afraid to be alone. "And I mean years. You would have been in school by then, gone to your first dance in your first grown-up dress. Years. And I went to a film, with a woman of my acquaintance," and his face lit in a smile that was positively boyish, cute.

She just stared at him, listened to him, powerless to do anything else, powerless to make herself stop trembling.

"I'd avoided horror films always."

"So did my father," she said in a croaking whisper.

"But, with this lady, I . . . we went to see the film. It dealt with werewolves. It was really very childish after seeing the real thing, and all the creatures did was attack their victims and knock them down. But I ran out of the theater and made it to the men's room and threw up.

"That evening, afterward . . ." he continued. How had he meant afterward? ". . . I started to read everything I had, from that entry in this American dictionary to books on mythology and — I just didn't have enough. Over the years since, I've tracked down every book and magazine article and every reference possible on the subject. So, you see, I'm a little obsessive myself. More or less of a macabre hobby, I suppose. Or supposed.

"I told myself they died. I told myself that to reopen things after all these years was madness. You see, they're part of the human racial subconscious, if there is that sort of thing, really. There have been medical and psychological studies dealing with similar symptoms, some attributing rare diseases, somatic conditions which manifest characteristics similar to lycanthropy, malfunctions of the pituitary gland, and the like. But there are differences between those who merely exhibit some of the symptoms and true lycanthropes, Dannie."

"Stop this. Please?" She just stood there, thinking that

135

she couldn't move if she tried. "Don't do this to me."

"But it would stretch plausibility beyond any reasonable bounds to suggest that the Nazis somehow recruited an entire unit of lycanthropes, trained them to be effective soldiers and fielded them as an SS group. Yet, if lycanthropes do exist, as I think they do, logic would dictate they'd be solitary individuals, most likely aware of few or no others of their kind, perhaps not even recognizing the true nature of their condition. Yet again, your father and I saw what we saw. The only rational explanation is the irrational one. Working from that, I've arrived at a theory that is more plausible than the myriad that I've rejected."

She heard her own voice asking him, but didn't want to be asking him anything. "What is your theory, Mac?"

He came up to her, gently touched at her elbow, said, "Let's return to the study. More comfortable in there." As he guided her from the room, she was surprised her legs still worked. He must have felt that, because with equal gentleness, he shifted hands at her elbow, his left arm going to her waist, supporting her. "The Nazis inspired almost religious fervor among the true faithful, and had the singular ability to enlist volunteers for nearly anything required." He hit the light switch, plunging the room into darkness, ushered her into the living room, let go of her for the briefest instant, closed the library doors, then was supporting her again as they crossed the living room toward the hall. "But such selfless devotion is not at all atypical for cults centered on personality, Hitler himself in the case of the Nazis. And, coupling this as a given with the extensive range of inhumane medical and pseudoscientific research, the theory is suggested."

She stopped walking, looked at him as they stood before the entrance to the study.

He smiled, his eyebrows shrugging. "It's only a theory, of course. But, what if the Nazis discovered, somewhere in Eastern Europe, say, one such legitimate creature, a true lycanthrope, a man who turned into a wolf for whatever reason. That's immaterial to the theory. But, important to the theory is that the cause of lycanthropy is in some way somatic, or at least what precipitates manifestation of the familiar symptoms."

"And?"

"Well, the legends of lycanthropy appear in cultures all over the world, throughout time."

"This is crazy."

"Hmm." He nodded, seemingly in agreement. They reentered the study and he sat her down in the couch, then went to the bar, taking a cigarette for himself. "What if the Nazis isolated the cause for this phenomenon? What if lycanthropy wasn't an old wives' tale, a legend, a story told to frighten nasty children but a chemical imbalance in the pituitary gland, for example? Or something else, but the pituitary gland, let's say, just for the sake of argument. What if the Nazis, from their captured specimen, were somehow able to duplicate the condition, or at least the manifested symptoms? Then they tested it," he said. He lit his cigarette. "They tested it in the same way they tested any number of crazy and deadly techniques on the prisoners in the death camps.

"And what if," Mac went on, "after the Allied invasion, when Hitler abandoned what modest restraint might have governed his decisions prior to D-Day, a corps of volunteers from among the SS was enlisted? What more logical unit than the Liebstandarte Adolf Hitler, after all, because the unit began as his personal guard? The effect of lycanthropy on someone already highly trained and highly motivated—perhaps even insane—and bent on killing the enemy would be that of creating a nearly invincible fighting man, an entire unit of such men. Especially if the effect could be controlled."

He crossed the room, stood beside the saddle again, flicking ashes into his cupped left palm. "And all of this ties in neatly with the actual events. The actual SS attack was clearly designed to stop the unit of which your father and I were a part. When the castle, where presumably the

137

SS unit was headquartered, was penetrated, they struck. After the war, when the castle was taken over by Allied forces—and I've read the secret reports—nothing was found there except human bones, and only fragments in fireplaces."

"Ohh, God!"

"Consider the blond. If the SS unit which lay in wait for us and was repelled, didn't become the werewolves, then what happened to them? And why was it that the leader of the SS unit had blond hair and so did the leader of the werewolf pack? And, these weren't real wolves, because they could walk just as easily on two feet like men, albeit hunched over, as they could on four feet, like animals."

"But—"

"I told you that ordinary bullets wouldn't kill them. I saw that several times. So did Evan. What if nothing ordinary kills them? What if a side effect that perhaps no one even anticipated was some sort of rapid, spontaneous tissue regeneration? And they never died, never even aged?"

She sipped from her teacup, then drank from it.

"What if Dr. Stein is really the Standartenführer, really the blond wolf? And he's still exactly as he was nearly a half century ago?"

Dannie knotted her hands in her lap. She stared at Hugh MacTavish. "If, ahh—if you are right," Dannie Hardy whispered, "then no matter how they did it, my father's death was murder."

"Yes. And when you visited Dr. Stein, you set yourself up as the next victim."

She shivered.

"But I have no intention of letting that happen."

"A heart attack . . . How—"

"The East Germans were very fond of cynanide gas guns. They fire a stream of the stuff and it's inhaled and the victim appears for all the world to have had a heart attack. Unless it's looked for, it invariably goes unnoticed in an autopsy. More likely, if indeed your father's death was engineered, they merely shackled his arms above his head—"

"There . . . there was a mark, a bruise on his right arm."

"And of course his left arm didn't work to any real degree. They might easily have . . . Hmm." He walked over quickly to the little table, stubbed out his cigarette, brushed the ashes from his left palm, took up the contents of the manila legal envelope again. He set everything down except the yearbook page. "Here's how, I'd wager: Dr. Stein helps out with football and wrestling and track so he'd be intimate with the machinery associated with physical training. Familiarity with such equipment would suggest to a would-be murderer simply taking a man with a known heart condition, shackling him in place so he couldn't fall, and setting him on a treadmill, then gradually but relentlessly increasing the speed and keeping it up and up, merely letting nature take its course."

She couldn't help it anymore. The tears just came and she hurt inside.

Chapter Eleven:

Sleeping Over

Fog was rolling in, just like in British movies. And she could see all sorts of shapes, gray and scary, lurking in the rolling mists like spectres.

Her head leaning against the windowframe because she was too emotionally drained to lift it, she didn't turn around when she said, "What will we do?"

She could see his reflection superimposed over the glass as he paced about the room behind her. "Going to the police is out of the question, isn't it? Werewolf stories are hardly more palatable to the authorities today than they were in 1945. Going to Professor Stein may imply that he's having you followed, if he is guilty and hasn't killed you already. So you may have led him or his henchmen here." The landscape seen through the window matched perfectly what she was hearing. This was a nightmare. "The thing to do now, of course, is to neutralize the enemy's potential for realizing what objectives he may have while at the same time finding the answers we require in order to strike back."

"If they can't die—"

"I didn't say they can't die, Dannie. I said conventional bullets, regardless of the caliber, seem to have no effect beyond knocking down one of the creatures and hence slowing its progress."

"But, the thing about not aging, never—"

"They may age so slowly it is imperceptible to us, or they may indeed not age at all. But if we accept as a given that at least some of the werewolf legends are at least partially based on fact, then perhaps some of the remedies suggested in those legends might prove efficacious."

She laughed, sniffing back tears. "Silver bullets?"

"Who knows."

"With all this cowboy stuff, do you have silver bullets?"

"I have no silver bullets, I'm afraid. But you're safer with me than you would be out there, Dannie." She wheeled away from the window and looked at him. "Unless dining out, I usually make my own dinner. If you're willing to gamble your digestive system—"

"You mean—"

Mac smiled. "Remember, I'm not only an officer and, to that degree, a gentleman, but I was also your father's friend."

"All of my things are at the hotel."

"You should call and say you won't be returning this evening, but don't say why. And, as to things, well . . . I may be a sixty-one-year-old bachelor, but that doesn't equate to being exactly sexually inactive."

It was an autonomic response. Dannie sucked in her breath.

He smiled more broadly. "I don't know whether I should feel complimented or offended, but I merely meant that there are new toothbrushes in the drawer in the lavatory and there's a footlocker in the closet in the spare room with some odds and ends of women's apparel left behind in my bedroom over the years. I noticed that Mrs. O'Shea recently had the contents of the footlocker cleaned and repacked everything. Perhaps she has second sight, but I'm more inclined to think it was compulsory neatness on her part; it's her passion. And, besides," and he gave her the full shot of the smile now, "the fog rolling up from the lowlands is already thick enough to cut with a knife."

She studied his eyes for a moment longer, then said,

"Yes, I'll stay. But if you're going to put me up for the night, the least I can do is make dinner."

It wasn't the full shot of his smile; she got that now "I was actually hoping you'd say that. My own cooking's terribly boring. Shall I get some wine from the cellar once you've settled on what to prepare?"

"That would be nice."

He ushered her through the house, pointing out this and that, each room seeming to have a character all its own, as if none of the rooms was really related to any of the others. Mac had, it seemed, eclectic tastes.

The kitchen was large, more like the rambling country kitchens of New England or the South than anything she'd expected to find in an English country home. But, of course, not many of those were epically proportioned two-story log cabins, either.

She surveyed the very American-looking freezer, noting that there was a microwave so thawing wouldn't be a problem. She wasn't the world's greatest cook, either, she'd always thought, but she could make a healthy, tasty meal from next to nothing on upward. All those years of cooking for her father as soon as she was old enough had helped there. "What were you planning on?" Dannie asked Mac.

"I was going to make spaghetti."

"Hmm." She walked herself through the kitchen, exploring the well-stocked shelves, found the pantry, examined its contents as well.

When she was completed, Mac leaned toward her across the counter and asked, "And, the verdict?"

"Pot roast with fresh vegetables and large flat noodles. Some chocolate pudding for dessert."

"I've a very satisfactory burgundy, not resiny-tasting at all, hearty yet with hardly any aftertaste."

"Wonderful. Now go do what retired Brigadiers do and let me cook."

He nodded, gave her a mock salute and, as he sauntered off, called over his shoulder, "If you need any help—"

"I know, I'm out of luck."

She liked him.

She really liked him.

And for a few moments, fear of the consequences arising from what he'd told her was just an abstraction at the edge of her consciousness, brushed away by the ordinary things of living . . .

Dannie Hardy knew her father would have liked the western room, but she liked this one—the dining room—best of all. The walls were of stone, and there was a massive hearth set in the outside wall, the front and rear walls set with high, darkly ornate stained-glass windows running nearly to the height of the cathedral ceiling. Clearly, the room consumed both floors of the house.

She imagined that in the morning, or the afternoon at sunset, the windows would be beautiful.

Massive wooden doors dominated the remaining wall. At the center of the room was the table. It was long, sized for two dozen or more men to eat and of rough-hewn wood. When Mac held her high-backed wooden chair and she'd remarked about the table as she'd sat down, he said almost dismissively that he couldn't find a table that really suited him, so he had made it himself some years ago.

Over the hearth were crossed swords, stout-bladed with protective guards that looked as if they would swath even the largest hand. He must have noticed her looking at them. "They're called Claymores, the traditional blade of the Highland fighting man. The one crossed under is an original that has been in my family for quite a few generations. The one crossed over is a duplicate of it, made of all modern materials. It's probably as stout as the original, more powerful, though no better. With it—the

143

replica—I've cleaved down a small tree, hacked through a chain, and once even shaved."

"Cut through a chain?" Dannie said incredulously, a forkful of her pot roast stopped halfway to her mouth.

"Your dinner is delicious, by the way. Anytime you wish to cook for me, there'll be no need to stand on ceremony. Rest assured of that. And, as to the chain part, you see I met a man who liked insane projects some years ago—a Scot much like myself, as a matter of fact—and we discussed the Claymore long and hard over several drinks. We arrived at the conclusion that to make something every bit as fine in these days of modern materials, a dramatic step would be needed. I helped him a bit and we crafted the basic blade from the same material used in hydraulic drill bits. Hard to give it a proper edge, to be sure, but amazingly durable."

"That's—"

"Different?"

"Yes."

She sipped at her wine. He asked, "How do you like it? The wine, I mean. Agreeable?"

"Very." She hesitated, then asked the question which had nagged at her from the first time he'd opened his mouth. "Daddy always said you were a wild young boy and—well, how did you?"

"How did I what?"

"You're one of the most well roundedly cultured men I've ever met."

Mac smiled. "Well, thank you very much, Dannie, but you're overly kind, I'm sure. You mean . . ." and he put down his wine, raised his fork, but didn't eat. "You mean, why is it that I don't sound like the dustman in *My Fair Lady* when I speak?"

Her cheeks flushed. She half nodded.

"I was always a voracious reader, ever since I was old enough to understand the printed word. I realized early on, however, that the primary problem for me was that I didn't sound that way . . . educated. Your father no doubt mentioned Forrestal, the young lieutenant in our unit?"

"A little. I don't think he liked him much, but he thought that he was brave."

"Accurate on both counts. Forrestal was brave, and he was also a twit. But, you see, he didn't sound like a twit. I, on the other hand, was well read, well informed (or, I certainly tried to be), yet I sounded like the ambassador from the Great Unwashed. There was this girl," and Mac smiled broadly, his eyes positively lighting up. "She was from a really solid middle class family in Manchester, and she'd been schooled in London for some years. We were keeping company." What a sweet way of putting it, Dannie thought. "She was the first person in whom I confided about my problem. She was a teacher, and I suppose the challenge was irresistible." Or Mac was, she thought. "So she undertook to help me."

"What . . ?" And she shut up; it was none of her business to know what had happened between them. Something romantic, she bet.

"She married another teacher several years later," Mac told her, as if somehow reading her mind.

She just looked at Mac.

He laughed. "I married, too. A few years after you were born. I was already an officer by then, that the result of a quirk of fate, really. Margo, the woman who helped me to sound educated, even came to the wedding. Her husband was the master of his own school by then and they were very prosperous. The girl I married, her name was Elizabeth, my wife. I've found it best to get awkward things out of the way as soon as possible. So, yes, Elizabeth was very beautiful. Hair that was almost black and eyes that were very blue and skin that was white and smooth. She looked as fragile as an exquisite doll in the window of some expensive shop. And, she was also very frail. I didn't know it, but her doctor had advised her against ever having a baby. But she desperately wanted one." Mac set down his fork, stared toward the crossed Claymores over the fireplace. "I accommodated. She died in childbirth and the baby—a son—died with her. I buried them both and decided never to marry again. That was twenty-two years ago and I kept my promise to myself. And it was a promise made for very practical reasons. There could never be another woman like her."

Dannie Hardy wanted to change the subject. She sipped at her wine. "Why did you have that sword made?"

"What?"

"The special sword, the one that is so strong. Why did you—"

"Why?" The faraway look that had been in his eyes when he'd first looked back from the fireplace was gone now. "Mainly as a lark, but also as a means of someday proving a theory I developed over the years. If I ever work it out, somehow I think you'll be in a position to know if my hypothesis proved out."

What did that mean? Dannie thought. She was about to ask when he interrupted her thoughts. "I'll get us another bottle of wine, if you'd like."

"Ohh, I don't know."

"Then a liqueur?"

"Maybe a glass of Scotch."

"It is whiskey, my dear. Not 'Scotch,' but I'll chart that off to your American upbringing." He smiled good-naturedly and stood up, going to the little bar at the far end of the room.

It was about the same size as the one in the cowboy room. And, as in the cowboy room, there was a piano near it. She laughed a little, imagining this place turned into a nightclub with piano bar. She was finished with her plate. "Do you play?"

"Most wouldn't call it that."

146

"Daddy tried lessons with me, but I was terrible at it."

"Perhaps you were too young and there was no motivation. Come here."

She stood up, set her napkin beside her plate, crossed the room. He had a glass in each hand, set them on the bar and came round to the piano, a baby grand, ornate-looking like the one in the cowboy room. He opened the lid on the bench before it and extracted a piece of sheet music. She expected that he would sit down and play something.; Instead, he almost ordered, "You sit there. Make certain you're comfortable."

She felt flushed again. "Really. I can't play."

"Find middle C."

She put a finger on the white key.

"Ohh, that's very good." He spread the sheet music before her. "Try this." The sheet music was for "Long, Long Ago" and she remembered struggling with it as a child. "Fingering is very important." And, he would touch a finger and then expect her to hit the note under it, occasionally gently rearranging her hands, taking her through half the song. "See?" Mac said at last. "You can play. I've generally found that when one sets one's mind to almost anything, it can be accomplished if one perseveres. There are a few exceptions. Pray as hard as I might, I couldn't save Elizabeth. Nor can I rewrite the past, perhaps having prevented what happened to your father, Dannie."

She looked up at him. He smiled. "Now let's have our chocolate pudding and a glass of whiskey and then you should go off to bed. You'll find quite a number of fascinating books in the library."

Bed? She wasn't really tired, but maybe he was. Despite his looking so hale and hearty, he was, after all, an older man. She stood up, took one of the glasses of Scotch, and walked across the room beside him, toward the table. "I thought I might read up on those legends you were talking about. Maybe there's one book with an overview that I might—"

"Such books make for bad dreams. I speak from experience." And then, as if dismissing any further discussion of such books, as he held her chair for her, Mac said, "I'll be up rather late. Some reading I must catch up on. Nothing to do with this, of course. And tomorrow, we'll need to form a plan of action." He took his seat near her. "A good night's rest is the thing now, and that will fortify us for things ahead."

She poured a few drops of cream onto her pudding and began to eat, feeling somehow she was about to be trundled off to bed while the big people did something important . . .

There was an ample supply of towels and she wrapped one around her hair to keep it free of the spray from the shower head while she soaked her body under the hot water. Of the two nightgowns she'd found in the footlocker, only one of them was something she'd feel decent in, the other so transparent as to be obscene. Just what kind of women did Mac have up to his home, anyway?

But that was none of her business. Dannie smiled, wondering what old Mrs. O'Shea thought about the Brigadier's nocturnal pursuits.

The nightgown — long and white and not only expensive-looking but very pretty in a lacy sort of way — hung on a hanger just inside the door. She was counting on the steam from the shower getting the wrinkles out from how it had been folded.

She shut off the water, toweling herself dry, taking the towel from her hair, slipping the gown over her head. It came to the tops of her feet. Slippers there were none, but Mac had evidently slipped into the spare bedroom while she'd been preparing dinner, leaving her a pair of heavy boot socks and a man's bathrobe. She left the bathroom, put on the socks and the robe — it was deep

148

maroon and heavy and came almost to her ankles—and looked at herself in the full-length mirror.

She laughed.

Still laughing, Dannie returned to the bathroom and began to wash out her bra, panties, and stockings so they'd be clean and dry for tomorrow. And it was while she was hanging up her things to dry that Dannie Hardy remembered she'd forgotten to put away the pot roast.

She'd taken off the man's bathrobe because she'd kept getting the cuffs wet. And they were wet still. But over the back of a rocking chair beside the window there was a Scottish plaid woolen lap robe. It was roughly square in shape and she took it, folded it into a triangle, and pulled it round her shoulders. She left her room, padding along the second-floor hallway in her oversized green bootsocks. At the head of the stairs she paused, listening. But there was no sound of movement. Perhaps Mac had fallen asleep.

She started down the stairs and toward the kitchen. It was easy to understand why her father had liked Mac so much, loved him in a brotherly way. Mac's personality was magnetic and his proclivity for taking charge wasn't abrasive, just something that was simultaneously natural and very comforting. Dannie Hardy could understand the reason why there was a collection of panties, a couple of bras, some stockings, and even a garter belt in that footlocker where she'd found the two nightgowns: Mac was irresistible, age not a negative factor at all.

As she found the British equivalent of Tupperware in an appropriate size to house remains of the small pot roast, she tried to imagine Mac at the age he'd been when he'd saved her father's life. Would she have liked him as much, all rough at the edges, the "ambassador of the Great Unwashed?"

Somehow, she thought she would have.

The roast away, a quick check of the stove that all the burners were off, and she shut off the kitchen lights, then

149

started back for the stairs.

But she passed the dining room and, when she did, she peaked through the crack between the doors.

What were the grown-ups doing?

She saw Mac, feet propped up on a hassock, asleep in one of the two big chairs near the fire, a book resting over his stomach as though he'd just fallen asleep. She felt herself smiling. She stepped through the opening between the doors, just to make sure that he was all right, no intention of going close enough to accidentally awaken him.

A pace inside the doorway, she saw the top of the small table beside the chair. The lamp was still lit and, in its glow, there was a longish, heavy-looking object.

She shrank back. It was some kind of a handgun.

Mac wasn't catching up on his reading by staying down here. He was guarding her. And that was at once sweet and terrifying . . .

Dannie Hardy rolled over and she opened her eyes. Her knees were locked so tightly together her legs hurt. Her hands, balled into fists and clutching her pillow, hurt as well.

She lay there, staring through the blackness of the spare bedroom darkness toward the gray of the fog outside her window. And she remembered what had awakened her, could see it again when she closed her eyes; so, she kept her eyes open.

A dream.

The creatures Mac had described to her had been coming after her. She'd been out in the fog, wearing the nightgown she wore and nothing else, running, seeing herself and at once inside herself like only one can experience a double reality in a dream. She ran, hearing heavy breathing behind her, the sound of running feet. And she turned around and there was Dr. Stein and he

150

laughed at her and reached for her and caught hold of her gown. She went to pull away but couldn't. She grabbed at his hand and, as she touched it, it changed, the fingers lengthening, hair growing across the back of the hand at a phenomenal rate, fingernails growing long and twisted and yellow and then it wasn't even a hand anymore.

She screamed for her father. Stein laughed and the laugh became a howl. Behind him, running out of the fog, a sword in each hand, she saw Mac, but it was as if Mac were running through wet cement or something, or maybe a swamp, because his steps never carried him closer to her.

The howl became louder, and in her dream she felt Stein's breath on her flesh and she screamed. And she shouted for her father again and, when she looked, Mac wasn't Mac anymore but her father, and his swords were gone and he was holding that little shiny handgun and he was running toward her but never getting closer.

She shouted to him to stop running before he had a heart attack and he told her not to worry, but his voice didn't sound right.

And there was a drumming sound.

She realized, as it got louder and louder, that it was the sound of her father's heart.

What awakened her was the sound of the drumming just stopping.

She sat up, shivering, pulling the covers up under her chin and back over her shoulders.

What if Hugh MacTavish, for all his charm, were insane? Her father had never told her about any of this werewolf stuff. Her father had been reading about the things before his death, but . . . She told herself she wasn't sleeping alone in the same house as a lunatic.

And she had a thought that scared her to death, making her shake violently. She remembered the old movies she'd sneaked seeing at girlfriends' houses. The werewolf

151

attacked the nice guy—that was what had happened to Lon Chaney, Jr.—and the nice guy, even though he didn't want to, became a werewolf. What if Mac had been bitten?

But, her father was all right—had been. And how could Mac have been an officer in the British Army all those years if every time there was a full moon he changed into some beast that ripped out people's throats?

Dannie threw back the covers, put her feet down on the floor, and sucked in her breath so loudly it was almost a scream.

The floor was like ice to her.

She found the socks draped over the bed's footboard and pulled them on, stood up, took the lap robe shawl from the back of the rocking chair by the window and wrapped it around her. As she looked out the window, she paused. Fog blanketed the ground, but above, oddly, the sky was clear and, predictably, as there would have to have been this night, there was a full moon.

She almost laughed.

But, out of the fog, there came a howl. It was like the one in her nightmare; or was this still a nightmare?

Chapter Twelve:

Just A Little Silver

Mac was no longer asleep in his chair. The book lay on the table and the handgun that had been there was gone.

Her left hand clutched the ends of the blanket shawl and her right hand shook.

Dannie Hardy sucked in her breath, threw back her shoulders, and walked toward the fireplace, taking up one of the pokers. There was something else odd about the room. She didn't know what.

Maybe it was the fire, all burnt out except for red-hot coals at the center that glowed.

Maybe that was it.

She started out of the room, clutching the poker in her right hand upright, before her, ready to lash out at anything that came after her. And where was Mac?

The hallway. Maybe Mac was in the cowboy room. She started across the small living room or sitting room into the main hall, still clutching the poker, her fingers numbing around it. She wanted to call out to him.

The doors to the cowboy room were open. She peered past them into the blackness, seeing nothing

She turned, thinking maybe she should look upstairs.

Something grabbed her, catching the hand with the poker in it in fingers as tight as a vise, at the same instant a second hand covering her mouth and nose and most of her face and she was pulled off her feet, into the blackness of the cowboy room, against something hard and warm, her shawl fallen away, her bare shoulders and back pressed against something that was scratchy She tried to scream. Warm breath against her neck and cheek. "Dannie, its me, Mac. Keep quiet."

The hand eased away from her mouth and for a split second she thought of screaming anyway. But Mac wouldn't hurt her; somehow, she knew that.

She breathed instead.

His hand eased on her right hand, which held the poker. Her gown was bunched up and her left leg brushed against something cold and hard. And Dannie remembered what was odd about the dining room. One of the two swords was gone from over the fireplace, the one that was made out of the same kind of steel used in big drills. The poker was taken out of her fingers. She just stood there, trembling. "Take this. Heavier than you think." She took it as he pressed it—the handle of the sword—into her right hand. She realized the tip of the blade had to be pointing into the floor.

She felt the blanket shawl being put up around her shoulders and her left hand clutched it to her chest. "You have a gun," Dannie whispered.

"I have several guns," he whispered back out of the darkness.

"Aren't modern guns illegal in England?"

"Most guns are illegal in England, but members of Parliament can't be expected to be both popular and bright, can they?" She didn't know what to say to that. He didn't give her a chance, though. "Bring the sword if you can, and be quiet and stay close."

She raised the sword a little and realized she'd need both hands because her right hand was already trembling with the weight. With both hands, then, she held the shawl around her and the sword in front of her, point down. He was moving, and she moved with him. "Where are we going?"

"To the kitchen to turn on the emergency generator. They'll knock out the power in a moment and, in darkness, they'll have a decided advantage."

But it was dark already and the light had still been on in the dining room and who were they?

As she dogged Mac's footsteps through the hallway, across the living room, she glanced into the dining room. Only the fire glowed there now. She started to speak, heard Mac say, "Shh."

They were in the kitchen, moving around the small table. She bumped the sword into a chair or something and there was a dull clang. "Shh!" Mac hissed again.

There was the sound of a door opening. The broom closet? There was a click. Then she heard something like a cough, not human but like a car's engine and there was a faint hum. "Wind power. Store the electricity in batteries," Mac whispered. "Now, hold on to that sword and stay with me. There's a master light switch located just around the kitchen door that will illuminate the entire dining room and hallway. There's one just like it beside the front door. Come on."

"Who—"

"Who do you think?"

"Jesus."

"Not Him."

"Do you have silver bullets in your gun?"

"As a matter of fact," Mac whispered, "and no disrespect to The Lone Ranger, silver bullets are too soft to be effective on a target and they won't feed reliably in a semi-automatic pistol." She didn't really understand what he was talking about. Feed? "I had these specially made; they're standard 180-grain jacketed hollowpoint .44 Magnums, but the cavity is filled with silver, ninety-nine percent fine. Expensive as anything."

She started to ask if his gun was like Dirty Harry's in the movies, but shut up instead.

They were back beside the kitchen doorway.

Why was he waiting to turn on the lights?

She started to ask him.

The howling sound came again, louder, then echoing all around them in the darkness, but not echoing, repeating.

She almost dropped the sword. Maybe, if they turned on the lights, whatever was outside would go away. What was outside? Those things?

"Mac?"

"Be afraid, but control yourself and you'll control your fear, be able to use it to stay alive."

"Be afraid" he'd told her? She was glad she was doing the right thing without being told, because she was more scared than she'd ever been in her life. She wanted to reach out into the darkness and touch his sleeve or something, but then she'd drop the sword.

She felt his hand on her shoulder and, in the split second before she realized it was his hand, almost screamed. She closed her eyes, inhaled, tried to control her body's trembling. Couldn't.

"Give me the sword. I have a place for it. You take this back." He took the sword from her hands and her arms trembled and she felt him stick the fireplace poker back into her fingers. Hadn't he left it in the cowboy room? She guessed not. She heard the sound of the metal of the sword scraping against something. Dannie huddled closer to Mac. "Be ready. And, whatever you do, stay close to me, Dannie."

She had no intention of doing otherwise.

A howling sound, louder than before. The sound of glass shattering and she almost screamed. Mac rasped, "Good girl. Squint your eyes against the light now!" She already had her eyes closed.

There was a flash of light and everything on the other side of her eyelids was hot pink for a second then orange, and she felt Mac moving beside her and opened her eyes too wide, squinting them against the brightness. The sound of glass shattering from behind her. She turned her head.

There was a roar right next to her louder than anything she'd ever heard in her life and her ears rang with it as a tongue of orange flame flicked past her cheek and something huge fell through the window and sprawled across

156

the kitchen sink and she finally screamed her lungs out. The thing was covered with hair all over and— There was a horrible scream from the thing and a crackling sound and the beast seemed to be shriveling up. "Mac!"

Mac dragged her around. "Stay with me, Dannie!" His voice sounded like it was coming to her through a seashell, her ears ringing still. She turned her head, saw Mac sprint through the doorway and she followed him, holding the fireplace poker in her right hand, her shawl clutched against her chest in her left.

The doors to the cowboy room, half open, smashed in splinters into the hallway, chunks of wood flying in all directions. Two more of the things, taller than men, almost upright, but hunched, massive shoulders bowed forward and long, apelike arms poised for balance. Above the shoulders, a head, not human. "Mac!"

She shrank back. Mac wheeled toward them, the pistol in his hand—big and black—firing, then firing again and again. One of the things shrieked and fell back. It was already starting to change.

This was a nightmare.

Dannie Hardy's mind rejected anything else.

The second one bounded toward them on all fours now, leaping through the air, a mouth like an impossibly huge dog held open wide with fangs more like those of a bear in a natural history museum, glinting white with saliva. Mac turned toward it, fired his big gun, the beast dropping to the floor, the couch overturning, a hole in the wall behind it. The beast was up, lunged for her.

"Mac!"

Dannie realized that her right hand and arm were drawing back and she lashed out at the thing's head with the fireplace poker as it came for her. Her right foot caught in the hem of her gown and she stumbled, the creature crashing into the wall in front of which a split second before she had stood.

It was up. She edged back into the corner formed by the wall and an overstuffed chair, the creature's mouth open

157

wide, hands that weren't hands reaching for her, eyes that weren't human but were hard and evil and deepset and black.

More glass breaking.

More shots.

A click. She'd seen enough westerns. Mac was out of bullets.

Dannie stabbed the poker toward the beast's eyes. One massive arm swung, a hairy paw with long claws at its end swatting the poker out of her grip, her wrist stinging with the impact.

She tried to pull back, but the wall was behind her and there was no place to go.

The creature's shoulders tensed and she knew it was going to jump onto her and kill her and— "Protect your eyes!" Mac's voice, her left arm already up in front of her face to protect her, she could just see Mac, his face a cruel mask, the lines in his cheeks drawn deeper than she had seen them before, arms over his head, the sword in his hands, swinging it, contact.

Dannie screamed.

The blade of Mac's sword seemed to hesitate, then continue on its path, a spray of blood and fur and flesh all around her, her eyes squinted against it, the beast's head severing from its shoulders.

She saw Mac reaching down to her with his left hand. His gun was stuck into his pants in front of his abdomen and the sword was in his right hand.

Mac dragged her to her feet and she collapsed against him.

"Sorry it took a moment. A fourth one came in through the window under the stairs. But they wouldn't have sent just four; that would be insulting. Come on. To the dining room! We're safer there."

"They . . ." She gasped for words, for breath. She looked down at the floor. Right beside her foot there was a head, becoming more human looking as she stared at it, unable to take her eyes away.

But then Mac was dragging her, around the corner of the living room and into his medieval dining room. He let go of her hand, doing something with his gun, the bloodied sword under his arm. Lights went on in the dining room and she stared, standing there, waiting for him to tell her to move. He held his gun in his left hand, his sword in his right. "Come on!"

"The . . . What about . . . Should we close the doors?"

"Just means they'll break them. Hurry. Toward the hearth there."

She caught up her nightgown, the shawl gone, her body shivering with cold, ran after him. He set down his pistol, reached up and handed her the second sword. This one felt lighter when she took it in her hands. "Here. The Claymore works better than a poker. Stay behind me."

She wanted to tell him something. She shook her head. His beautiful stained-glass windows. Did he think they were too high? "Windows?" That was all she could manage.

"Plexiglas on the outside, just like the great cathedrals of Europe."

She huddled beside him, finally just sinking to her knees, the sword still in her hands but the blade clattering against the floor.

Mac's eyes were on the door. She looked up at him. "What's happening?" Dannie pleaded.

"I learned to find hope in adversity years ago, Dannie. Until a moment ago when I got three of them with silver-tipped bullets and cut the other one's head off, I wasn't even certain they could be killed."

Dannie tried to swallow, gasped the words, "Your theory about the sword."

"Aye. Rest easy. We'll make it through!"

There was more of the howling now and, outside, beyond the open doors connecting the dining room to the hall, she could hear the sounds of things breaking, things being thrown about. "Got them miffed a bit, Dannie. They'll be coming. Best stand up now."

She nodded, tried to say something, couldn't.

And, as she looked toward the door, she saw them, four of them, huddled close together, some standing on their hind legs like men, some on all fours, one of them pawing the floor, howls coming from them.

The one closest to the center rose up, its right arm or what should have been an arm clawing the air.

Dannie looked at Mac.

"Be brave, girl!"

Tears welled up in her eyes, spilled hot across her cheeks.

She clutched the handle of the sword in both her hands, standing as close to Mac as she could.

And something stranger than anything else she'd experienced this night happened to her then: her hands suddenly stopped trembling. Mac expected her to be brave, stood shoulder to shoulder with her against this enemy, just like he'd done with her father almost five decades ago. "Talk to me, Mac."

"What about?"

"Anything. Please?"

"All right. All right. I was very pleased with the performance of my gun. The Israelis make some fine weapons."

"It looks like a very nice gun."

"Ohh, indeed it is."

"What kind of gun is it?"

"A Desert Eagle .44 magnum semi-automatic with a six-inch barrel and an eight-round magazine."

"It's loud."

"Yes."

"Daddy's gun was smaller."

"Really. Most handguns are. Be ready, Dannie."

The creature at the center reared back and howled. The others breathed heavily, tensed, readied themselves. "I'm ready."

"They'll move in four different directions. Remember, they still think like men but have the added advantage of a wolf's natural cunning."

"Right."

The one at the center howled again.

There was a sound like a thunderclap by the window toward the far end of the dining room and she looked toward it. The stained-glass window was intact. The Plexiglas was working.

There was a howl from outside.

There was the sound of something breaking from beyond the dining-room doors and in the next instant a fifth one of the beasts had joined the other four. Like nearly all the rest, it was covered with hair, like the rest the hair generally dark, ranging from brown through black. Only one of the beasts had a coat which was nearly blond, and that more a sandy brown.

So none of these was Dr. Stein.

If somehow she survived this and Mac survived this, the thing still would not be over. Not until—

The central one of the creatures howled, a different pitch, as if the howling were a form of communication, like speech. And then all five of the creatures were in motion simultaneously.

Mac fired his pistol, then fired it again and again and again. One of the creatures began tumbling in midair as it leapt toward her, fell, the table vibrating under its weight, the body skidding across its length, changing even as she watched, becoming human again. Another of the things dropped to the floor a mere yard from her as she raised her sword, ready to hack at the thing.

And still another sprang toward Mac this time, coming at him from the left, Mac taking a step back, shielding her, thrusting his sword outward, impaling the beast through the chest. There was a loud whimpering sound like a dog being hurt and the beast fell, rolled across the floor, yelping.

A fourth creature came out of nowhere, Mac shoving her back, the creature's fur brushing against her bare arm as she screamed, hacked at it, the creature shrieking pain. Mac fired, a bullet splitting through its skull, the creature

161

rolling away, beginning to change.

And Dannie was thrown back, her sword clattering to the floor, skidding away from her as the fifth beast impacted against Mac's body. Mac's right fist still clenched the pistol and he beat at the thing with the gun like a club, the creature's left arm backhanding Mac across the chest, sending him flying into the hearth, hot coals spraying up around him as the beast wheeled toward her. Dannie crawled back across the floor, reaching for her fallen sword. The beast lunged toward her, forelegs or arms or whatever they were extended to full length, its body airborne. She screamed as her hand found the sword, but too late she knew.

There was the thunderous roar of a pistol shot, and then again and her ears rang with it as she looked toward the thing and it fell, hitting the floor, sliding across it, the transformation to human form starting already.

Mac was standing beside the fireplace, his sweater smoldering, his face black and dirty, the gun in his hand, but the gun odd-looking, as if some of the parts were on it wrong.

And, behind him, the beast Mac had impaled with his own sword rose from the floor, pushing outward with its huge front paws against the blade, coming from its chest now, dripping blood, a sound, human and animal at once and neither and both and terrifying, issuing from its black leathery lips, drool pink and frothing oozing from between its glistening fangs. The creature was on its hind legs, swayed, steadied itself.

Mac turned and it leapt toward him.

"Mac!"

The beast was on him, Mac punching at it with his fists, the flurry of blows having no effect it seemed. But then, as the creature's jaws went to snap over Mac's face, Mac's right fist punched upward, catching the beast in the throat, the creature rolling away. Mac struggled up to one knee. The creature was up on all fours, spittle drooling from its fangs.

162

And then it vaulted toward Mac, its powerful hind legs merely seeming to flex and then the beast was sailing through the air toward Mac. Mac let go with his left fist, obviously stunning the creature, its head snapping back, but not deterring the creature. And Mac was down, the beast upon him once again, jaws snapping for Mac's neck, Mac's hands on the creature's throat, struggling with the thing, trying to keep the jaws of the hideous thing from snapping over his jugular.

Dannie was standing up before she realized it, the sword Mac had given her and she had lost now in both her hands. Images flashed through her mind: as a little girl, Daddy letting her try the axe at the little cabin they'd rented in the Adirondacks, Arnold Schwarzenegger in one of his barbarian movies, a look of unremitting wild rage in his eyes, and Mac, the sword in his hands, swinging, cutting off the head of the beast that had been about to kill her.

Dannie hauled the sword up from the floor in a wide, ragged arc from behind her right shoulder, smashing it downward with all the force of her body behind it, falling hard to her knees on the hard cold floor as she brought the sword down over the creature's back and through fur and flesh and felt the blade catch in bone and there was a shriek, the beast spinning away from Mac, the sword torn from Dannie's hands.

The sword flew across the room, impaling itself into the floor, vibrating. The beast stood on all fours, howled, and the howl became an almost human scream as the creature sagged in the middle and collapsed, the transformation—Dannie screamed—starting. The muzzle of a wolf began to shrink, the crackling sound again as bone seemed to visibly shrink before her eyes and matted hair withdrew into pink human skin and hunched shoulders raised, only to slump forward, blood a bright red wash across a back contorting, twisting, a man writhing for an agonizingly long few seconds, then still, dead on the floor.

Dannie knelt there, staring at it. A human face, hand-

163

some, the muscles still twitching, the jaw still retracting, the eyes big and brown and staring blindly, dead.

Mac was on his knees beside her.

She looked at him, afraid to ask.

Mac smiled at her. "It didn't bite me. And close only counts in horseshoes, hand grenades and nuclear explosions."

She started to speak.

There was a voice, human, from out in the hall. "Brigadier!"

"You're as brave as your father, and that's not a compliment I give lightly," Mac told her, doing something with his gun, a loud clicking noise as he pointed it toward the doorway.

"I was scared to death."

"All the more reason to commend your bravery," Mac said hoarsely.

Mac's clothes and hands and face were covered with blood and when she looked down at herself, the lacy white nightgown was streaked and splotched with red and brown. Her arms seemed covered with it—blood.

She began to tremble.

Mac was up, in a kind of half crouch as the shout came again. "Brigadier?" Mac's gun was pointed toward the doorway. And, into the opening, stepped a man. He was slightly built, little more than her own height, shaggy blond hair spilling across his forehead. He had very serious-looking dark eyes, the eyes all the more intense-looking because his complexion was so fair and yet well tanned. "This is a bloody mess, Brigadier!"

Mac leaned forward, lowering his head, and for an instant Dannie was afraid he really had been seriously injured, or worse. But then she realized he was laughing, and the laughter seemed to grow inside him as it came and, his voice barely under control, Mac said, "Dannie Hardy. David Mallory, master of understatement."

Chapter Thirteen:

Allies

Dannie Hardy showered for what seemed like forever; but, no shower or no amount of soap could ever be enough to wash away the blood of the—she said the word in the shower under the steamy hot spray and shivered: "Werewolves." When she closed her eyes, she could still see the way they had changed right in front of her like that, and the metamorphosis was somehow more frightening than the threat of death their attack had placed her under.

Seeing their bodies change.

She shook her head, trying to clear her mind of the image and she couldn't.

After they had all stood around for a few moments and done nothing but stare at one another and breathe (except that Mac had reloaded his pistol and commented that the load he just put in it was the last eight of his silver-tipped bullets), David Mallory asked, "Are these the ones you were worried about, Brigadier?"

Mac had merely nodded, then said, "We'll have to move the bodies. Then board up the windows they broke. If nothing else, we'd freeze overnight without that. In the garage there's some wood we can use."

"Shouldn't we call—" she started to say "—the police?" She didn't, in a flash of realization knowing that would have been insane. There were nine dead bodies in the house, all naked as jaybirds (had she ever seen a jaybird?) and some of the bodies were decapitated and the floor was slick and sticky with blood. One didn't just call the police under circumstances like that. What she wouldn't have done for a Polaroid camera just then when the beasts—when they still looked like beasts instead of men—had attacked, and then photos of them as they changed back. That would prove to the most skeptical person . . . what? That a group of Nazis in their seventies and eighties could change themselves into werewolves, but when you killed them they automatically changed back?

She hadn't mentioned police at all.

Mac said, "There's a spot in the storage barn out behind the house that'll do nicely for them with any luck; they'll have compatriots still outside who'll whisk the bodies away." And then his eyebrows danced up and he smiled. "I can hope, can't I?"

Mac told her to get to the shower immediately. She refused, saying she wouldn't unless he would be in the house. David Mallory had refrained from laughing, but he'd smiled a bit as he put his gun away under his very British-looking trenchcoat. So, instead, while the men hauled off the bodies and even the pieces of bodies, she screwed up her nerve, found a scrubbrush and some pails and set to work on hands and knees to wash away some of the bloodstains. The men finished their grisly work and joined her, telling bad but clean jokes to relieve the tension, whistling even, all the while cheerfully obliterating evidence that would prove vital to a police investigation. Dannie realized they were all certainly mad by now.

As the men finished boarding up the windows, each of them still armed, she brewed a pot of coffee (but she couldn't help thinking of the beast which had thrown itself through the kitchen window only to be shot with a silver bullet and fall dead in the sink). And, by then, she was freezing cold to the point of her feet being numb and goosebumps so large and profuse on her arms and legs that she felt covered with them.

Then came the shower.

And now, as she stepped out, dried herself, wrapped a towel around her hair, and pulled on the borrowed robe—the nightgown was ruined, of course—she wondered just what would be coming next . . .

Wearing a pair of Mac's sweatpants (too long and cinched so tightly at her waist that she could tie the cord in the back) and a sweater (miles too big, drooping down at one shoulder or the other and the sleeves bunched like huge muscles above her elbows) Dannie Hardy sat on the living-room couch. What was broken was swept up or put away, but she avoided looking at the overstuffed chair near the kitchen door because that was where one of the things had almost killed her and Mac had chopped its head off.

A Claymore was on the floor beside her feet, just in case, and that didn't help, either, even though the blood had been cleaned off.

David Mallory, the skinny blond man not much bigger than she, sat in a chair opposite her, a cup of coffee from the second pot brewed that morning in his hand. This pot was brewed by Mac; he made better coffee than she did, Dannie conceded.

Mac was still absent from the room, upstairs showering, she surmised. David Mallory cleared his throat and she looked at him over the rim of her coffee cup. "I'm a friend, I suppose you might say, a friend of the Brigadier."

Dannie nodded, looked back into her coffee.

She heard whistling and looked up again, Mac doing a rendition of "The Ballad of Paladin" as he came down the stairs, a gunbelt of some kind hanging from his shoulder and the other sword in his left hand. For the first time, as she looked over at David Mallory, she noticed or

167

thought she noticed, a bulge under his brown tweed sportcoat. That would be his gun. What was he doing here? And, what good was a gun anyway unless David Mallory had silver bullets, too.

Mac stopped whistling, just stood between them. He was dressed in black sweatpants, a gray sweatshirt, and track shoes, his bald pate gleamingly bright from the shower. He set the gunbelt down at his feet and the sword beside it as he took a cigarette from David Mallory's pack on the table, then took David Mallory's windlighter to light it with.

"Do you want your cartridges back, Brigadier?"

"No, David. Keep the four I gave you for now."

"Yes, sir."

That answered her question about silver bullets anyway. As if resuming a conversation dropped seconds before, Mac said, "David here was one of the best pupils I ever had."

"Your student?"

"In the SAS, although he wasn't a member. The people David used to work for and occasionally still does sent him through, as is their habit at times."

"Who?"

Mac smiled. "In England, we have the Official Secrets Act, which covers a multitude of socially awkward explanations. For the last two years . . ." Mac went on, exhaling smoke, "David's been rather heavily involved in private security work for multinational corporations. I'd suspected there'd be trouble possibly and asked David to come round and help out. He's a good man in a fight, and better still, he has marvelously keen eyesight, so I reasoned he was probably the only man who could see well enough to come up from London in all this fog." He stood behind David Mallory now, clapping the younger man stoutly on the shoulder. For an instant, Dannie thought David Mallory would blush. "And besides, David owns a .44 Magnum revolver, which will use the same

168

ammunition as my Desert Eagle, so he could use the silver bullets, too."

"How many are left?" Dannie asked, feeling practical for asking.

"Exactly eight," David Mallory told her in his slightly congested-sounding voice. "Four in the cylinder of my Smith and Wesson and four in the magazine of the Brigadier's pistol."

"And, what then?" Dannie asked.

"I think we're relatively safe for the rest of the night," Mac said, coming around from behind David's chair, taking the end of the couch opposite her, crossing his long legs. He looked at his watch, one of those big black-faced stainless-steel watches divers wear. "At least for what's left of the night."

"Just what happened?" David Mallory asked.

"Didn't you tell him?" Mac said, turning to her.

"I thought you'd told him," Dannie said honestly.

Mac stubbed out his cigarette. "Werewolves, my dear fellow. Werewolves."

"Werewolves," David Mallory repeated, then started to laugh . . .

The sun was nearly risen. She could see that through the only window visible from where she sat which hadn't been smashed out during the night's attack. And she was happy for the coming sunlight. Weren't werewolves supposed to be all right during the daytime? Wasn't a full moon what started them?

Mac was talking to David, including her, but she didn't understand half of what was being said anyway even though she tried to listen. "It seems clear that even major caliber cartridges loaded with silver-impregnated bullets aren't an instant guarantee of bringing down one of the creatures before it can kill. The one I stopped through the kitchen window was a head shot. I got another one in the dining room with a bullet to the head. The silver must be some sort of poison to them and would seemingly have to get through the bloodstream to a vital organ before death ensues. But, when combined with a major caliber, if the bullet is placed right, the effect is to drop the beast and, before it can move again, the silver takes its effect. The Claymores, on the other hand," and he gestured toward the one David had lain across his knees, "is instant when the head is severed from the body or the spinal cord is severed, as Dannie proved when she got that one off me in the dining room."

Dannie shivered, hunching her shoulders in the borrowed sweater.

"Do you think, Brigadier, that there's some more rational explanation—"

"For this?" Mac asked, his voice rising almost into laughter. "Hardly, although I wish there were."

"So, then, if I shoot one of these things with an ordinary round of ammunition, or stab it merely, the damage automatically heals?"

"It would seem so, but correspondingly, when the head is lopped off or the spine is severed, the damage is irreversible. I wonder if a limb lost while in the werewolf state would regenerate?"

"Interesting theory." David nodded, lighting a cigarette.

Dannie stood up, fists balled beside her thighs. "Both of you stop this! I don't care if we cut one in half and we have two of them! What the hell are we going to do?"

Neither man answered her and she just stood there, looking at them, feeling her cheeks start to flush and feeling more foolish by the minute.

At last, Mac spoke. "We have to regroup, Dannie. Another attack in the force of the one we endured would be unsurvivable, even with the able assistance of David here. As soon as it's fully light, we'll reconnoiter, see if the bodies are still there or have been spirited away, look

for any signs of their clothing or by what means they arrived here, things like that. Then we'll get on with the
business of striking back. Sit down."

She sat down. "They can't touch us now that the sun is
up, can they?"

And then Dannie remembered the story Mac had told
her yesterday—it seemed a much longer time ago than
that—about how the beasts attacked the men of the Allied commando unit when the sun was rising and pursued her father and Mac through the daylight hours.

And then David Mallory said something which she
found oddly comforting from a man who up until a few
hours ago was a total stranger to her. "They'll never get
you, Dr. Hardy, not while there's a breath left in the
Brigadier's body or mine. I pledge that."

She looked at David Mallory. He smiled for the first
time.

Mac, suddenly closer beside her, an arm around her
shoulders, said, "He's right, Dannie. They'll never get
you while we're alive."

She sat there, listening to them talk some more. She
smoked a cigarette she took from her purse. She heard
talk about using a camera to photograph the dead men if
the bodies were still there, so some sort of identifications
could be worked up. It all sounded perfectly normal, perfectly everyday. Fingerprints. Passports and international
drivers' licenses and car rental receipts and things like
that. It was the stuff she read about in mystery novels,
heard about in movies. David had been some sort of spy,
she assumed. And Mac had been his teacher? She remembered her father giving her talks when she was a
teenager about watching out for what sort of crowd she
fell in with.

And she wondered now, what kind of crowd had she
fallen in with indeed?

Chapter Fourteen:

Detectives

"It seems clear that the creatures can control the metamorphosis from man to beast," Mac announced.

David nodded, but said, "There has to be some other explanation besides werewolfery in the twentieth century."

"When you think of it, David, please let me know," Mac announced, then took another Polaroid and handed it to her while it developed.

She stared at the ever-more-clear photograph of a severed human head set on top of a bale of hay and she wanted very badly just to barf.

Evidently Mac had all the photographs he needed, taking two distinct sets of each body. As soon as the photos were completely dry, she removed them from the bale of hay on which she'd placed them and put one of each into two separately marked envelopes. It was typical, whenever there was at least one man and a woman, the woman got stuck with the clerical work or the cooking or whatever and, although it galled her sometimes, she accepted it as the way things worked in life. While she dried, sorted, and packaged Polaroid photos, David Mallory performed a task she didn't envy at all, however. Using a small kit from his car, he fingerprinted each of the dead men and, using an odd-looking camera, he photographed the insides of their mouths. After photographing for dental records, then fingerprinting, he took hair samples from each corpse, building a small envelope file for each of the dead men.

172

They left David to finish his mildly disgusting work and began to search the woods along both sides of the road.

Dannie felt proud of herself, because she found the car first, about midway between the house and where the ranch road met the public road.

The car was a Jaguar, much like the one she had rented and, she theorized, rented as well. Mac quietly said, "I hope you're correct, Dannie." The car was locked. Mac told her that likely the keys had been left under a rock somewhere or hanging from a tree branch, since werewolf skin didn't have any pockets. "Too bad werewolves aren't marsupials, eh?" She didn't like his humor this morning but assumed he was making the attempt to keep up her spirits so said nothing about it.

On the backseat were five neatly folded piles of men's clothing. "Why only five?"

Mac looked at her and smiled. "Because there are four piles folded similarly on the backseat of the Mercedes I was just about to mention I'd found parked on the other side of the road. It was locked, too." He seemed to be studying the vehicle, bending over, peering inside. Then he straightened himself up and took her by the hand, gesturing with his head toward the ranch road. She went with him.

Once on the road, they moved up and down along it, finally stopping just as David Mallory drove up. His car was pretty, she thought, a white Saab 900 Turbo convertible, the convertible top and what she could see of the upholstery chocolate brown, but the top up against the brisk morning wind. "Find them?" David asked, getting out.

"One car over there, a Mercedes, a Jaguar right through those trees and over that bracken." And Mac stooped slightly, gesturing, David's eyes following. Dannie could see it, too.

"You're thinking the vehicle might be rigged with plas-

173

tique or something against tampering," David said matter-of-factly.

"Ye-ss," Mac drawled. He took the big black pistol from the holster at his right side. "I'm changing magazines, Dannie," he told her, as if guessing at her perplexity. "No sense wasting the few cartridges we have remaining to us that have silver-filled cavities in the bullets. I'm going to shoot through the window of the Jaguar on the driver's side, and with any luck the bullet will exit through the passenger-side window. If there's a booby trap of any sort rigged to go off when the car is opened, this will set it off."

"The Brigadier hopes," Mallory interjected.

Mac looked at David and smiled. "Yes. The Brigadier hopes." His gun reloaded with one of the things from a pouch on his belt, he advised, "Close your ears." Then Mac bent over the hood of David Mallory's Saab, resting his elbows there.

"Watch the paint job, will you, Brigadier?"

"I'm more concerned about the brass hitting the windscreen, but as you will." Mac's right first finger moved and she squinted her eyes and held her fingers more tightly against her ears, but could still hear the shot.

The glass on one side of the Jaguar seemed to implode, while the glass on the other side exploded outward. But, evidently, there was no bomb.

Together, they started toward the car . . .

"Very professional," David announced, everything from the inside of the Jaguar spread out on its hood. "Everything that has a label was purchased from mass merchandisers; no driver's licenses, no credit cards, nothing."

"Won't the license plate tell us something?" Dannie suggested.

"Indeed it will, and we'll get the names of these men as well. If they're Americans sent here by Stein, or local

174

men in Stein's employ, either way we'll know. But all of that will take time, time in which Stein can launch another attack against us. He'll use greater care this time, and he'll succeed if we let him come to us. So we have to take the attack to him instead."

"Why do I think I won't like this?" David Mallory asked.

Mac clapped David on the shoulder. "David, David. These creatures must be stopped, of that we're all agreed. And evidently Dr. William Stein feels that we must be stopped, too. Which means, of course, that confrontation is inevitable until one side or the other achieves victory. Anyway, I understand that the Christmas season in what our American friends call New England is a time of rare beauty. There's a thrill in store for us all, lad."

"America? We're going to America?"

"Yes, the land of opportunity, where the streets are paved with gold — and hopefully there's enough silver just lying about for us to fabricate some ammunition with which to kill these bloody beasts before they kill us."

Chapter Fifteen:

Almost Christmas
Not Far From Connecticut

They'd flown separately, for security reasons as both Mac and David Mallory had explained to her, waiting for each other's arrival in as much crowd as could be found at Kennedy ("There's safety in a crowd if you use it properly," Mallory had told her) and then taking separate taxicabs all the way from Kennedy to LaGuardia, once there taking another taxicab to the train station, killing better than two hours there and taking a commuter train to Highcliffe. Her Jaguar was parked at the station just as she'd left it except for the addition of seven or eight inches of snow on the roof and, after David had inspected it ("Could have planted explosives.") mercifully gotten out of the web of public transportation.

But any thought of returning to her apartment was ruled out, just as earlier thoughts of going to her father's apartment, which she still owned, were dismissed ("They'll be looking for you, for all of us; and, although they wouldn't think we'd be obvious enough to go to either flat, they would have to have both locations under surveillance," Mac had said.).

They drove, instead, to the nearest mass merchandiser which sold sporting goods.

Inside, using cash rather than credit cards, Mac and David purchased stout-looking hunting knives, flashlights, batteries, all sort of accessories. And they had her purchase two shotguns. "You know what you want. What do I know about a shotgun?"

"Neither of us is an American citizen; to purchase a firearm, aside from its being illegal, would be impossible since I.D. would be required," Mac explained patiently.

"What about silver bullets?"

"The shotguns won't stop them, but with heavy slug loads, we'll at least be able to slow them down a bit."

She merely nodded, doing as she was told, paying with cash, buying two identical-looking guns called Remington 870 Wingmaster Pumps and virtually cleaning the clerk out of ammunition called 12-gauge slug loads.

Burdened with their new possessions, they returned to the Jaguar, David sitting in the backseat inspecting the equipment they had purchased and loading one of the shotguns. Mac told her, "I need a telephone." By now, automatonlike, she didn't even question, merely found the nearest convenience store and parked while Mac went off through the freshly falling snow and started using the telephone.

David said barely a word to her while Mac was gone—which was a considerable amount of time—and she turned on the radio, drifting from easy-listening stations through sixties oldies tunes through classical. "There. Rachmaninoff. I love Rachmaninoff," David told her.

"I hope you'll be very happy together," Dannie snapped back but left the station alone.

After about twenty minutes, Mac returned. "Well children," he smiled, getting into the car and pulling off his blue knit stocking cap (he looked like one of the Greek fishermen she'd seen as a child on one of her trips to Europe with her father) "there is positive word. We have the equipment we'll need—at least for the initial stages—coming to us. And we'll also have our information. But, that's all tomorrow. And, as I make it, about a hundred miles from here near Hartford. So, we'll find a place to spend the night."

"My apartment?"

"Hardly," Mac said dismissively . . .

When Dannie Hardy awoke, she felt more embarrassed than she ever had in her life — except for the time in high school when she'd been wearing a brand-new straight skirt and the back seam totally ripped out. This time, however, the source of her embarrassment was considerably higher along her anatomy: her head. It was resting against David Mallory's shoulder.

"Hello."

She looked up at him, sat bolt upright, then tugged her skirt down and just stared straight ahead.

There was a yawn from the backseat of the Jaguar and she heard Mac say, "Time to get rolling and have some breakfast."

She wanted to urinate, very badly, but there weren't any facilities in the clearing to the side of the road where they'd pulled off for the night and she felt grubby enough from sleeping in her clothes without starting out the day with wet thighs. Where there would be breakfast, there would be a bathroom. She forced her concentration off her kidneys, turned down the passenger-side visor and worked at restoring her hair and her makeup.

They'd driven through to about thirty miles outside of Hartford, found an old farm road that would have been more accessible with a Jeep than a Jaguar and Mac had gotten behind the wheel, driven them in, branches scraping across the coachwork all the way. Mac assured her that her car's wax job would protect the paint.

After a few bounces on the undercarriage, he stopped. For about an hour, as snow piled up on the windshield and she became progressively colder, they discussed what lay ahead of them. Mac eventually switched to the backseat, saying something about old bones and muscles needing to stretch out. David Mallory came forward, volunteered for the more confined position behind the wheel. Soon conversation ended, both of the men drifting off easily to sleep, it seemed. But, correspondingly, it seemed to her that she took forever dozing off. And her dreams were haunted by giant, hairy, spectral shapes with blood-dripping fangs coming at her out of the woods.

And, one of them, its fur was blond.

When Mac volunteered to drive them out, she was mildly surprised the car wasn't bogged down so hopelessly in the night's snowfall that it couldn't move. Once they'd slipped and slid and stalled their way to the main road, it took another ten minutes before finding a roadside place to eat.

The ladies' room wasn't too bad and, after doing what she had to do, she found a dry spot on the sink to set her purse and tried again to fix her hair, wanting desperately to be able to wash it but knowing that would have to wait.

The smell of breakfast when she'd walked into the diner with Mac and David Mallory had been enough to make her feel like throwing up. All that was missing, she told herself, would be having her period a couple of weeks early . . .

"They're gonna have my ass, Mac."

Hugh MacTavish studied Dominic Centafari for a moment, smiled, and told him, "I'm sorry to disappoint you, Dom, but I don't think anyone really wants your ass."

Centafari was short, stocky, and muscular, reminding Mac oddly of Captain Erskine, the American who'd led their unit into battle against the SS unit in 1945. "Were you ever a boxer, Dom?"

"A little, in college."

Mac nodded. Captain Erskine had boxed, and though neither man had boxer's scars on the face, the build and even the way the eyes moved were consistent with other pugilists MacTavish had met.

Centafari made a motion with his head toward the mud-splattered light-blue Ford sedan in which he and another man whom Mac had never met had driven into the shopping center parking lot. It was too early in the morning for more than a few cars to be there, employees, most likely, MacTavish theorized. Mac looked back at the Jaguar, Dannie behind the wheel, Mallory beside her. "Stay here. I won't be more than a moment."

Mallory nodded, Dannie just looking exasperated. It was hard on her, MacTavish knew, but she was a good soldier no matter how unused to the drill.

MacTavish fell in behind Centafari, the man slowing, letting Mac catch up. "What the hell you need this shit for?"

"By shit, do you mean the weapons or the papers?"

"Hell. Both."

"Well, the papers are to facilitate our movement, of course, make us appear less conspicuous. The weapons are in case we inadvertently become conspicuous."

"You must have a lot of pull with Admiral Helsberg."

Mac grunted something noncommittal. He'd never met Admiral Helsberg but knew his reputation. Helsberg, as interim director of covert operations planning for the American Central Intelligence Agency, was Dominic Centafari's immediate superior. But MacTavish had spoken with Helsberg's superior, Stanley Becker. Becker's name, let alone the agency for which Becker was the chief planning officer, if recognizable at all to Dominic Centafari, would be shrouded in mystery.

But Becker pulled the strings, strings Hugh MacTavish desperately needed tugged when he'd started his telephone calling from that pay phone outside the convenience store. After purchasing their immediate needs for getting through the night should it come to violence that soon, the real preparations needed tending to.

They stopped beside the trunk of the blue car, Centafari's apparent partner, a tall, very muscular-looking young black man whom Centafari didn't bother introducing, hung back by the driver's side door. "Just don't get caught with this shit," Centafari warned, opening the trunk and taking out a briefcase. The briefcase made the meeting in the parking lot look like some sort of American television drug deal, MacTavish thought. But he took the briefcase anyway. "You do, there's gonna be a lot of explaining."

"Which shit, Dom? The fake paperwork in the case or the weapons?"

"Agh," and Centafari hunched his shoulders deeper into his coat and just shook his head. "The keys are in there, too. Leave the Jaguar and we'll get it taken care of."

"Don't trash the lady's car, Dom. It's a nice car."

"We got a place."

MacTavish nodded, wondering if Dom's American gangster facade was really that, or genuine. He'd met the fellow when Dom and seventeen other men from CIA's Covert Operations Division had come to the UK to train with British Secret Intelligence, as was occasionally done, each learning from the other. MacTavish, on the other hand, had been in Scotland to teach—principally, how to kill people quietly and efficiently and, of late, without the risk of infection when an artery was preremptorily opened.

Killing used to be so much simpler, Mac thought.

"Okay, the other stuff's in the car, just like you ordered. You know how hard it is to get hold of a Chevy Suburban with the big engine in it at this time of year?" Mac didn't, but he waited a moment and Dominic Centafari told him. "The last year's models are all sold out and the new models are all special orders, so they're spoken for."

"I'm sure it was pure hell, Dom. That's why I'm so pleased you were sent with it, because if anyone could get me what I needed in this country, I just knew you could." Likely, Centafari had had nothing at all to do

181

with getting the documents and the equipment, including the car, but there was no harm making the chap feel important.

Dominic Centafari shrugged his burly shoulders, grinned, said, "Hell, Mac, what are friends for, huh?" MacTavish offered his hand. Dom took it. "I was asked to find out when we know what's going on?"

MacTavish assumed that Becker had given CIA the impression, but only that, that he—MacTavish—was Stateside on official business for Her Majesty's Government. There seemed to be no logical reason to alter that now. "As soon as I've got it organized, Dom. This is big, and I won't be able to pull it off, even if I wished to, without your people coming in."

"Terrs?"

Terrorists? "In a manner of speaking, the worst kind. But I can't say anything else. Need to know and all. Except this. Your people will be kept on top of the situation." And then, still clasping Dom's hand, looking quickly about them, MacTavish said in a low whisper, "It's a job that's been brewing up for a long time. Originally, your people and mine were involved with it. That's the reason for the American girl with us."

"She one of our people?"

"I can't tell you who she works for but you'd recognize the name." Hugh MacTavish had learned, years ago as an enlisted man in the Special Air Service, and even before that in the Commandos, that being left in the dark only bred suspicion. But a little tidbit of information, however genuine or not, made those involved in the lower echelons of an operation, or even at its periphery, feel included, feel satisfied. And, besides, Highcliffe was a well-known institution of higher learning, so he wasn't actually lying when saying that Dom had likely heard of it.

"We'll be waitin', Mac."

"Thanks, Dom." And he released the man's hand, nodded to the black chap standing beside the driver's side, then walked back toward the Jaguar.

Chapter Sixteen:

Girding For Battle

"Gee, Sis, whaddya pack for? A trip to Europe?"

Dannie just glared at David while she held the door for them as they carried in the luggage from the new car. Hugh MacTavish found the whole thing rather amusing. He set down two of the lighter weight cases, David Mallory insisting on the heavier ones out of deference to age. There was an interesting relationship developing between Dannie Hardy and David Mallory, as would have been obvious to anyone; but, as to its nature he was uncertain and preferred to not even hazard a guess.

MacTavish started back toward the car, rubbing the palms of his gloveless hands together for warmth. Fresh snow squeaked softly under his shoes, was moist-tasting on his lips. The Suburban—he'd given no color preference—was actually quite pleasing to the eye, a deep battleship-gray on the roof, bonnet, and the upper portion of the sides and rear where the snow wasn't covering it, then a gleaming midnight-blue below that, the blue well splotched with salt and mud stains. The most important item of its appearance, however, identified its origin as Ontario, Canada.

The Suburban, what an American Special Forces officer had once called a "cowboy Cadillac," was equipped more or less identically to the one garaged at his home, except for the absence of some specially built hiding places that this Suburban would be perfectly adequate without. He brushed snow off the lock, powered down the rear window again, then reached inside and pulled up on the tailgate release, then swung the tailgate down.

MacTavish reached into the back and took two more suitcases, this time two of the heavy ones. He was stronger than David Mallory anyway, regardless of the father-son age difference. "I can take those . . ." And David added "—Dad" rather lamely.

"That's all right, Son. I have them." And Mac felt his face seam with a grin as he looked at young Mallory. "But you can take Daddy's keys and close the car, if you'd like."

David Mallory shot him a deadly stare, then started to laugh as he took the keys. They'd registered as Hugo McNally and family, daughter Delilah and son Donald, taking adjoining rooms at the Holiday Inn sixty miles from Sutton College. Not the world's best deception but good enough to buy a little more time.

"Your dead friend's daughter—I don't think she likes me," David said, his voice hushed to a whisper.

"She's under considerable pressure; I don't think she's ever had people coming after her to murder her before."

"And of course we're old hands at that, aren't we?"

"Some of us older than others."

David closed and locked the car and then fell in beside him as Mac started the hike across the snow-packed parking lot toward their rooms. MacTavish had wanted a spot he could back into and drive out of quickly with a good head of steam if needed. So he'd parked for practicality rather than convenience.

"Say, Dad . . ." David Mallory began as they trudged back through the snow toward the door Dannie still held open. "How about a coupla pizzas?"

"Great idea, Donald! Why don't you find the nearest place which delivers." On his few trips to America, always too spur of the moment or too secret (usually both) for him to look up Dannie's father, he'd discovered that delivery pizza, rather than bread, was the true staff of life . . .

The television worked. She was almost sorry that it did, not so much because she didn't like the movie—she liked it quite a bit, really—but because watching this man so physically dissimilar to her father yet in other ways so much like him sitting glued to a horse opera reminded her that her father was dead. And that still made her want to cry. It was a Chuck Norris movie, which she'd seen before (with her father, and at least three times), Norris playing a modern-day Texas Ranger.

When the pizza man knocked at the door, Dannie immediately got up to answer it, taking the money out of her skirt pocket. "Wait, Sis!" It was David Mallory ordering her around again and he was getting on her nerves with this "Sis" crap he persisted in. She looked back at him and he was disappearing into the adjoining room with the shotgun he'd kept beside him while he and Mac watched the movie. "Now, go."

She went to the door, looked through the peephole, saw the Domino's uniform and the thermal pack for the pizzas and opened up. The man made some remark about the weather, she paid him, gave him a tip, thanked him when he said to enjoy her pizzas. Dannie closed the door behind him.

She looked at the television screen. Chuck Norris seemed in terrible trouble, but she was confident enough that he'd survive that she sat down and started eating . . .

"Two of the men were Sutton College alumni," Mac said.

"Surprise, surprise!" David said, but emotionlessly, his voice back to that irritating low-key monotone again.

"Two of the others are from Hambricke. I gather that's some sort of technical school near Sutton?"

"About two miles away, Mac," Dannie supplied, nibbling at a piece of pizza crust. "Sutton lets Hambricke use some campus facilities."

"The gymnasium, I bet." Mac nodded.

"What about the other five?" David asked.

"Either British nationals or they entered the country illegally. So, nothing yet," Mac told them. He twisted the top off a bottle of Michelob for her as she reached for it, without even waiting for her to try herself—so what, she usually couldn't do it—and handed it to her. "And nothing physiologically unusual in the autopsy reports, either. Not yet, anyway. They're doing complete blood workups and tissue sample things, but who knows." He chewed on a piece of pizza.

After they'd gotten safely set in their rooms, Mac working his way through the television's cable channels and David Mallory searching the telephone book for a source of pizza, she'd gone into the adjoining room, closed the door behind her but not locked it, stripped and showered for a very long time. She changed into a comfortable gray skirt and matching pullover and her slippers, her hair barely dry but semi-presentable. Mac would understand, and David—who cared?

But David was nowhere in evidence. "Beer run," Mac told her matter-of-factly, without her even asking.

She looked over Mac's shoulder for a while, advised him, "This is a terrific fight scene coming up."

"If I had ten men who could fight like that, I could have invaded the Falklands all by myself."

"Were you there?"

"Yes." He said nothing more then.

After a while, she went back to her room, finished drying her hair, put on a little lipstick and a pair of white cotton anklets because her feet were cold, then rejoined Mac. David had already returned, was dialing for the delivery pizza.

Mac had opened one of the suitcases—one of the heavy ones—as soon as they'd entered the rooms and closed the doors. It was the same case he'd opened when he'd first unlocked the car Mac's friends had provided for them. There was a gun in it, big and black and identical-seeming to the one he'd used in England.

He watched the movie while they waited for the pizza,

then afterward, while they ate, he kept the gun beside him.

It was on the bed next to him now as he sat, cross-legged, sipping at a beer. "With this definite link to Sutton College and this Hambricke institution, the evidence that Stein is our man is even heavier. I am not prepared to say for certain that all of those men who attacked us are part of the original unit from 1945, but almost certainly that is at least partially the case."

"What if they don't live forever? What if Stein is the original leader's son or something?" Dannie asked.

"I suppose that's possible, but somehow I don't think so."

"Why are they here, for God's sake?" David asked. "I mean, if they are all that powerful—"

"Then what?" Mac said, swallowing some beer.

"Then, well . . . they must be up to something besides waiting around to avenge themselves on the only two survivors of a battle that took place almost a half-century ago."

"Forty-five years, to be precise. And I agree. And, even if revenge were the motive—and that's hardly justifiable since they won, actually—why go after Dannie when they already got her father? On the off chance she'd be able to prove something—what? Any evidence of what originally happened to turn ordinary humans into creatures that can become werewolves is lost or buried in some unopened Nazi file. Stein and his people had to be worried that Dannie's potential for interference, however minor, could somehow upset their apple cart. The question is, what's in the cart that's so important?"

She wanted to scream, except that wouldn't have done any good at all.

"And here's the kicker." Mac smiled, rolling his beer bottle between the palms of his hands. "Five out of the nine bodies had subtle but detectable scars from plastic surgery, right where an SS number would have been tattooed." And he pointed to the location on his arm. "Right there. We have to go to Sutton, meet in the open with this William

Stein, while at the same time we attempt in secret to discover how the transformation is initiated, and what we can do to stop whatever it is Stein and his SS men are planning. Only when we have irrefutable evidence can we get some help, and nothing from regularly constituted authority, of course, because that would be admitting that such things as werewolves existed, which is something neither the American Government nor Her Majesty's Government would ever do. It will have to be from the clandestine agencies if we're to get any help at all."

She wanted to ask a question, felt almost as if she should raise her hand. She sat cross-legged at the head of the bed, legs and feet hidden under her clothes. She cleared her throat. Both men sat toward the foot of the bed, Mac in a chair, David on the edge of the bed itself, what remained of the second pizza in the center of the bed between them. She cleared her throat again and Mac looked at her. It sounded stupid, and Dannie regretted saying it as she said it, but the words were already coming. "They just wait for a full moon, like the other night, don't they?"

David stared at her, as if he knew something she didn't, but she didn't think that he did.

Mac, his voice low, filled with almost fatherly indulgence, said to her, "Dannie, you see, after I had that experience at that movie theater, seeing that werewolf movie, and realized that the only way to rid myself of the ghosts I carried around in me was to understand them better, one of the first misconceptions I dismissed was that business about the full moon. It seems that in some cases of werebeast transformations, the moon indeed does play a part, perhaps its gravitational pull, much as a woman's menstrual cycle follows lunar cycles. But a full moon isn't always necessary, in fact may not be necessary at all, to trigger the transformation from man to beast."

She nodded, not knowing anything to say, feeling like a freshman sitting in by some horrible mistake at a graduate seminar in celestial mechanics or particle physics. No syllabus she'd ever seen had offered a course in werebeasts and, if it had, she wouldn't have taken it . . .

There were no more lectures about lycanthrophy and, despite the fact that on one level she needed to know more and knew that she did, on another level she was, for the moment at least, happier in her ignorance.

Instead, the topic of discussion moved to another area with which she was totally unfamiliar: weapons.

Mac and David Mallory opened the cases Mac's friends had left for them in the car. Outside of movies and television and the like, she'd never seen so many things associated with violence. But she forced herself to ask questions. "What's that?"

She knew what it was—the big black gun like the one Mac had used at his house when the werewolves attacked, but she didn't remember what it was called.

"A .44 Magnum Desert Eagle. The trouble is for all of these guns, we don't have silver to tip the projectiles. Yet. And, I didn't dare ask for ammunition to be made up for me that way, because my associates would have thought that I was crazy. Tomorrow, silver is the first order of business."

"How will—"

"I'll show you." And Mac opened another of the cases on the bed beside him, this one quite heavy-seeming, too. Inside the case were tools of various sizes, some of them looking like pliers, some of them looking like molds, hollow on the inside. As she stared at the contents of this first case, she heard movement beside her and turned her attention toward it. David was opening another of the cases. There were cannisters, the markings on them revealing them to be gunpowder. "We'll melt down our own silver— ninety-nine-percent fine—and remanufacture the bullets supplied me in these containers." And he pointed to the contents of the first case. "Then we'll manufacture our own ammunition, powder, primers, and that sort of thing.

These are only simple tools, so the volume won't be high, but for our purposes it should be adequate."

In another of the cases, there was a revolver, something very professional and deadly-looking about it. David Mallory took it into his hands. "That gun David has," Mac went on, "is a Smith and Wesson revolver, stainless steel, in the same exact caliber as my semi-automatic pistol. You see, my handgun fires revolver ammunition even though it's a semi-automatic. At any event, it was hard to come by — David's gun. Mine is a standard production item. David's tastes are a little more exotic. See the way the grip is rounded?"

It didn't have pretty wooden handles like her father's little gun had had, these black and rubbery-looking instead. "I see."

"They don't come from the factory that way, so my friends had to look up a gunsmith or pull it out of some existing service."

"This is pretty well-fired-in," David said noncommittally. He was inspecting the gun in some detail, then did something which momentarily shocked her. He put the gun up beside his ear, the fingers of his left hand touching at the gun delicately while his right hand pulled the trigger. "Action job. Sounds good, nice and smooth, too."

"Let me," Mac said, taking it from David, putting it to his ear, evidently listening to something inside the gun, then holding the gun up to the light, looking at it. "The cylinder, Dannie, that's the part where the cartridges go, should be free of wobble and there should be similar amounts of light visible on top and on the bottom and, most importantly, even."

She didn't have any idea what he was talking about.

"Witness protection shotguns," David announced, taking two stubby-looking versions of the guns she'd bought for them from another case. "A little handier to carry around." David shrugged out of the gray cardigan sweater he wore and pulled on a black holster of some kind, a shoulder holster but not anything like the kind James Bond wore sometimes in the movies. After a moment, he had one of the two shotguns suspended from the holster under his right armpit. He snapped the shotgun from the holster, the gun making a clicking sound as he pointed it toward the wall. "Yes, this'll do nicely."

There were knives, too, very long ones that looked like something Arnold Schwarzenegger would have used in a movie. She knew that somehow she was supposed to take some comfort from all of this elaborate preparation for defense, but she didn't . . .

The next morning was bright and the sun shone and the sky was clear and blue and, somehow, Dannie Hardy felt better. Mac was already gone when she awakened, off to "buy some silver," David told her. She showered, wanting a run but not wanting to be alone, instead just standing under the hot water a while longer than usual. She brushed her teeth, her hair still wrapped in a towel, then laid out her things. Since she didn't know what kind of a day to expect, she tried to dress for all contingencies: A midcalf-length brown wool tweed skirt with pockets, the pair of boots with the more sensible heels, a comfortable long-sleeved cotton blouse with a collar that tied into a bow and camel-colored cardigan sweater she could button for warmth, leave open, or remove altogether. She dried, brushed and arranged her hair—up—and rejoined David to go down to the hotel restaurant for breakfast.

As she entered the room, her fur coat over her arm and her purse slung from her shoulder, David was already dressed, of course. But, instead of sitting there impatiently, he seemed to be studying the contents of a large manila envelope; various pieces of paperwork spilled out on one of the beds. "What is it?" "It" was probably none of her business, but she asked anyway.

"I'm memorizing a background."

"A background?"

"Yes, you see I'm to be infiltrating Sutton College as a

fellow named David Huston, a Canadian, working on my second master's degree, specializing in Europe during the Nazi period, something else the Brigadier arranged for me. Too close to the end of the term, of course, but I'll audit a few classes, among them one of Dr. Stein's, supposedly in preparation for the new term."

"How did Mac's friends here set something up like that so quickly?"

"Not his friends here, but friends of both the Brigadier and myself back in London accomplished it, probably through friends of theirs in Canada."

"But isn't it going to look suspicious, David? I mean, what if you were identified when you entered the United States?" She realized, oddly, that she was genuinely worried for him.

"Sometimes, in work like this, one wants to be noticed, and quickly. That's the case here. With any luck, they'll have spotted us at the airport, either Heathrow or Kennedy, or perhaps when we picked up your Jaguar at the train station, although if it had been the latter I should think they would have tried hitting us by now. So, when I show up auditing one of Dr. Stein's classes after the holiday break, Stein and his Nazi friends should know just what I'm there for."

"You could get killed," Dannie said flatly.

"That is a distinct possibility, but hopefully I won't."

"Hopefully you won't?"

"Yes. Interested in breakfast, were you?"

She let him help her with her coat, but she was shivering despite its warmth.

Chapter Seventeen:

The Wolf In His Lair

They'd rented another motel room for the operation of manufacturing their special ammunition, paying in advance and abandoning the room by midnight with a hopefully adequate supply of 180-grain .44 Magnum handgun ammunition and twelve-gauge slug loads for the two witness-protection shotguns, all tipped with silver. The shotguns—at least Mac hoped—should prove particularly devastating, a larger amount of silver in the hollow cavity at the tip of the projectile than possible with the handgun rounds.

The shotguns had nothing more than a healthy-sized pistol grip for a stock, and the barrel of each gun was sawed back to just over twelve inches.

Like David Mallory, Hugh MacTavish utilized a shoulder holster-style sling specifically designed for police or clandestine operatives (mostly fighting the drug trade) and manufactured by an Arizona-based firm, finding the assembly quite comfortable. The 12-gauge pump did not protrude beyond the bottom of his sportcoat and he wore a slightly longer winter coat over that now as he moved along the sidewalk at the center of the Sutton College Commons toward his meeting with Dr. William Stein.

It had been a simple matter, really, to arrange the rendezvous, despite the fact that classes were out for Christmas. Stein was evaluating a soon-to-be-published biography of Adolf Hitler and was using his office for the task, allowing him to work with the wrestling team as well (which was already into its season before the Christmas holidays). After securing the silver needed for their special-purpose ammunition, he had rung up Dr. Stein, tracking him to the Athletic department, declined to leave a return telephone number with the student who'd answered the call, tried again when Dr. Stein was expected, and gotten on to him very quickly. They'd exchanged few words, just made the appointment to meet, not in the history department offices but, rather, in the small gymnasium where the wrestlers worked out immediately following the day's practice the next morning.

Dannie had been talking in her sleep from the next room, and Hugh MacTavish had remained awake for quite some time, worried that the strain was becoming to great for his old friend's daughter, and too nervous to fall off to sleep himself because of the meeting with Stein.

For a while, as he'd driven to the college, he'd considered leaving the shotgun in the car, going in weaponless lest he suddenly lose all self-control and simply murder the man on the spot. But, more for Dannie's safety than his own lest he should be captured and by the use of drugs forced to reveal where she and David were, he took the gun anyway.

He stopped before the library, asked directions of a man uselessly shoveling the still-falling snow, turned right, and headed toward the gymnasium. The flakes were large, soft, and Sutton College, except for the constant scraping of the snow shovel on the library steps, was totally still.

It proved unnecessary to even enter the gymnasium. Dr. William Stein was there, waiting for him.

Despite the fact that Stein wore a fedora hat pulled low over his eyes, Hugh MacTavish recognized the face from forty-five years before.

"Brigadier?" As Stein spoke, Stein looked up and MacTavish saw the eyes, their unreal blueness.

"Yes." MacTavish balled his right fist, wanting to grab

195

for the shotgun beneath his clothes and end this now and forever.

Stein didn't extend a hand, nor did MacTavish.

"I thought it might be more pleasant to walk about the campus a bit while we spoke, Brigadier. I felt you might enjoy seeing the sights, even find it more comfortable than the gymnasium."

"That's very considerate of you, Doctor." MacTavish nodded, pulling the snapped-down brim of his own fedora lower over his eyes against the snow.

"The snow actually feels almost warm, doesn't it?"

"Yes." MacTavish nodded.

"You're sure . . . well, a man your age, of course, I wouldn't wish to subject you to any discomfort."

"Actually, I've found that a brisk walk every day helps to prevent constipation." MacTavish smiled.

Stein laughed and they fell in beside each other and began to walk, at first back along the path over which MacTavish had walked alone, but passing by the library steps where the janitor still so fruitlessly shoveled away still-falling snow, toward the far end of the commons, Sutton's generally modern architecture in stark contrast to the occasional building such as the library, which was neoclassical. Stein would occasionally comment about this architectural feature or that, or again about the snow.

MacTavish stopped walking at last, Stein stopping, too. MacTavish lit a cigarette. "I'm sure you don't remember me from those days, do you, Dr. Stein?"

"May I have your word as an officer that you are not, as they say these days, wired?"

MacTavish genuinely laughed as he exhaled. "You have that word, Doctor. Or, should I say Herr Standartenführer?"

Stein smiled good-naturedly. "Should I assume that you are armed?"

"You should indeed."

"With more of your amusing silver bullets?"

MacTavish allowed another smile as he exhaled. "I shouldn't think that your nine dead comrades found them that terribly amusing, Stein. By the by, is that your real name?"

"That hardly matters, does it? Why are you here?"

"You and your kind exterminated my unit forty-five years ago, and recently caused the death of a very dear friend. That's reason enough, but I feel I have an obligation as a member of the human race to make certain that you are destroyed forever, all of you."

Stein chuckled a bit, smiled, scuffed snow from his shoes. "Shall we?" They began again to walk. Stein said, after a long pause, "You have given yourself a most ambitious undertaking, Brigadier MacTavish."

"I've always liked a challenge."

"Ahh! I see. By the way, Brigadier, just how old were you at the time we last met?"

"I'd lied about my age and was always rather on the tall side. I enlisted when I was fourteen. I was sixteen then."

"You appear to be in marvelous shape, if I may say so, for a chap your age."

MacTavish smiled. "Well, thank you very much. That's most flattering. Weren't planning on testing my cardiovascular endurance on a treadmill, were you?"

Stein laughed. "You really are most amusing, Brigadier. I imagine you are also curious."

"To a degree, yes."

"Do you have a theory—about us?"

"Please correct me if I'm in error, but the only thing that seems to make any sense at all is that somehow the old legends about werebeasts are true, or at least true enough that such a thing as a werewolf exists in nature, and, further, that in some way or another the Nazis found one."

"Yes?"

"Synthesized the blood or some ingredient in it and

asked for volunteers, of course after it was tested on persons in the death camps."

"This death camp business is a lot of crap, MacTavish. We killed a lot of Jews, but who cares? Except the Jews. I find it so hypocritical that people who felt exactly as we did suddenly became so piously supercilious and condemnatory. We merely had the courage and organizational abilities to do what every other civilized race had wanted to do for centuries, exterminate a pestiferous subhuman race which usurped economic and other freedoms with the intent—"

"I've really heard all that masterrace absurdity before, Stein."

Stein shrugged his shoulders, his smile gone. "Actually, you guessed at what happened surprisingly well, MacTavish. It all did begin by chance, really." They reached the gates at the far end of the commons near where MacTavish had parked the Ford he'd rented earlier that morning under another set of false I.D. They started back on the opposite side. "It was in Poland, in 1939, shortly after our glorious victory."

"Some might call it a slaughter, tanks against horse-mounted Polish cavalry."

Stein laughed again. "Yes, how many Polish cavalrymen does it take to stop a tank? It's a joke. Try to answer it."

"I can't think of an answer."

"All of them!"

MacTavish looked away for an instant; if he'd had any doubts before this, he knew now that Stein was totally insane, just hanging on to a veneer of humanity for his cover and for his ego. "You were telling me how your people got into this, Stein."

"I was." Stein nodded as MacTavish looked back. Stein dug his hands into his pockets, looked down at his feet as he walked, then began again. "There are many advantages. I could be walking about here totally naked and, albeit I'd be cold like anyone else would, I would never suffer the risk of frostbite, pneumonia, even the common cold. I haven't been sick since 1944, MacTavish. It's really quite remarkable. Ohh, I've come down with a mild case of sniffles, mind you, but it's been gone within an hour. Cut myself on something and the cut is healed in minutes. It's like being a god, MacTavish."

"How nice for you. And do the disadvantages include difficulty in flossing the human flesh from one's teeth the next morning, or just a little more beard to shave?"

"I can see that you little realize what I and others like me represent, MacTavish. And that displays your inferiority. I mean no personal offense. But think about it, MacTavish. How many good years do you have left? I mean, you appear hale and hearty, but can you run as fast as you did when you were sixteen? I can, only faster. Do you find the flu a little harder to avoid each year, lingering longer each time you contract it? I don't, because I'm never ill. Do you worry about cancer with that cigarette?"

MacTavish dropped the cigarette, crushed it under his foot. "Make your point, Stein."

"Uncomfortable? Joints stiffen, don't they, and it's a little harder to get up in the mornings or fall asleep at night, isn't it? That is age."

"That is normal."

"For you. Not for me. Not since 1943 have I aged a single day. When I made my first transformation, an old wound sustained on the Russian front used to bother me now and again when it was damp. Afterward, the wound never bothered me again. Even the scar from it healed perfectly, MacTavish. Perfectly!"

"You were telling me about the process."

"Think to learn some secret weakness about us, do you, MacTavish? Well, there is none. You can't ward us off with garlic, have a curse thrown on us or anything else."

"You forget silver bullets, Stein."

"And beheadings, yes. But there is not enough silver to shoot us, and few men are sufficiently skilled or reckless to get so close as to dispatch one of us by severing the head. I will tell you any secret you wish, because we are invulnerable."

MacTavish wondered how fast he could get the shotgun out and use it? Faster than Stein could transform and rip out a throat? Probably.

Stein stopped walking, looked at MacTavish. Stein was an inch or so shorter, MacTavish noticed, his shoulders well set, the shape of his neck displaying that he was into bodybuilding. And, MacTavish wondered, just how good was Stein the man, not the werewolf. Stein said, "There was a small group of Polish resistance hiding out in a remote wooded area, not far from what is today the border with Czechoslovakia. They were heavily armed. A force of Wermacht was sent in after them. The patrol vanquished the Polish resistance, of course, but was attacked during the night by what was described only as a 'creature.' Two men were killed and one of the bodies was torn limb from limb, as the report went. The officer in charge of the patrol, a young lieutenant, insisted that he personally had shot the creature at least five times but to no apparent effect. He swore to the accuracy of his men, as well. The report suggested that the creature had been shot at least eighteen times.

"SS leadership for the area became aware of the incident and were, as you might imagine, intrigued." And Stein positively beamed then. "The Führer called me personally to his offices in Berlin. I was but a Haupsturmführer then. The Führer was most intrigued by the possibilities such a creature suggested."

"Why you, Stein?"

"Why was I selected, you mean?" Stein began to walk again, MacTavish beside him As they neared the library, they began to retrace their steps, the janitor still shovel-

200

ing uselessly at the falling snow. "I was an historian before the war, but my field was the history of science. Therefore, I was well versed in the various scientific disciplines, of course, and I'd always had a passion for things folkloric. I possessed the perfect qualifications. Rest assured I am not only uniquely qualified to serve here as a full professor but I also have the appropriate academic credentials, MacTavish."

"I'm very relieved to hear that, Stein. Truly."

Stein laughed his soft, almost internal laugh again. "We traversed the area where the creature had attacked, even utilized aerial reconnaissance. There were a few intriguing sightings which matched somewhat the descriptions taken from the survivors of the Wermacht patrol. But these sightings would always turn out to be nothing but a wild animal of some sort. I personally supervised the interrogations of several hundred peasants in the vicinity, solid subhuman wretches to be sure, but nonetheless there was the occasional intriguing reference to werewolfery, something which prior to that time I had dismissed as folklore and nothing more, the ravings of stimulus-starved dolts.

"In the end, there was only one thing to do."

MacTavish stopped walking again, just looked at Stein. "And what was that?"

Stein smiled. "You are SAS, Brigadier. I know what your people do, have done. Don't attempt such a holier-than-thou attitude with me, sir. You would have done the same."

"What did you do?"

"I had gathered up a dozen from among the peasant population of a village near to the actual attack on the Wermacht patrol, ranging in age from infants to older adults, male and female. They were made to run for extended periods throughout the day, kept in confined areas with only sufficient ventilation that they would not pass out. They were denied toilet facilities, and neither were

201

they allowed to bathe. All of this, of course, was calculated to strengthen their human scent.

"As a young man, my parents wealthy, I had the good fortune to hunt in India and in Africa," Stein went on, picking up the walk, MacTavish falling in with him again. "It was common practice when attempting to snare a predator to stake out a young goat or calf, using this lesser creature as bait. The same system seemed the best means by which to take this creature whom we stalked, making it come to us. We returned to the site of the Wermacht patrol's encampment that night when the creature attacked. The peasants were staked out strategically in hopes that their presence, augmented by heightened human scent, would attract the creature, of course."

"You're wrong."

"What?"

"I wouldn't have done it that way, Stein."

Stein shrugged his powerful shoulders, picking up the thread of his narrative. "That first night, nothing happened except that one of the smaller children died of exposure." MacTavish touched at his side where the shotgun hung, his right fist balling. "Uncertain that the creature might not be tempted by carrion, the child still had potential usefulness to our endeavor. During the following day, we again exercised the hostages, denying them toilet or bathing facilities. Prospects seemed bright because there was to be a full moon, and I naturally thought, if indeed such a thing as a werewolf might exist, then perhaps, too, the folklore concerning full moons and all might have validity as well. In the case that blood might attract the creature, great care was taken to inflict wounds upon a percentage of the subjects which would neither bleed so rapidly as to kill nor so slowly as to close on their own. We were very thorough."

MacTavish lit another cigarette, his hands shaking, not from the cold but the company. "Then?"

"We waited. At midnight almost precisely, a peasant

202

girl with razor cuts made over both breasts, along her forearms and thighs, was attacked. The blood evidently helped to attract the creature. Obviously we were intrigued, observing the attack for several minutes. When it seemed the creature was through or nearly so, we closed in to apprehend it.

"This proved extraordinarily difficult," Stein said, sighing. "Two of my men were killed, one other injured seriously. We had steel-mesh-reinforced nets ready, as well as gas. We were, after a brutal fight, able to subdue the creature. Even nearly unconscious, it struggled at the net, fought to be free, growling, evidently reliving this attack or another one in its dream state. And then, when morning came, there was the most astounding transformation. All of us were actually moved as the body returned to human shape, the body hair was drawn in through the skin or molted away. The unfortunate fellow was a Russian schoolmaster who'd fled to Poland to avoid being drafted! How do you like that, MacTavish?"

"How amusing." MacTavish nodded, inhaling.

"And here is the fascinating part. The man was obviously exhausted from his night's ordeal and from the transformation itself. But the minor wounds the creature sustained during the struggle to apprehend it were in no way evidenced on his body. In fact, his body was essentially perfect, not a single blemish on the skin, not a bruise, the body with a fine symmetry."

"Then what happened?"

Stein smiled, taking a cigarette from his coat pocket, asking, "Do you mind?"

It took MacTavish a beat to understand that Stein wanted a light. MacTavish took out his old Zippo and handed it to the man. Stein lit the cigarette, handed back the lighter, said, "Thank you," exhaled. "Where were we? Yes. I questioned the schoolmaster extensively without full satisfaction. But I did not wish to risk using harsher means."

"What happened to the rest of the people you'd used as bait?"

Stein shrugged his shoulders. "They were kept for some time lest the schoolmaster should transform and need to feed once again. And that very night he did. We had the foresight to plan for this thankfully. We had a cage that was assembled on the spot, constructed of the strongest Krupp steels available."

"Yes, nothing but the best."

Stein ignored the remark, went on. "I planned doubly well, reasoning that if the schoolmaster were shackled he might sustain injury during the transformation. I introduced one of the peasants through a secondary cage and the schoolmaster, now transformed, killed the fellow instantly.

"But a curious thing occurred then," Stein went on. "Do you recall that one of my men had been injured?"

"I hadn't realized I should be anticipating a quiz. But I do recall that, yes," MacTavish told him.

"Well, the man—a young Rottenführer—had recovered very well during the day. And now he, too, began to transform. It was evident that when the schoolmaster had transformed, it caused him some physical discomfort. But the young man who had been injured went through the tortures of the damned."

"Rather like you'll experience in the afterlife, you mean?"

Stein smiled. "Very humorous, Brigadier. Very humorous, indeed. But, whether you believe me or not, it was quite terrible to see the fellow suffer so horribly. He killed one of the two men I set to guarding him, anticipating there might be some similar reaction, and escaped into the woods. We hunted for him through the night to no avail. And that was interesting in and of itself, since here was a young man from Hamburg who had little skill as a woodsman yet evaded us as skillfully as a wild animal. We found him at last, but not until the next day,

204

wandering about in the woods, naked, exhausted, scarred from a fight of some sort with a wild animal. And here is the very odd thing, MacTavish." Stein seemed about to burst with excitement as he spoke. "Within an hour of finding him, even the deepest of his lacerations had nearly healed. I interviewed the young man extensively, but he remembered little about his experiences; I had the distinct impression that the shock of what happened to him almost totally robbed him of memory. He continued to be disoriented throughout the day, slept a great deal when permitted. The schoolmaster, however, when persuaded, remembered all which had happened, nor was he at all so tired. Evidently, the effect of the transformation was more easily handled with experience."

MacTavish wanted to say "Practice makes perfect" but didn't. They were nearly to the gates again, MacTavish putting out his cigarette, stuffing his cold hands into his pockets now.

"That next evening, the young Rottenführer was confined in a similar cage I had flown in expressly from Berlin. Both of the men transformed to creatures. When both were offered prey in the form of two powerfully built fellows from among the peasant group, both killed, the schoolmaster with greater efficiency, the young Rottenführer with greater brutality. It was fascinating, and of course we had lights set up and preserved the attacks on film for the Führer to view since he had already contacted me—me!—during the day by special messenger commending my coded report recounting the activity of the previous night. I was under orders to return to Berlin at once with the film."

They stood beside the gates on the other side of which MacTavish had parked the rented Ford. "And?"

"You could not realize what it was like to be in the Führer's presence."

"I can guess," MacTavish offered.

"You joke, you make fun, but he was beyond human.

It was as if an aura surrounded him. One was in the presence of a true god in the flesh of man, MacTavish. You know only what the so-called Allies wished known of the Führer, and most of that is lies. There was no more courageous man, no more intellectually persistent man, no greater man. After he viewed the film three times, he questioned me for several hours, eager for even the slightest detail I could provide. And he commanded me to take personal charge reporting only to him of this important project."

"To synthesize whatever it was which made the transformations possible? Supersoldiers for the Reich?"

"Yes, if you must put it that way. It was determined that blood and tissue of the schoolmaster and the courageous young Rottenführer be studied, analyzed, that their transformations be observed, that more subjects should be bitten by the creatures and saved, if possible, from death, so they, too, could be studied as they transformed. The end in mind, of course, as you say, a supersoldier, one who would be invulnerable to injury. At that time, no one suspected that the condition also conferred immortality."

"Immortality? You really think you'll never die, Stein?"

"I was born in 1910, Brigadier. You were born in 1939, I assume?"

"Yes."

"Which of us, MacTavish, looks older? You at sixty-one, or me at seventy-nine?"

Hugh MacTavish had no answer.

Stein put out his cigarette, looked down at his feet again, then up into MacTavish's face. "The finest minds available were brought in on the project. And I had personal control. My reports to the Führer never went beyond his inner circle, nor did even those who worked on the project—because the research was segmented, only the overall scientific director knowing the true scope of the research—ever knowing the ultimate goal.

206

"The cause of the transformation," Stein said softly, "was eventually discovered. Without the proper scientific background, you would not fully comprehend. Suffice it to say, there were some similarities to the rarely encountered malady known as porphyria, but only similarities. Fortunately, to aid in our research, there were any number of test subjects available. There were some fascinatingly bizarre results, yet the true answer, the true key evaded us until February of 1943. We had been missing the forest for the trees, to paraphrase the old saying. We had been ignoring the reality of the situation. The ultimate soldier was there before our eyes. The werebeasts themselves. We already knew how to bring about a transformation, and how to prevent a transformation. I can tell you this. The technique involves high-frequency sound waves, but you would never find the frequency even if you, too, were immortal. Once the ingredient from the blood of the werebeast is injected into the subject, after the first transformation, the sound waves can be used to bring about another or prevent another, however one wishes. The moon's gravitational effect on the bloodstream effect was no longer at all of consequence.

"Think of it, of what you have set yourself against, MacTavish. An-all-but-invulnerable soldier, trained to the highest degree, motivated beyond normal human limitations, able to increase in both size and strength as well as endurance and speed to heroic proportions otherwise beyond the scope of humanity. Such a soldier is capable of wreaking immeasurable destruction against even the most powerful enemy, Brigadier. And what injuries might be sustained would be healed within minutes, hours at the most, so he could fight forever."

"Why did you have yourself injected, Stein?"

"I volunteered, knowing that in doing so I would be aiding the cause of a greater Germany. From among my own division, the Liebstandarte Adolf Hitler, ten times the number of volunteers required stepped forward, not

207

one of these besides myself knowing the true nature of the life for which they offered themselves. When, at last, those fortunate few from among the volunteers were selected, not one of the men after being informed failed his duty, showed any fear. The volunteers were injected and went through their initial transformations and had mastered transformation, as I had before them, by spring of 1944.

"Then it was too late." There was a catch in Stein's voice, and a dullness suddenly in his eyes as MacTavish listened, watched, shivered. "The Führer, acting on the advice of inferior men, held us back from going forth to resist the invasion of Europe. We were relegated to a part of the Werewolf program." He smiled, laughed. "Humorous, isn't it, that we really were, yet the program incorporated thousands who were not. They fought, many of them, but we fought only once for we were held in reserve. That is why your unit, forty-five years ago, could not be allowed to pass, to take back word that we were there.

"By then, we had been ordered to remain hidden at all costs, to wait until the hostilities had ceased, then to strike."

"Why didn't you? Strike, I mean, at the Allies' backs," MacTavish asked him.

The smile again, then Stein stared down at his shoes, began speaking as he looked up again toward MacTavish's face. "I decided that the Reich would best be served if our superiority should remain a mystery, Brigadier. I anticipated the conflict which would arise between the United States and its allies and the Soviet Union, never really an ally at all during the war. But I knew nothing of the advent of nuclear technology. From the objective perspective of an historian, it is indisputable that the coming of nuclear weapons technology altered the flow. You chided me over what are popularly called 'death camps' for the damned Jews. What about the genocide perpetrated by Britain's ally, America, on the Japanese, just because they were yellow instead of white? Would Truman have ordered the dropping of a nuclear bomb on white Europe? I think not."

"Harry Truman was many things, but I never interpreted any of his actions as racially motivated. Right or wrong, the bombings were perceived as a means of bringing about an end to the war in the Pacific, a means of saving more lives than they cost. There's no comparison to what your people did."

Stein merely shrugged his shoulders, evidently shrugging off any debate as well. "At any event, by the early 1950's, I had a strong suspicion that we were, indeed, if not immortal, aging at a vastly slower rate than lesser men, my men and I. And warfare between the United States and the Soviet Union seemed inevitable then. We bided our time. But again I had miscalculated how one single event could disrupt the flow of history."

"You sound like a bloody Marxist," MacTavish told him. The snow was falling more heavily now and MacTavish wanted to get this over with. He was all but determined to kill Stein on the spot. But Stein had to know that, didn't he? MacTavish's eyes had been drifting across the commons, up and down each building, looking for a possible sniper or some other trap. After all, Stein had been the one to insist on walking out here.

Stein continued his story. "The war between the United States and the Soviet Union did not occur because of the threat of mutual annihilation. I had to rethink my plans. And, during the sixties I became sure. I realized that the age-old dream of eternal youth and vigor had been fulfilled and that I and my men had all the time in the world to wait until the moment was perfect. Consider that—time enough to wait for generations if needed. You have no time left at all. One day, very soon, traumatic illness will strike you, perhaps, or even something as simple as pulling a muscle while performing an ordinary ac-

209

tivity you have performed every day of your life. Gerontology has become a fascinating subject to me, observing the natural degeneracy of the human species while knowing all along that my body and mind are as they have ever been and ever shall be, thanks to that which sets apart the blood which courses through my veins."

"You'll never win," MacTavish told him, realizing it sounded lame, because in a very real way Stein had already won, but in another way they had lost and were lost from the very beginning. MacTavish ran it through his mind how he would step back as he drew the shotgun from the holster beneath his right armpit. It was a very fast rig to use. He would simply shoot down Stein and run for the car. If he got that far.

And Stein's words in the next instant echoed Mac's own thoughts of a second earlier. "I have already won, Brigadier MacTavish. That is why I take the time to speak so freely with you. The key was giving the Werewolves the ability to control their actions, to change from one state to the other at will. Once we had achieved that, your doom was sealed, yours and that of men like you. Even if you were somehow able to convince a person in high authority that this were all true, that we really did exist—which you cannot do—by the time any action could be taken, it would be too late because we would merely accelerate our timetable, a minor inconvenience for us, nothing which would work to your advantage."

"And what if I kill you now?"

Stein's eyes changed. But there wasn't fear in them, almost a glowing about them instead. "You carry a weapon under your coat. How many shots? A shotgun, isn't it? Five rounds?"

MacTavish said nothing.

"The man shoveling the snow." MacTavish could still hear the senseless scraping. "There is a man just on the other side of the hedgerow there." And Stein pointed toward the far side of the very modern Fine Arts Building.

MacTavish had thought he'd detected movement from there earlier, dismissed it to the back of his mind. "Others of my men, all like me, are watching you. Let's say you are very adept at killing, Brigadier. Let's say you kill me with one of your silver bullets before I am able to rip your throat open or split you at the sternum and tear your heart from your chest while it still beats And then, assuming five rounds, you are able to kill the man shoveling snow, the man behind the hedge, two others. By the time you have begun to reload or run toward your car, the others will be on you. Perhaps you have a large knife and think that you will be able to sever a head, save yourself. Perhaps you get one more. The others will shred your body and devour it. And, killing me, if you are thinking of some supreme sacrifice for the good of all mankind, will likewise cause but a ripple in the new stream of history, because my plans have been lain for some time and I am no longer required in order that they come to fruition.

"So, you have a choice." Stein smiled, almost good-naturedly. "You can enjoy a last few days of life until I come for you, or die this instant. Who knows, perhaps in those last days you can think of some way in which you can destroy me." Stein chuckled a bit, looked down at his shoes again, then up into Mac's eyes. "Perhaps you'll have the time to fuck that little girl, Dr. Hardy."

Hugh MacTavish didn't think about it, took a half step backward on his right foot, turning his left shoulder inward as his fist snapped out, hocking across Stein's jaw, sending him to the snowy pavement.

MacTavish stood there, in the next instant realizing it was over. He grabbed for the shotgun.

Stein lay on the ground.

The janitor was sprinting across the commons at unnatural speed, there was a blur from MacTavish's left as the one from behind the hedgerow started toward him, movement from the other side of the Fine Arts Building,

211

a figure in an overcoat running from the parking area beyond the gates.

And Stein shouted, "*Nicht jetzt!*"

The janitor stopped in his tracks, shouted, "*Was ist passiert, Herr—*"

"*Nein!*"

MacTavish, the shotgun in his hands, poised to fire into Stein's chest, rasped, "*Ich verstehe nicht!*"

The others had frozen in their tracks now and, as MacTavish's eyes shifted right and left, he saw more of them in the commons, a dozen at least, more than he could possibly have killed.

MacTavish looked back at Stein.

Stein, still on his back in the snow, gloved left hand rubbing at the right side of his jaw, answered, "Your accent isn't half bad, MacTavish. But I imagine you've spent time with GSG9 and had plenty of opportunity to polish it."

MacTavish still held the shotgun.

Stein stood up, dusted off the snow. "You loosened a tooth, I think." Stein smiled. "But it will be fully restored in less than an hour. If you intend to kill me, do it now. If not, leave. I have more important matters to which I must attend. And . . . I apologize. I hadn't thought an old man's feelings concerning a young girl could be so close to the surface."

Hugh MacTavish kept the shotgun in his hands, looked at Stein hard, whispered through clenched teeth, "Just remember, Nazi *ubermensch,* it was an old man's fist that knocked you on your bloody arse."

Keeping the shotgun beside his right thigh, his finger inside the trigger guard, ready to fire, Hugh MacTavish turned his back on William Stein and walked away, murmuring to himself,

> He that fights and runs away
> May turn and fight another day;

212

But he that is in battle slain
Can never rise and fight again.

. . . unless, MacTavish thought, one were a werewolf.

213

Chapter Eighteen:

Explanations And Incredulity

Richard shook hands with Mac first, then with David Mallory, Richard eyeing both men suspiciously.

Dannie ran her palms down along the legs of her blue jeans and sat down on the couch, crossing her legs. She supposed it was natural to compare the three men. After all, men compared women to one another, didn't they? Mac was the tallest—and despite his age, the best-looking—of the three. David and Richard were about the same height, David perhaps a half inch taller, or maybe just looking that way because, despite reasonably broad shoulders, he was slight. Mac had the least hair, bald on top, of course, that close-cropped fringe of gray at the sides. Richard's hair was going, at once gray and away. There, as it concerned hair, David was the clearly best equipped, that shaggy blond mop of his that always appeared scrupulously clean yet uncombed.

Richard sat down on the couch beside her, but only after Mac took one of the armchairs and sank into it. That left David still standing. He fixed that by perching on the arm of the other chair.

"What the hell is going on, Dannie?"

She looked at Richard, then looked at Mac.

Mac cleared his throat. "Well, Doctor, have you had much experience in your psychiatric work with persons who think they are werewolves and really are?"

It was not an auspicious beginning . . .

* * *

They talked for more than two hours, Richard listening mostly, asking an occasional question to clarify something Mac said, never once offering an opinion.

As Mac described his interview with Dr. Stein in the Sutton Commons, Dannie watched Richard's eyes widen. But still, he made no comment.

She had been the one to push for Richard's involvement, knowing that he would be worried that supposedly she had returned from London but was not at her apartment; and she had pushed to return to her apartment as well. To her surprise, Mac had almost enthusiastically agreed to both requests, but the latter on the stipulation only that he could find an apartment or hotel room near to her, since he considered counteraction by Stein's Nazis imminent.

She'd wondered then, as she did now, if somehow she were being used like those poor people Stein had used, as bait for the wolves?

She shivered at the thought.

Drinks. Everybody needed a drink, she told herself. And knowing that Mac liked wine and beer and that David liked anything, it seemed, she withdrew, excusing herself to the kitchen. Since she was there anyway, she took out some microwave eggrolls and started heating them. Richard's rum collins took the most trouble, because he was very particular as concerned the proportions of the ingredients.

The microwave beeped that the eggrolls were ready and she was just about to put them onto a little hors d'oeuvres plate with a toothpick reservoir at its center when she heard Richard start to laugh. "You can't be serious. Now come on. I've got as good a sense of humor as the next man. Brigadier? Like on *Doctor Who?* And is this young man—David, wasn't it?—is he a time traveler or something? This is rich! Do we get to see the monsters in the foam rubber suits?"

Dannie Hardy closed her eyes for a second.

Without opening them, without even turning around, she announced, "Richard, this is for real, dammit!" And

215

dropped toothpicks all over the counter. It really was real . . .

"Ohh, she's in danger, all right," Richard said, leaning forward on the couch, a vein in his forehead that she had never noticed before standing out, pulsing. "She's in danger from lunatics like you two putting a lot of shit into her head about Nazi conspiracies and werewolves and men born in 1910 who look like they're still in their thirties. Tell me something about you, Brigadier . . ." Richard sneered the word. "Just why did you retire from the British Army? Wasn't for psychiatric reasons, was it?"

Dannie bit her lower lip.

David cleared his throat and looked away.

Mac, his voice with the slightest tremble to it — rage, not age, she knew — answered Richard. "I served Her Majesty's Government on active duty from 1943 until 1985, sir. Forty-two years. In that time, I was married and lost a wife. In that time, I'd taken so little leave time I could keep the same pair of civilian shoes for years and never wear them out! I retired because to have continued on in the SAS would have been ludicrous. I have never lived outside of the Army in my entire life, sir. And I'd bet my sanity against yours any day of the week. Let me tell you something. You're so bloody concerned with Dannie's safety, well, so am I and so is my time traveler friend, as you call him. And when the monsters show up, they won't be wearing rubber suits. They'll be flesh and blood and sinew and bone and have fangs over two inches long. But one thing they won't do is die, unless we hit them with one of these!"

Mac's right hand slipped under his sportcoat and he drew his gun. Richard sat back. Mac took something out of the bottom of the handle section. "This is called a magazine, Doctor. And this . . ." He pushed his thumb along the top of it. "This is called a cartridge. The front end, here," and he stabbed the tip of the cartridge into his other

216

hand, "is called a bullet. When the gun is fired, the bullet travels down the bore of the weapon and, if you've done your part and the gun and ammunition combination do theirs, the bullet hits its target. If this were an ordinary bullet on the end of this cartridge, one could shoot at these bloody werewolves all day long and it wouldn't have any appreciable effect. I've seen them shot with submachine guns, machine guns—there's a difference—what they call assault rifles these days, ordinary handguns, seen them stabbed with bayonets and beaten with fists. They don't die unless you do one of three things. Hit them with a bullet tipped with silver, like this one," and he threw the thing across the space between him and Richard, Richard reflexively catching it. "Or you take a large knife or a sword and either cut off their fucking heads or sever their damn spines. Ever hear of salamanders? They lose a limb, it grows back. You shoot out one of these damned Nazi's livers and it heals itself. The damned things are immortal unless you kill them in the right way. What I'm saying, Richard, is that if you value Dannie's life as much as you protest to value it, what you'll do is help us to guard her, help us to prepare for the attack they'll make.

"I brought us back here at Dannie's request," Mac said, his voice calming, "because I realized that this would be a more built-up area, that their attack would have to be more blatant, therefore easier to spot, perhaps easier to repel. And she needed some stability because all of this has been a great shock to her. You can hopefully provide that stability since I gather the two of you are engaged or something like that."

Dannie felt her cheeks redden. What were she and Richard, anyway?

"My point, Richard," Mac said, his jaw hard-set, "is that when they come, we'll need every man. If you are right, and this is all some figment of our imaginations, then all you'll do is waste a little time and have the final satisfaction of saying that I'm crazy as a loon. If you're wrong, how will you feel seeing Dannie's body dismembered and

217

disemboweled on the living-room floor?"

Mac lit a cigarette.

Richard said nothing.

And then David spoke and Dannie looked at him and was surprised at what he said. "She's a lovely girl, Richard—bright, attractive, '. . . the perfect woman nobly planned.' If you love her, you don't have a great deal of choice, do you?"

Richard's voice sounded strained. "This is madness, utter madness; but, I'll help."

Chapter Nineteen:

No Time

Mac left to get some sleep. It was natural, she supposed, for a man his age to be tired. After all, she was. Richard was up long into the night after the meeting in her living room, pacing the floor of her bedroom while David lay asleep on the couch outside. "Why the hell does he have to stay here?"

"You don't know how to shoot a gun. He does, so go to sleep, Richard." Richard came to bed, wanted to cuddle; she obliged for a time, but was too exhausted to make love. In the morning, Richard tried again and this time there was no reason to refuse him and she was scared from the nightmares which had beset her sleep anyway and wanted it just as badly as he did.

When they finally exited the bedroom, there was a note scrawled on a stick-up message blank pasted to the kitchen countertop. "Gone to take care of business. Keep Richard with you. They won't attack during daylight hours, probably." No signature, just a big letter "D" . . .

Mac pulled on a pair of sweatpants he'd left on the empty bed that was nearest to the door and picked up the sawed-off shotgun. "Who is it?"

There was no secret knock because secrets like that could be pried out of people, nor was there any code phrase prepared, and for the same reason. "It's David, sir."

David's voice sounded natural enough, not under duress. Nonetheless, Hugh MacTavish held on to the shotgun as he approached the door from an angle. Cautiously, lest he should be shot through the door or, for that matter, the thin motel room walls, he peered through the peephole. He was careful there, too. There was the case in West Berlin once, in the days before the Communists had started dismantling their wall, where an SIS man, new to the field, had been killed looking through a peephole such as this. A pneumatic pistol with a carbide-tipped dart the thickness of a straight pin was fired through the peephole, into the unfortunate fellow's eye and, because of the slight angle (the East German agent was a woman, hence shorter), right up into the brain.

But, as far as MacTavish could tell, David was alone.

MacTavish slipped the chair from under the knob—it wouldn't stop anyone, but it would make noise breaking right enough—and then removed the safety chain. He turned the knob.

"Good morning, Brigadier," Mallory said cheerfully enough.

"Yes, David. Good morning. Have you had breakfast?" Mac closed the door behind the younger man, reset the chain, and shifted the shotgun into his left hand.

"Just some juice at Dr. Hardy's after I showered, sir."

"Well, then you should join me; I shan't be a moment." And MacTavish handed David the shotgun. "She's hot," he noted as he started for the bathroom.

A quick shower—and showers were quicker with so much face and so little hair to wash—and he slipped into clean clothes and stuffed the rather out-sized Desert Eagle pistol into his pants, emerging from the room for the second time this morning.

The first time had been more than an hour earlier, the long-bladed cold steel Magnum Tanto knife strapped under his sweats for a long run. He reasoned that the likelihood of an attack in force during the daylight hours would be remote and, after punching Stein in the jaw, he was convinced that the werewolves were just as vulnerable

220

in human form — albeit not as mortal — as anyone else. Hadn't they fallen, been grievously wounded in the battle in the woods that afternoon forty-five years ago? Yes, they healed fantastically quickly, but they could still be knocked down, temporarily immobilized.

"I'm planning on going by Sutton to arrange for my matriculation, Brigadier."

"Bad idea, David," Mac told him as they reached the end of the mazelike corridor and started for the lobby, toward the restaurant. "When I'd thought we had more time, your possible penetration of their group, or your possible discovery, both seemed attractive for different reasons. Either way, you'd be inside, if they didn't just kill you outright, of course. But I've reappraised the situation since then. Remember what I told you Stein said?"

"Sir?"

"That even if we got someone to believe us, by the time anyone could act to move against them, it would be too late? I don't think that was bluff. It was a simple statement of fact. I want you, instead of going to Sutton, to get back to Dannie and this Richard fellow, right after we breakfast. Richard seems a bit anal retentive, but we shouldn't jump to conclusions about him. And, obviously, they care for each other, he and Dannie. That's more than many people have today, so it's worth a great deal. While you do that, staying with Dannie and Richard, I've made arrangements to go to Washington, for a head-to-head with some persons there I can trust. I don't know how long it will take me to convince them that Stein is what he is, or even if I'll be able to. Yet that's the only chance we've got, really. The only other alternative is to track these men down — Stein among them — and kill them in their human form, which will be easier, and one at a time."

"The odds for success, especially since we don't quite know how many of them there are at this time, aren't very good."

"No, but we'll have no other choice. Or, I should say, I will have no other choice. You needn't —"

"Forgive me for interrupting, Brigadier, but whatever you require of me, I'll do. I'm as committed to this as are you."

MacTavish clapped the younger man on the back.

They crossed the lobby, turned toward the restaurant, and fell into the short queue in front of the hostess desk.

A lovely young girl with a small waist and an amply endowed chest approached, pushing a wave of auburn hair back from her forehead. "How many in your party, sir?"

"Just the two of us," MacTavish told her, smiling. She smiled back. At his age, he reflected, that was decent encouragement. He turned to look at David. "At any event, our friends might come visiting tonight or the next night, but it will be soon. See if Richard can get her out of there. She needed that one night in her apartment for sanity's sake, but there must be someplace safer. He's a local. He should know. Enlist his aid. I'll give you a number to memorize where I can be reached in Washington. Do what you can, what you have to do, until I return or get word to you. All right?"

David nodded.

MacTavish watched the hostess as she signaled for them to follow her. He would have followed her even if she hadn't been showing them to a table . . .

MacTavish sipped at his decaffeinated coffee. David, with a younger man's appetite, had gone back to the breakfast bar for another helping of eggs, potatoes, and another full rasher of bacon. Where did David put it? Probably where he himself had put it thirty years ago. David had asked a question, and it deserved an answer: "If I'm to be the ground man, Brigadier, while you're in Washington, could you fill me in a bit more on what to expect when our friends come. I've never even seen a wolf outside of a zoological park."

MacTavish had seen both real wolves and werewolves. He took a bite from his plate, the eggs a little rubbery-

222

tasting because they had cooled. The gun he'd shoved into his trouser band, large under any circumstances, felt awkward there, but .44 Magnum was the minimum caliber he would trust to put one of the beasts down long enough for the silver to enter the bloodstream and do its deadly work.

"You have your work cut out for you, David. The ordinary adult wolf can run as much as seven stone or a little better, the females only slightly lighter. The heaviest wolf on record, according to what I've read, was an Alaskan male at better than eleven stone."

"What a bruiser!"

"Yes."

"There aren't that many places where one encounters wolves these days, besides Alaska and parts of northern Canada, correct?"

"Their range is broader than that, actually, but in years gone by, even until quite recently, wolves were in far greater abundance. That chap that Stein told me about, the Russian schoolmaster, God knows when he was bitten, but wolves weren't at all uncommon in central Europe where they found him, so that in essence was a natural cover for werewolf activity. And an adult male can range from five feet to six and a half feet in length, so it closely approximates the size of a man.

"But there are many differences," MacTavish went on, "between Stein's men after transformation and the genuine article, a real wolf, as well as many similarities. A wolf's elbows—on the front legs—turn inward and its paws turn outward. Our friends' forward limbs work like human limbs, with the elbows rearward and outward. But, the hind legs seem to change jointedness, the knees bending rearward, as in a real wolf or other four-legged animal."

The waitress came with the offer of more coffee and MacTavish abruptly ceased his dissertation, David filling the void with, "So you really think the Superbowl will be that cut and dried a thing, such a boring game?"

The waitress disappeared and MacTavish smiled. "Who's playing? Has it been decided yet?"

223

"I've never liked American football, so I wouldn't know. Maybe we can ask Stein."

"Umm, good idea, David." MacTavish nodded.

"You were telling me about our friends."

"Yes . . ." MacTavish began again. "In the genuine article, a real wolf, the tail or brush will generally run from a little better than a foot to as long as twenty inches or so. With Stein's chaps, the tails tend to at least that length or longer. A real wolf has four toes on the hind feet and five on the front, but that fifth toe doesn't touch the ground. Wolves move light on their feet, and Stein's men move that way as well. But, unlike a wolf which can only truly walk on all fours—I suppose they're capable of two-legged movement awkwardly for short distances, like trained dogs in a circus—Stein's men will move and even fight from a four- or two-legged stance."

MacTavish sipped at his fresh coffee, then went on. "I've had no opportunity to examine the feet of Stein's men while in the lycanthropic state, but a real wolf has large, calloused pads and blunt, nonretracting claws. I'd say, from the nature of Dannie's father's wound when he was grabbed by one them as we escaped the castle forty-five years ago, that the claws on Stein's men aren't much sharper. The fangs, on the other hand, seem larger than those of ordinary wolves."

"How big are those of an ordinary wolf?"

"They can reach two and a quarter inches, David. Stein's men have fangs that are considerably longer, and the heads are vastly larger. A real wolf has forty-two teeth as opposed to the number in humans."

"Thirty-two."

"Yes. As the jaw expands to form the werewolf's muzzle, the number of teeth may increase as well, then retract when transforming back into human shape. The pain of the first transformation must be maddening, seem as though it will never end."

"If a chap weren't mad to begin with, he'd be that way afterward."

"You may well have a point, David, but the key to their entire operation in the past and their current plan is that they can control themselves, at least to a degree."

"You mean through the sound waves that they utilize for changing back and forth."

"More than that, I'm afraid. Either through familiarity with the metamorphosis or through some other means, they are able to be at once beasts and men. With no means of comparing our self-made lycanthropes to the poor devils throughout history who've been unlucky enough to survive an attack and become transformed against their will, there's no telling whether or not, when the lycanthropic state is induced naturally, the human being inside is to one degree or another in control of his faculties.

"My observations of Stein and his men forty-five years ago," Mac continued, "indicated almost the same degree of military organization in the werewolf form as in human form. The others collected themselves round Stein—the blond—and waited docilely for his command. That may have been merely by body language or somehow verbal, although I'm more inclined to suspect that it's body language. The growls and yips and what-have-you may have had some meaning, and the howling prior to the attack at my house was definitely some sort of rallying cry.

"The thing to remember, David, is that when they are wolves, they can basically only perform as wolves. There'd be no facility for one of them to pick up a weapon of any sort and use it, even if the knowledge to use it were in the creature's head. They have to be fought as if they are animals, not people. Have you ever been attacked by an animal? I know that's an odd question, but have you?"

"I was bitten by a dog when I was a boy; nothing serious though, barely broke the skin. And once, when I was in the Service, I had an encounter with guard dogs, Doberman Pinschers, but I made it to my car before they could get me."

"I've seen dogs attack a man; you were lucky. And once,

225

during a training exercise, where we were to infiltrate a government facility where guard dogs were employed, one of the German Shepherds suddenly went bad. For a moment, I was paralyzed with fear, because it brought back all those memories with Evan Hardy during the war. The thing's jaws were closing for my throat and I punched the muzzle of my pistol up against its left ear, closed my eyes, and pulled the trigger."

"Would head shots work on these creatures, do you think?"

MacTavish shrugged his shoulders, swirled his coffee round in the cup. "I don't know. I've seen them shot straight in the heart and lungs. Nothing. If the heart and lungs are capable of regeneration, the same might hold true for the brain. But severing the head does kill, as does severing the spine. If—when they attack, remember one thing, David."

"Brigadier?"

"A gun will eventually run out of ammunition, but a knife doesn't. You'll have my weapons, all but a large folding knife I'll ship as luggage once I'm traveling by air between New York and Washington. But your supply of silver bullets will still be rather limited. Never be without a substantial knife."

"I'll remember that. But I wish you weren't traveling without a gun."

"The bother outweighs any potential advantage." MacTavish hoped so, at least.

Chapter Twenty:

Different Directions

Dannie Hardy didn't like the idea of moving; she didn't like the idea of Mac disappearing on them, either. Although she trusted David's intentions, he couldn't possibly be as competent at protecting her as Mac had proven to be. And Richard was back to being outraged and unbelieving.

"We should just pack up and get out of Dannie's apartment? Well, you're half right, Mallory. You should get the hell out of here. I've had it."

For some reason, both men—Richard and David—were standing in the kitchen almost toe-to-toe beside the refrigerator, glaring at each other as if they were about to come to blows at any moment.

"The Brigadier's orders were—"

"You get it straight, Mallory. This Brigadier of yours doesn't order me around. And he doesn't order around my girl, either! Have you got that?"

She was oddly flattered that Richard had called her his "girl," but then she looked at David, felt suddenly sorry for him. It was time to intervene. "I'm packing. We're leaving. If Mac thinks we should, then I guess we should, Richard." Richard just turned around and looked at her, as if somehow she had betrayed him by not agreeing with him, his eyes dull, staring, pain-filled. "I'm sorry, Richard. You're not a man of violence. I think that's one of the things I love about you." Did she love him? She'd never been quite certain of that. "Mac and David are. These creatures are a real threat, Richard. I've almost been killed by them. And, God forbid, if you ever see them you'll believe. And if we can keep them from getting to us by moving to a different place . . ." She didn't finish her statement, merely gestured helplessly with her hands, turned away, and went into the bedroom to pack; she'd just finished unpacking . . .

He left the Suburban in the hotel lot, both sets of keys given to David. The massive yet fast vehicle might well prove useful yet, and leaving it in David's care was better than parking it at the railroad station.

Much the same philosophy was behind Hugh MacTavish taking along no firearms. There was no security at American railroad stations like there was at airports, so he could easily enough have carried a firearm aboard the train to New York; but, once he reached LaGuardia about to board an aircraft, he'd either have to go to the bother of checking the gun as baggage (which, traveling as an American now with his new I.D. might not be that difficult) or ditch the weapon in a trash container or just check it into a locker. And, in Washington, the gun would be a distinct handicap. Although the streets of Washington, D.C., were among the most potentially deadly in the world, he would be entering government buildings which all had electronic security. Some types of electronic security could be defeated right enough, but that took preparation that he didn't have the time to bother with; and, he was coming as a friend, not an infiltrator.

The overwhelming thing was that David could use the other pistol, might need it.

The result, as he left the taxicab and started into the train station, bag in hand, was that his only weapon was a large lockblade folding knife. The knife was a B&D Trading Company Fazendeiro. Large, the lock secure and the blade fast enough into action if one knew how, it was a type of knife he'd used before. Once he'd gotten it from

Centafari as part of the collection of weapons he'd requested, he'd done two things. Immediately, while Dannie had been showering in the next room, he'd touched up the knife's edge, making his shaving sharp. The next day, when he and David had by then secured the silver and were fabricating a limited supply of silver-bulleted ammunition for the two handguns and the shotguns, he'd used coarse-grit sandpaper in conjunction with a heavy rattail file and a ballpeen hammer to make indentations in the blade flats, well away from his fine edge, and along the spine. These depressions he filled with silver. The knife was not big enough to use as he'd used the Claymores against the beasts, but with the silver, if he could get the knife into the creature, he might well be able to kill through poisoning . . .

David had everything planned out, carefully it seemed. They called a taxicab and took the cab to the bus station. At the bus station, although David said it would be better to split up from a standpoint of throwing off someone following them, they stuck together for safety and shared another cab, this one to Highcliffe's areawise small but quite busy shopping mall at the edge of the city.

"Couldn't your imaginary Nazis be watching the bus station, Mallory?" David had answered, more civilly than Richard had asked, saying that indeed they probably were and he had planned for that. At the mall, they found the greatest crowds possible with which to mingle, the pre-Christmas shopping days an asset. David left them for a period of time, telling them to meet at a predesignated spot in ten minutes and to make certain they were not followed. If they were, don't make the rendezvous, try again in another ten minutes.

The Suburban pulled up, and just throwing their things inside, David was out of the lot as quickly as if they were being chased. She wondered if just maybe they were. As they turned into street traffic, he told them that this "es-

229

cape route" was something Mac had worked out. Then David asked, "Your aunt's apartment is close to the river, you say?"

Richard didn't answer David for a second, then said, "Yes. What's the matter now? Are we being stalked by The Creature From The Black Lagoon, too? Or is it werefish?"

David said nothing. Richard, in the middle seat beside her, put his arm up and she assumed she was supposed to lay back against it and did. The apartment belonging to Richard's aunt seemed like a nice enough place to her way of thinking; she'd been there once for dinner, and several times with Richard, just looking in on the place. It was well furnished and immaculately clean.

Richard's aunt habitually wintered in Florida; she'd broken a hip years back in a nasty fall and always left before the icy streets and sidewalks came, only returning once it was well into spring. And she knew that Richard's aunt Louise wouldn't mind their using the place in a good cause, had even asked that Richard occasionally spend the night there. Usually Richard spent the night elsewhere, in Dannie's bed. Dannie nuzzled more closely against him, telling herself this would all somehow work out, that before she knew it, Richard and she would be back to their normal lives together, back to routine. Classes to teach, papers to grade, nice long weekend evenings and even longer mornings in bed. She wanted that very much, anything that was normal . . .

There was one thing Hugh MacTavish envied of women: the little compacts in which they carried their face powder. He didn't fear for a shiny nose, but there had been occasions in his life when the excuse to look into a mirror so he could see behind him would have been welcome. And this was one of those times.

Certain he wasn't followed from the hotel, if indeed he were not alone now his "tails" had picked him up at the train station. He'd anticipated that the stations would be

230

watched, but the next nearest town with a train station or small airport was Sutton, which could prove worse than Highcliffe. In Sutton, Stein and his men would be on home ground and harder still to combat. The only other alternative had been driving down to New York, but that would have been inviting disaster. At least, with other persons around, Stein's aggression would have to be at least slightly restrained, any attempt more circumspect.

Hugh MacTavish, relatively certain that he'd been "made," leaned back and closed his eyes, equally certain he would need the rest.

Chapter Twenty-one:

How Sweet Fortress

"Too many windows," David Mallory announced as he moved about the apartment, one of the little shotguns in his right hand. He paused by the windows.

"Why don't you just lower the shades?" Richard asked him.

"If anyone was able to follow us, which I doubt, we'd be telling them instantly just which apartment we were in. No. We'll stay well back from the windows for a while. We can lower the shades later. Good commanding view of the intersection from here. If only I had some sort of long-range weapon it would be better."

"What would be better? Richard persisted.

"Chances of killing them if we spotted them coming for us."

"You mean, you'd just open fire, unprovoked? You talk about these creatures of yours as beasts. For God's sake, what are you?"

David turned away from the window, pointed the shotgun away from Richard as he spoke. "Only a fool waits to be fired upon when he's being stalked by a mortal enemy, Doctor. If everybody waited for the other person to shoot first, then there'd never be any violent conflict at all, would there? And that would certainly be nice and all, but reality tells us there's violent conflict anyway, every day. Who starts it, then?"

"Men like yourself?"

David's usually impassive countenance showed a look of

total disgust and he left the room, Dannie could hear doors being opened and closed, imagining him checking inside every closet, even under the bed.

She went toward the kitchen, hoping Richard would take the hint and bring along the suitcase they'd packed with food so she could get something going for dinner . . .

Dannie Hardy was washing out a pot to boil water in so she could start making the spaghetti and the kitchen sink faucet was at an odd angle to the basin. She wore a light-blue denim dropwaist jumper with a very full skirt that came to her ankles, a loose-fitting long-sleeved navy-blue knit top under it, the shirt buttoning up the front to a low, round neck, like a man's old-fashioned longjohns, the long sleeves pushed up past her elbows, There were water spots splashed all over her dress from the sink so she went in search of an apron.

Hanging neatly in a little broom closet were several of them, perfectly pressed, maybe even starched, but all of the same type, the kind that you slipped your arms through and then buttoned up the back. The hell with that, she thought; but it was either an apron or ruin her clothing. She selected the least nauseating-looking print, took it off the hanger, and put it on, only buttoning enough of the buttons in back to keep the thing from falling off. Then she returned to the sink.

As she washed the pot and the strainer, her attention was elsewhere, watching as David—with admirable patience, she had to admit—was trying to teach Richard something about one of the two full-sized shotguns that had been stored under the seat of the Suburban. They had smuggled the guns into the apartment building, the guns partially taken apart.

She rinsed out the pot for the last time, set it on the drainboard, and worked on the strainer. This done, she set it aside for later, then turned the hot water off and started to fill the pot two-thirds of the way to the top with cold water.

She put the pot on the stove. There was nothing from which she could create a salad and nothing else to serve as a side dish. There was a microwaveable chocolate cake mix, however, but she wouldn't worry about dessert until after dinner. It was ridiculously quick and simple to make anyway. She went back to the sink and washed out three coffee mugs and three glasses for wine, her feet feeling damp through the soles of her navy blue tights. The sink had splashed onto the floor, not just her.

She wiped her hands on the dish towel, wiped off the coffee mugs and glasses, too, then took off the silly apron.

There was coffee going and she poured a cup for herself. "Anybody else want coffee?"

Neither man answered, even acknowledged, so she shrugged her shoulders and dismissed it. If they wanted coffee but were too "busy" to answer, they could damn well pour it for themselves.

It was good to get her damp feet onto the carpet where maybe they'd dry. Richard was telling David, "I have no interest in using a gun. I hate guns, Mallory. All they are for is death and destruction."

"A gun is a tool, like any other, Richard. If the man or woman behind it uses it for good, it does good; if it is used for evil purposes, it accomplishes evil. But only as an instrument, as an extension of the will of the sentient being behind it. If Stein and his werewolves strike, what do you propose to do? Philosophize?"

"Fine, all right? You point the damned thing and pull the trigger until it's empty."

"No. You point the thing, stroke the pump rearward — rather like the slide on a trombone — and then pull the trigger. Then you pump the action again before you can pull the trigger again."

"Right. Point; pump; pull. I've got it."

"I give up. Philosophize instead. That way, you'll bore them to death!" And David stood up and walked toward the windows, never quite standing too close . . .

234

The burnished, dully gleaming colors of Grand Central Station was part of an image of New York he had obtained over the years from American films. Except for his arrival in New York with Dannie Hardy and David Mallory, and for now, he had never visited "The Big Apple" in his life, although it was a city which had always fascinated him. He knew the right names—Waldorf Astoria, the Empire State Building, Statue of Liberty, Rockefeller Center, Radio City, F.A.O. Schwarz, Tiffany's—all of them. He had very few mental images with which to connect them. He smiled, wondering if Audrey Hepburn, always one of his favorites in American cinema, had really breakfasted at that famous jewelry store? And what decided the giant gorilla King Kong to abandon the Empire State Building, on his second, more recent trip to New York, for the twin towers of the World Trade Center?

Talk about a fatal attraction for heights.

Two men, at least, followed him, and he wondered whether they would strike here, amid the crowds of people going in all directions to and from trains, or on the street? His right hand rested in the pocket of his winter jacket, on the Fazendeiro folding knife, his left hand holding the suitcase. There was nothing much in the bag—some underwear, hose, a few clean shirts, and his shaving and toothbrushing gear, all of which could easily be replaced. But he'd packed along two rather large books picked up the previous day in a used-book store, the content immaterial to him, the size and weight the important thing, giving the bag he carried sufficient weight that it could be used as a weapon.

He passed a piece of dark plate glass and caught a full view of the crowd immediately behind him.

Two men definitely, about twenty feet apart, about ten yards back, both of the men fit-looking, good-looking, about thirty years old at the most, one of them very blond, almost as smooth-skinned as a woman. They wore business clothes, the blond bare-headed, the darker-haired one, almost as fair skinned as the blond, wearing a suede leather fedora.

MacTavish quickened his pace slightly just to be sure. They quickened theirs just as he caught their reflections again. One of them—the dark-haired man—had his right hand stuffed into the outside pocket of his short overcoat.

MacTavish's mind raced. If they made a hit—perhaps something as conventional as guns—right here, there was always the chance of slipping away into the crowd, but the location posed as many problems as solutions. Quickthinking police action could seal the escalators going back and forth to the trains, could seal the entire structure.

MacTavish looked toward the exit. He was walking west, toward Park Avenue. There should be taxicabs hovering about the station, but he wasn't certain of that. In the cinema, New Yorkers always found taxicabs but seemed to have a difficult time of it. There was something about when it rained the situation always being worse, he seemed to recall.

The two men, Stein's men, would perhaps have been able to call ahead, or had some sort of radio gear which allowed them to communicate with a getaway car of some sort that could be waiting outside.

MacTavish decided. They would strike as he exited Grand Central Station.

MacTavish eased his pace, no need to rush the thing, because the longer it took to come down, the more tension his two assailants would experience, hence the more likely they'd be to make some slight but hopefully telling slip. Mac reached the doors to the street, part of a huge two-way crowd, for a second losing sight of both men, then picking up the dark-haired man.

Where was the blond?

MacTavish quickened his pace again, to throw off their timing.

On the street, bells tinkled, men dressed like Santa Claus with red pots hung on frames before them wishing

236

passersby Merry Christmas, one man on each side of the entrance.

Mac's nostrils flared as he sniffed the cool early-evening air, like an adrenaline rush in itself after the stale hot air of the train and the station. He angled toward the dark-haired man, assuming that the blond one was on his other side. And going toward the one with dark hair would make the blond-haired chap's job more difficult.

There were no taxicabs near the curb on either side of the street, cars zipping past to angle downward, beneath the bowels of the building it seemed. He was at the base of some enormous canyon, buildings towering on three sides of him, stretching as far as the eye could see to the north, headlights on in the twilight, the sounds of horns blaring.

He knew as soon as he realized he'd gotten caught up in marveling at the city that he'd made a mistake; would it prove fatal?

MacTavish's right hand closed around the knife, ready to pull it, open it.

There was a sound like a cough to Mac's right and MacTavish threw himself down to one knee as a woman somewhere behind him screamed and a man not eighteen inches from him clasped his chest and fell flat on his face to the dirty concrete. MacTavish's brain calculated angle and trajectory as he threw the suitcase up to protect his face and upper body, a second and third coughing sound, the case vibrating in his hand.

MacTavish saw the blond now, the dark-haired man out of sight.

There was a semi-automatic pistol in the blond's right hand. The blond shouted into the crowd, "Out of my way!" A woman moved too slowly. He shot her in the face and she fell. The pistol was fitted with a suppressor, long, shaped like a diminutive automobile engine muffling device. The blond pointed the pistol toward MacTavish.

There was nothing else for it, MacTavish knew, but to attack. If he tried fleeing into the crowd, more innocent blood would be shed. MacTavish, his body low, as much of it as he could get profiled behind the suitcase, launched himself toward the man. Two more shots. MacTavish had already mentally catalogued the gun, one of the double-column magazine high-capacity Beretta .380s, perhaps half its rounds spent. Another shot as MacTavish impacted the blond-haired man, no sensation of impact through the suitcase, MacTavish with no idea of where the bullet struck until he heard a man shout, "Jesus! I'm shot!"

MacTavish's body slammed the blond-haired man, at the same time the bag crashed against the blond-haired man's torso, MacTavish's right knee twisting around inward and smashing up into the groin. *"Sheiss!"* The blond wasn't happy. MacTavish's left hand loosed the bag, letting it fall, then caught the man's right wrist, twisting the silenced pistol upward, another shot firing, hot brass pelting MacTavish on the left cheek just below his eye.

MacTavish had the knife in his right hand, no time to open it, but used the butt of it instead like a kubotan, smashing it to the blond man's left temple.

The blond's eyes widened and the right wrist went limp. MacTavish fisted the knife like a roll of coins, punching upward toward the base of the blond's nose, to smash the ethmoid bone upward into the brain and finish him. Mac's blow missed as the blond's face turned away, MacTavish splaying the nose to the side instead, blood spraying as the body went rigid and started to fall.

MacTavish reached to the sidewalk for the pistol. There was still the dark-haired man. The suppressor-fitted Beretta in his left hand now, the hammer cocked, his eyes moved through the crowd. There was suppressed pistol fire to his left and he wheeled toward the sound as a standard pistol shot cracked the cold air.

He saw the dark-haired man then, hatless now, pumping another pair of shots into the chest of a uniformed New York City policeman.

The dark-haired man turned away, toward MacTavish.

MacTavish shouted to the men and women around him, "Get down to the sidewalk, if you please!"

The dark-haired man pointed his identical pistol at arm's length like a bull's-eye marksman. MacTavish didn't sidestep, just fired from his left hand at chest level, then fired again. The dark-haired man's arm sagged slightly. There was the coughing sound again, a mechanical scraping noise part of it, a chip of concrete flying up about two rads from MacTavish's left foot.

MacTavish fired again, the dark-haired man's body already spinning round, like a ballet dancer, and then just falling, the pistol discharging once, then again into the concrete sidewalk.

MacTavish breathed.

Behind him, two sounds. A child shrieked. And there was the howling sound he had heard in 1945 and again only days ago at his house in England.

MacTavish turned round.

The blond-haired man's transformation was half completed. It was then MacTavish noticed the thing in the blond-haired man's right hand. It looked identical to one of the objects he'd found in among the clothes in one of the two cars the Nazis had used to drive to his home. It looked like a solar calculator.

The blond had the thing pressed to his right ear.

"Damn!" MacTavish shouted, "Out of my way!" He charged toward the partially transformed killer, skin tearing, bleeding, healing before his eyes, clothes flying from the body, the face distorting beyond human imagination, the jaw distending, a crackling sound, the howl again.

Hair sprang up in patches, then more patches, the patches closing with each other, a dense bright blond coat with dark splotches, almost the same as Stein—not quite.

MacTavish stopped three feet away and shot out both of the creature's eyes. There was a hideous, half-animal, half-human sound. The beast swiped its giant left forearm toward MacTavish. The arm was half human, half animal, claws bursting from the fingertips as the fingertips themselves darkened almost to black, calloused pads appearing as the hands themselves seemed at once to shrink and grow, twist, become animal.

MacTavish tried to fire, only then noticing the slide locked open, the pistol empty. MacTavish hurtled it at the beast, the knife unopened, still in his clenched right fist. MacTavish pinched the blade outward between thumb and first finger, snapping it open, then threw himself toward the werewolf as it tried to stand. MacTavish averted his eyes, raking the blade of the knife across the tree stump-sized neck just beneath the jaw, gouging the knife into flesh so the silver might have some effect.

The beast hurtled him back as it stood, MacTavish falling against two men, all three of them collapsing to the sidewalk. The beast swung its massive right arm, then shrieked as it stumbled to its haunches, collapsing, the transformation that came with death beginning.

From Mac's left, there was the howling sound again.

MacTavish pushed himself to his feet.

The dark-haired one, lurching toward him, in full form as the wolf, seeming to gain strength by the second, stride broadening, speed increasing.

Two uniformed police officers came from MacTavish's right, toward the street, one of them grabbing MacTavish, a gun to MacTavish's chest. "Don't move, asshole!"

The second officer pointed his gun at the werewolf. "Halt! Halt!"

"Shit!" MacTavish snarled, twisting away from the police officer holding him, left hand simultaneously snapping outward and upward against the gun, the gun discharging but upward, Mac's body twisting right, his left knee smashing against the policeman's testicles. The policeman crumpled to his knees.

As MacTavish twisted the gun loose of the policeman's right hand, MacTavish looked up. The werewolf vaulted toward the second cop, so rapid in its movements that if MacTavish had blinked, what occurred would have been over. The beast's front paws impacted the officer's chest, driving him down, the handgun discharging at least three times into the beast's chest, the werewolf's jaws snapping

240

closed over the policeman's throat, a snapping sound.

The werewolf reared its head, the police officer's neck still clenched in its teeth, the head severed from the torso. The werewolf swung the head once right and once left, blood still spraying from the body under its feet. And the beast flung the head into the crowd.

MacTavish was already in motion, someone reaching out of the crowd to grab him, stop him, MacTavish straight-arming the anonymous man in the chest. MacTavish stumbled, fell to his knees. He looked back. The werewolf snarled, barred its three-inch fangs, then vaulted toward him.

MacTavish turned away, scrambled to his feet, threw himself over the body of the werewolf he'd already killed, wrenching the knife from the dead man's throat, praying there was enough silver left on the blade.

As MacTavish tore the Fazendeiro free and started to turn, still on his knees, he could feel the fetid breath of the second beast come at him in a nauseating wave.

MacTavish tucked his chin down to protect his throat, cocked his left elbow, and put the wedge of his arm in front of his face, then punched the knife upward and forward the split second before the beast was upon him.

MacTavish's right arm took the full force of the werewolf's weight, pain seizing Mac's wrist and forearm, his body rocked back as the creature crashed onto him, rolled over him, the knife twisting out of Mac's hand, his own body rolling over right, his right shoulder wrenching, maybe dislocating.

A howling, so piercingly loud Mac's ears rang with it.

MacTavish lay flat on his stomach on the sidewalk. His right hand and wrist and forearm tingled. He stood, his gaze transfixed.

The werewolf's body was changing back, to human form.

MacTavish rubbed his right arm, looked around him. People stared, but there was almost total silence except for the traffic noises on Park Avenue, except for the wailing of sirens, perhaps a minute away.

For some odd reason, MacTavish realized he'd lost his hat.

He swallowed, his voice low, his eyes shifting from one nameless face to another as the crowd closed around him. "It will be all right now. They were after me. Only those two of them were here. You'll be safe from them."

He had to run, disappear into the crowd, throw away his blood-spattered winter coat, find a taxicab to LaGuardia.

But Brigadier Hugh A. MacTavish addressed himself to the crowd once more. "I promise you this; while there is breath in my body, they will not live to destroy you."

He shouldered his way into the crowd and through it.

No one screamed. No one spoke. No one even murmured.

And then—it was the strangest thing—someone from far off in the crowd began to clap his hands, and then someone else joined the first, and another, and soon, as Hugh MacTavish escaped from their midst, the applause rose to a roar, even more thunderous than the howl of the wolf which still echoed in his ears.

"Not bad for sixty-one, MacTavish!" MacTavish said under his breath. He wasn't thinking of the applause, although he couldn't ignore it; but, what he took pride in was that he had in his trouser pocket one of the devices, which looked for all the world like an ordinary, credit-slim solar-powered calculator.

It was the device which allowed the werewolves to transform.

The sirens grew louder. MacTavish walked faster, but didn't run.

Chapter Twenty-two:

The Beasts Come

The moon was all but full still. It frightened her. "Don't be afraid. From what Mac says, I doubt the moon really has much if anything to do with it, Dannie."

She turned her head around and looked up into David's eyes.

He smiled at her. "It was a fine dinner, really."

"Spaghetti sauce out of a jar? You should taste pasta when I have some ingredients. I, ahh . . . that's not cooking. It's warming up stuff."

"Then should I say you warm things very well?"

She looked away from him, laughed a little. She reached into the slash pocket along the left side seam of her dress, found her cigarettes and a book of matches. But, before she could strike a match, David had a lighter out, rolled the striking wheel under his thumb, the flame flickering before her.

She thrust the tip of her cigarette into the fire and inhaled. "Thank you. Why doesn a man who doesn't smoke carry a lighter?"

"For people who do."

She laughed. That felt good.

The dining room was dark, only a worklight on in the kitchen, so it was safe, David had told her, to stand beside the window.

Richard was in the shower. He had just worked out with the set of weights that he stored here in his aunt's apartment.

"Do you love him?"

"He's a good, gentle man, yet he's strong."

"Fine. Do you love him?"

"If I didn't, I should, so what difference does it make?"

"If you loved him, it would make a difference," David said.

She inhaled, exhaled smoke, watched it bounce against the window glass, ricochet toward her for an instant, then rise, dissipate. "Are you also a guide for the lonely hearts?"

"No. Just an ex-British agent trying to make a living in the private sector."

"I thought you couldn't talk about things like that?"

"If the werewolves attack us and we die, who's to worry? If we survive and defeat them, then we'll be heroes, won't we, and no one will care. Anyway, you have an honest face."

"What did you do in the Secret Service?" Dannie asked him softly.

"Ohh, secret stuff."

They both laughed. "No, really! What?"

"Some things I liked, and some things I didn't. I was on the young side when I got involved."

"And?"

"And. And, what?"

"Well, why did you quit?"

"I wanted to do something else; got tired of people telling me to do things; thought there was money and opportunity and a future in doing private security."

"Is there?" Dannie asked him.

"There's money in virtually anything, but the trick is finding out how to make it. And who's to say anything about the future?"

"You and Mac are good friends."

"Yes. He's the father I don't remember, really. Sounds terrible, doesn't it? Like a line out of a low-budget film? I mean, well—"

"What do you mean?" She turned around, looked away from the moon, looked at him. He had pretty, dark eyes.

"You're beautiful." The back of David's right hand

brushed against her cheek, so incredibly gently. He walked back into the darkness, crossed from it into the diffused light of the kitchen, and picked up the bottle of wine, poured some into a glass.

Dannie Hardy felt numb watching him. She closed her eyes, lowered her head, stood there breathing shallowly, softly . . .

"Central, this is 201, proceeding on suspected — holy — Central, we have — look out, Harry! Jesus!"

There was static and the transmission was gone, the red diodes on the scanning monitor flickering on in sequence, at last one lighting as a currently broadcasting frequency was found. "Central to all cars in the vicinity of the Highcliff House. Code Fourteen. I say again, Code Fourteen. Proceed with caution." The message kept repeating. David flicked the toggle switch beneath that band's position, blocking it out. He'd explained how the scanning monitor, another piece of equipment that had been given to them at the same time they were given the guns and the Suburban, worked. It continuously searched for active frequencies, and frequencies with constant traffic could be temporarily locked out.

She'd been sipping wine for the last forty-five minutes or so since dinner, sitting on the couch with Richard and David, just watching the little red lights, the apartment in relative darkness, the only illumination the kitchen worklight and a candle beside the scanning monitor. The sirens had started up a half hour ago and were still going, even louder now, and David had turned on the monitor and the first of the police and fire department reports began coming in. At David's insistence, she'd pulled on her boots, gotten her warm three-quarter-length parka and her sweater and gloves and scarf and put them nearby along with her purse and a small shoulder-strap-fitted athletic bag.

David had said, "We might need to move in a hurry." He'd suggested she change to pants. She'd told him she could run just as well dressed as she was but had packed her running shoes in the athletic bag along with a set of sweats just in case.

Richard had refused to get his things together, saying, "It's night, it's Christmas vacation for twenty thousand college kids. What the hell do you expect except police calls?"

David had changed into something that approximated a uniform, she guessed, loose-fitting black trousers bloused over army boots, a black, long-sleeved placket-front knit shirt with a collar, a heavy-looking black sweater with cloth patches at the shoulders and elbows; a black army jacket was laid out nearby. There was also some sort of a back pack and a cloth shoulder bag, with a strap on it, about the size of a woman's purse. "Are you through playing monster chaser now?" Richard had asked him. "Let me guess, now . . . I know! You're James Bond, right?"

To David's credit, he ignored Richard.

Dannie wanted to tell Richard to knock it off, just to stop, but instead she listened, in her mind assembling the pieces of the horror story she was hearing coming in over the scanning monitor. The machine found an active frequency again, catching it in midtransmission. ". . . damn right, Ernie. There were three fire trucks and an ambulance on the scene when we got here, and by the time we had the minicam rolling, one of the firetrucks was called away. Some kind of damn riot or something near the Highcliff House. One of the cops on the scene said he'd heard maybe a half-dozen people were killed. The building here is a loss. All they're trying to do is contain the fire now to keep it from spreading. If Pam isn't back with the tape in about another two minutes or so, beats hell out of me what happened to her."

The transmission paused, the monitor continued scanning. A woman's voice, a police officer, Dannie guessed. In the background was something which sounded like static. But Dannie realized it had to be gunfire. ". . . know what the hell they are, but they're covered with fur and they're damn bulletproof and they're killing people, pulling 'em out of buildings and ripping them apart. They're moving north along Chester Highway, about to enter the city. About a hundred of them. And some of them are aww—" The transmission cut off, the monitor scanning ahead.

Richard said, "I was wrong," then stood up, presumably to get his things. There was a very worried look on David's face that worried *her* just to see it.

Dannie locked her hands over her knees. If she could have seen her knuckles, she knew they would have been white . . .

Hugh MacTavish was just off the bus which carried passengers back and forth between the terminal and the various aircraft. He surveyed the crowd, looking for hostile faces and one friendly one in particular.

The man wearing the black leather knee-length coat who caught MacTavish's eye took off his tinted glasses with his left hand, extending his right hand as he walked toward MacTavish through the Dulles terminal crowd. Some indefinable something about Bob Magee, the ease, the grace with which he moved perhaps, had always reminded MacTavish of the film actor Sean Connery, either that or of a cat burglar.

Hugh MacTavish took the offered hand. "Magee. How come you don't seem to get any older?"

They clasped hands still, the man named Magee saying, "Clean living, I suppose, Mac. I'll lie, too; you look great. Where's your coat?"

MacTavish shrugged, stuffed his hands into his trouser pockets. "Trash can in an alley near the Pan Am building. Nice coat you're wearing. Let's see, where was the last time we met?"

"Brazil, in Rio Grande do Sul, wasn't it?"

"And the time before that in Rothenburg." MacTavish laughed. "You seem to get around the world nearly as much as I do."

Magee exhaled slowly, his eyebrows cocking upward. "I'm working on my frequent flyer's discount. Pan Am Building, you say? You know, that's odd that you should say Pan Am Building, because come to think of it, there seems to have

247

been something very peculiar that happened on the Grand Central Station side around rush-hour time, earlier to-night."

"Really?" MacTavish smiled.

"Something about two naked corpses, a couple of critically injured New York's Finest, a couple of dead ones, too. And, wouldn't you know it, the whackos are everywhere. Because there was some stuff about creatures that were all furry and everything."

"Really? And I missed it! Perhaps that's what all the commotion was about as I was leaving. I was in a bit of a hurry. Could have been rats."

"Maybe. Why'd you get rid of your coat, Mac?"

"Spilled something on it."

Magee nodded, shoved his hands into the pockets of his coat. "Do you have a bag?"

"No, no." MacTavish smiled again. "I did, but talk about odd things, it developed quite a number of holes in it as I was carrying it along from the train."

"Moths?"

"Perhaps, but I'd never seen moths like that in England."

"New York moths can be very aggressive," Magee said as they fell in beside each other and started out of the terminal.

"Perhaps it was rats," Mac offered. Magee lit a cigarette, MacTavish lighting one of his own. "Still in the gun business?"

"Aren't I always?" Magee smiled.

"It's nice the way my friends at the Company thought of you coming by to pick me up. I hadn't realized we had that many mutual friends."

Magee laughed good-naturedly. "What company is it they're with? The fella who called me's just a guy I bump into every once in a while."

"Virginia-based firm."

"Tobacco?" And Magee gestured with his cigarette.

"Quite diversified, I've always understood. Just where are we meeting our mutual friends, by the way?"

"Office building down by the Potomac, not too far from

where I work." They stepped out of the terminal, MacTavish shivering with the sudden cold.

"What a coincidence!"

"I thought so," Magee agreed.

They found a cab, MacTavish telling Bob Magee, "Treating me to a taxicab ride no less! How generous."

"Shut up, or I won't find you a coat." Magee climbed in after him, telling the driver, "Alexandria, friend."

MacTavish leaned back in the seat and closed his eyes . . .

The sky where the horizon line would be glowed orange and yellow as far as she could see in any direction. And she knew what she was seeing were fires, burning out of control.

All the lights in the apartment were out, and the scanning monitor was dead, just like the television, the clock on the microwave oven, the clock on the VCR—no power.

At first she'd wondered why they didn't just leave, David and Richard and herself, run for it, but then Dannie had started thinking about the police and fire calls they'd been picking up throughout the last few hours. Where could they go? No one had used the word "werewolf" yet, at least not over the radio, but every once in a while "creatures" or "beasts" or "some kind of fuckin' animals" would creep in. The things were everywhere.

And she realized from watching David's face that he'd miscalculated and they were in even worse trouble somehow.

No stations could be picked up over the battery-powered radio, except for a hard-to-understand AM station from New York State somewhere. The normal stations, the golden oldies one she listened to, the ones that played elevator music and hard rock and everything in between, they were all broadcasting nothing but static and whistles, as if their transmitters had been knocked out or the broadcast facilities just abandoned.

She told herself that maybe it was just the power loss responsible, but she knew many of the stations had reserve power, and the civil defense bands would have been broadcasting. But there was nothing.

David hadn't planned for this. He'd planned for an attack on them, not an all-out attack on the entire area, an uprising. She knew that as she watched the worry in his face when the moonlight through the curtains or the glow of their single candle would catch his features.

All of the streetlights were out and every houselight and business sign and everything in all directions was darkened. When she looked along the streets intersecting below the windows of Richard's aunt's corner apartment, the only light was the glow of the fires.

Heavy clouds scudded across the moon and snow was falling, gentle-seeming, in bizarre contrast to the tales of destruction she had been privy to via the scanning monitor, but the snow taking on the yellow-orange glow of the fires as it touched the streets and sidewalks, imparting a surreal quality to the night. It was as if somehow everything surrounding this darkened apartment in which she cowered from the night was the landscape of a nightmare.

Fires burned only a block or so south of them. She could see the fires raging as she parted the lacy curtains with her hand and peered through the window. No more, however, were there the sirens of emergency vehicles, coming to put the fires out. On the scanning monitor, before it had stopped working, someone had used the word "firestorm." Fires would burn so hot that the updraft they created bred its own winds and the winds spread the fire and created more heat to increase the winds and spread the fire still more.

She had felt the gravity and perhaps the hopelessness of their situation most of all, oddly enough when David had donned his shoulder holster, checking the load in his handgun, then putting the gun back under his left armpit. Richard hadn't made any cracks whatsoever about spies or private eyes or anything. Instead, he'd asked, "May I have a gun, Mallory?"

David gave him one of the shotguns.

Richard inhaled so loud that in a woman it might have been interpreted as just short of a scream.

Dannie left her window looking toward the river and went to stand beside him, never doubting Richard's courage because even though she had seen the beasts before, from dangerously close, she felt like screaming now. Behind her, she heard the by-now familiar sound of David getting one of the shotguns ready to fire.

As she looked over Richard's shoulder, she saw the stuff of nightmares, but worse, she thought, than anything any human mind could create, no matter how tortured that mind.

An army of them moved along the street just below the window closest to the kitchen. Some of them trailed bloody human limbs in their mouths, barely walking on two feet or all fours, sated on human flesh to the point of physical exhaustion it seemed, lurching from one side of the street to the other, drunk on human blood. Others of the beasts bounded through their midst, leaping through storefronts, into doorways, in the next moment dragging out human prey, sometimes still alive. Her stomach started to go, but if she ran into the bathroom to throw up, she'd be alone in the dark. She told herself not to throw up.

The beasts were pressing on toward the river, it seemed to her, because when the beasts at the leading edge of the phalanx reached the corner at which the apartment was situated, they were turning. That didn't make any sense. She tried controlling her voice enough to speak, when David, flanking her on her left side now, almost whispered, "It's like they're coming for us, specifically, isn't it?"

She noticed now, with the paralysis of detachment, that many times the beasts would not kill, merely batter and taunt the human victim, then bite, then cast aside the body. "They're making more of themselves."

She hadn't really realized she'd said it aloud until David answered her.

"Yes," David said, "for tomorrow night perhaps, if there is a tomorrow night, if the fires don't consume everything in Highcliffe first."

"The car. Maybe if we could make it to the car . . . ,"

Richard began.

"The car is parked by the river. We'd never make it to the river through them now. I miscalculated totally what they would do so now we have to wait." And he gestured toward the creatures filling the street.

"You miscalculated? So then, we should wait? What's to say you're right this time?" Richard said, an edge to his voice Dannie didn't like.

"I expected, if anything, an attack, like the one which took place at the Brigadier's estate. I hadn't realized that Stein and his people's big plan was so close to being launched. But this is proof that it was We can't run now. We'll have to stay here, fight it out and wait for just the right moment, then make a run for it. I count over sixty of them out there."

Dannie looked back into the street. David was probably right, but there seemed to be more, hundreds of them. She realized her fists were balling in the fabric of her dress, opening and closing.

She was scared.

"They did all this to get us," Dannie whispered.

She looked at Richard, could see his face remarkably clearly because the light from the fires reflected off the fresh snow, the light as bright as a full moon's. She wanted him to say that such a remark was an expression of paranoia, just born out of terror.

Richard didn't say that. He didn't say anything.

But David spoke. "We'll have to make it out across the roof, but only when there's a chance they won't spot us. And, until then, we'll have to defend this place. Dannie, look around in the kitchen and see if you can find any combustible petroleum-related product—"

"Lighter fluid?"

"My aunt doesn't smoke."

"Maybe she used it for spot remover, Richard."

"Richard, you take anything combustible you can find and stoke it into the base of the hearth there. If they bashed away the chimney, they might be able to come through it and get at us so we'll want to be ready to ignite instantly."

"All right."

David said nothing else, setting to work instead. She watched him for a second, looked at Richard, wondered if she was going to die.

Then she started for the kitchen.

She set out another candle in the kitchen, with shaking hands lit it with a match, flicked the match into the sink. She dropped to her knees in front of the sink, her dress ballooning out around her. The candle in her left hand, she began searching for anything that would make a fire start to burn quickly. She found something, brass polish.

She didn't bother closing the cupboards, nearly caught the heel of her left boot in the hem of her dress as she stood, then still holding the candle, ran toward the fireplace. Richard was throwing magazines and newspapers into it, and she helped him.

She looked for David. He was pushing furniture in front of the door. "Richard. Go help him. I can do this."

"All right, Dannie." He picked up his shotgun, went to help David.

"David? Do you want me to pour the stuff on now?"

"Not yet. If it saturates in too much, we might not get a good, fast fire. Wait until I tell you."

She knelt there, waiting.

She looked at David. He had Mac's big black pistol in one hand, one of the little shotguns in the other.

She thought she heard noise on the roof.

"David!?"

"Not yet." He was beside the windows. "There must be three dozen of them just closing in around us, the rest of them going on toward the river."

"Then we're cut off," she said.

"Don't give up."

Richard. She saw Richard, one of the shotguns in his hands, the other leaning against the couch beside him.

"Pour it on now, Dannie, then get over here," David ordered.

She obeyed, sprinkling the brass polish over the newspapers and magazines as widely as she could. "Should I light

253

it?"

"Not yet. Get over here and bring your candle." She got up, went to join David by the windows. "Hold this." He gave her the second little shotgun. She didn't know what to do with it. Why hadn't someone thought to teach her? And she looked out the window, tears welling up in her eyes as she did, her throat too choked for her to scream.

Some of the beasts were climbing up from the street along the downspouts and over the rough-surfaced bricks. She could see others disappearing through the entryway, actually inside now.

Again, there was noise on the roof.

"Point; pump; pull. Right?" Richard shouted to David.

"More or less. Just keep shooting and try not to miss; we don't have that many rounds tipped with silver."

Dannie Hardy found her voice, but it didn't sound quite right as she spoke. "What can I do?"

David looked at her. "When I tell you to, run over to the hearth, throw the candle in, then get down on the floor between Richard and me. Don't lose that shotgun. It's stoked with silver."

"How do you shoot it?"

"That'd break your wrist with a barrel that length if you weren't used to it. If you have to, work the pump back and forward, evenly. And all the way back, huh? Then anchor the weapon beside your hip so where you face the muzzle of the gun faces, then just hold the weapon down hard so it doesn't snap up into your face, and pull the trigger. If you need a second shot, repeat the process. All right?"

"Yes."

"Go and stand by the fireplace. Be ready."

"Yes."

There was more noise on the roof now.

Glass shattered behind her, one of the windows on top of the street, the sound of David or Richard firing a shotgun, a howl so terrible that her stomach wrenched with it. David shouted, "Be ready with that candle, Dannie!"

She couldn't help herself, looking back.

The body of a werewolf in midtransformation lay half inside the window, draped over the sill, a hideous-looking wound in the creature's chest.

More noise from the roof. Louder now.

Bricks began falling down the chimney. "David!"

"Not yet!"

Pounding noise from the doorway, as her eyes flickered toward it, some of the furniture piled there against the door starting to dislodge.

More bricks down the fireplace.

There was a rush of air past her face, warm air from inside the apartment. That had to mean that enough of the chimney had been knocked away that there was an updraft.

She was just about to shout to David, ask him if it was time yet.

And then, David called to her. "Light it, Dannie!"

As she bent toward the fireplace, the candle blew out — blew out in the draft. Bricks were crashing downward now, impacting the base of the hearth and bouncing away with terrible force, one of them just missing her head.

"Dannie! Get back!" It was Richard's voice.

She started to edge away.

More bricks fell. From above her, she heard one of the creatures howl. More glass broke behind her. Pistol shots in response; she was amazed that she could tell the difference between the sound of a handgun and a shotgun. In the left slash pocket of her dress, she still had her cigarettes. And a book of matches.

Dannie dropped to her knees beside the hearth, bricks falling faster now, and huge clouts of snow from the roof as well. In a second, she knew, the first of them would be able to force himself inside. She grabbed off three of the matches from the book, striking them as one, simultaneously, then touching them to the rest of the matches. She threw the burning matchbook into the fireplace and threw herself in the opposite direction as she scrambled to her feet.

There was a roar, and for an instant she was terrified that somehow her dress had caught on fire.

She looked down at her clothes as she dropped to the floor behind the couch, near Richard. Her clothes were not in flames and she was amazed at herself that she'd remembered—subconsciously, it had to be—to pick up the little shotgun David had given her.

There was a terrible scream, human but not human, like the screams she'd heard when the beasts had attacked Mac's home outside London. But this sound came from within the upper recesses of the fireplace.

The flames were rushing upward faster than she had thought possible.

She looked to her left.

All of the windows were shot out now. The fire was sucking air in through the windows. What if the roof caught?

David stood his ground beside the glassless window-frames, firing his little shotgun from the hip as one of the beasts lurched through an opening and toward him. The broken glass surrounding David caught the firelight and glowed red.

"The door's about to go!" Richard shouted.

"Get your things; be ready to leave fast," David ordered.

Dannie was already shrugging into her coat and scarf, slinging on her purse and the athletic bag.

Just above her there was a ripping sound, then a crash, and as she looked to the ceiling, smoke was curling just beneath it. She realized the roof was on fire. Hammering sounds, as if objects were being pounded against the roof. From the fireplace there came another shriek, and as she looked, she screamed; in a storm of steaming bricks one of the beasts jumped through the flames, its body like a torch as it lurched out of the fire and toward her.

Richard stepped between her and the werewolf and there was a thunderous roar as Richard fired the shotgun. The beast fell back; Richard fired again.

David shouted, "Don't waste the silver! If you hit him, he's dead or dying!"

The rug near the hearth was in flames now, catching from the body of the beast. And, amid the flames, she could see the transformation back to human form taking place, cries of pain that were more human by the second coming from it. And there was a sound like a gust of high wind and the body of the creature was devoured.

The smoke in the apartment, despite the open windows, was acrid-smelling and dense, mingled with what she knew had to be burning flesh.

"Look out!" Richard shouted, pushing her back. A portion of the ceiling three or four feet square collapsed just in front of the hearth, a plume of flame instantly sucked upward out of the debris toward the new source of air. Flames were advancing across the carpet, too, now, toward the windows.

As her eyes followed the flames upward, she saw something that her mind for an instant refused to believe. One of the werewolves jumped into the flames from the roof above, crashing down into the center of the room, its back, the left side of its body, already partially consumed. Fangs bared, it lunged for Richard.

As Richard raised his shotgun, Dannie trying to work the pump on the one in her hands, there was a pistol shot from behind her. The creature fell back into the flames.

Richard wheeled away from it, shouted something she couldn't hear, and raised the shotgun, the gun firing less than a yard from her face, her left hand up to shield herself. Her ears rang with the sound and the concussion hit her like a slap.

A werewolf half into the apartment through one of the smashed-out windows just behind David fell.

David shouted something Dannie couldn't perfectly make out, her ears ringing so badly now all sound was as dull a roar as the sound of the fires burning around and above them.

Richard grabbed at her.

She stumbled after him as he ran toward the windows.

There was a roar louder than any other. From behind them. She turned her head around, the door bursting inward, the furniture stacked against it skidding away on all sides, werewolves bounding over it. Richard was saying something. She fell. She looked up. One of the werewolves dove toward Richard's throat. Richard stood his ground. The wooden part of the shotgun snapped forward in his hands, hitting the creature in the side of the head, the creature falling away for an instant, stunned. Richard took a step back, fired into it point-blank. Another creature flew against Richard, knocking him down.

Dannie worked the pump on the little shotgun and pushed the end of the gun up against the creature's back and pulled the trigger.

The gun fell from her hands, her fingers suddenly numb, her right wrist aching like a bad tooth.

David was dragging her to her feet, shoving the shotgun back into her hands. He wheeled toward the door, fired Mac's big black pistol, fired it again, bringing another of the creatures down, a second one vaulting over the sofa.

Dannie screamed.

David threw the pistol at the creature's head, hitting it, the beast falling back for the tiniest fraction of a second. David ripped the little shotgun from her hands and fired it into the beast's face.

Tears streamed down Dannie's cheeks.

Richard was up, to his knees, trying to stand.

David killed another of the creatures coming through the door, turning around then and shoving her bodily toward the windows, Richard beside them.

Dannie could barely hear her own voice as she shouted, "In the windows!"

Richard's gun went off directly beside her and a were-wolf—black-coated, blood clotted in its fur—fell back through the window opening and was gone.

She looked at David. He was loading one of the little shotguns. She'd watched as he'd loaded a shotgun before. You stuffed the bullets or whatever they were into the bottom of the thing.

He was shouting at her.

She could tell that but couldn't make out the words.

Richard was climbing out onto the window ledge. David shoved her toward the windowsill. She hitched up her dress, climbed up, stepped out.

More of the beasts were in the street below. One that she could see was climbing up the downspout toward them.

David stepped out through the window opening, firing one of the little shotguns, a tongue of flame leaping from it again and again and again.

Richard was walking along the ledge.

Dannie followed close behind him, the ledge narrow, slippery under her boots. She closed her tearing eyes for a moment, blinked them clear, edged after Richard.

Flames licked through the window openings behind her now, David so close to them she expected his clothes to catch fire at any second. He waved for her to go on.

They were near to the downspout, and the beast was nearly to the level of the small ledge. Richard braced himself against the wall, fired his shotgun, missed. The beast's fangs glinted in the light from the fires. Its fur was reddish brown, the color of the dog she'd played with when she'd go with her father to the cabin they'd rented in the Adirondacks when she was just a little girl.

She called out her father's name.

The creature's right forepaw touched the ledge, grabbed for her ankle. Dannie kicked at the thing, her boot hitting the beast in the right eye. The head whiplashed back and then forward, the jaws snapping shut inches from her foot as she recoiled.

And her ears popped.

She could hear the crackle of the fires now, and the howling of the werewolves.

Richard was trying to pump the shotgun with one hand while he clung against the building wall with the other.

The beast grabbed for her as it seemed to leap upward, onto the ledge.

She felt the crack of the pistol shot, the beast reaching for her with its right forepaw as she recoiled. And suddenly there was a hole just like a third eye, between the other two at the bridge of the beast's saliva-dripping muzzle.

The creature howled as it fell back into air, the transformation already starting.

She closed her eyes, looked away.

"Dannie! We've got to get onto the roof!" David's voice sounded like it was processed through some sort of echo chamber, like electronic music.

"The roof?!"

"Follow Richard!"

Richard was already climbing, the shotgun somehow stuffed through his trouser belt and hanging beside his left leg.

She looked back again.

Another of the creatures was on the ledge, this time behind David. "David!"

David, his pistol in his right hand, didn't turn his body, just moved his hand to in front of his chest, looked at the creature, and fired.

The beast fell toward the street.

Dannie reached the downspout, Richard nearly to the roof. She didn't have the strength of a man, not enough strength in her hands and arms to climb like that. But somewhere inside her, she heard another part of herself saying that she was lighter than a man, more agile than the average man, was in good shape from running and aerobics and—Dannie grabbed onto the downspout and her eyes scanned the building wall for a foothold. David—it had to be David—had his hands on her, shoving her upward ahead of him.

She was moving upward, a toehold against a metal clamp that held the downspout to the building wall, another where some of the mortar between the bricks was eroded away.

She looked up. Richard was partially visible. She could hear gunfire.

She looked down.

Her stomach went crazy and she felt faint.

David's hand was on her butt, pushing her upward.

She kept climbing.

Her right hand reached for the edge of the roofline. As her fingers touched the concrete lip, something closed over her forearm and she screamed, "Help me!"

She was flying for an instant, then crashed down hard onto the roof, the breath knocked out of her.

Brown eyes, impossibly large; hair almost the same deep auburn as her own.

Hulking over her.

One of them.

Drool fell from its fangs and onto her left boot. It reached down for her.

Richard interposed himself between them, pumped his shotgun. Nothing happened.

The beast was on him, Richard wrestling against it, the beast tossing him away like a rag doll. Dannie was on her feet, shaky, not even knowing how she'd stood up.

Fires burned everywhere on the roof, the smells from them making her at once faint and nauseated. She edged back. The creature dropped to all fours, moving slowly toward her, head cocked to the side, mouth wide, fangs glistening. A low growl issued from deep inside it.

She stopped, feeling the lip of the roof just behind her right heel.

If she took another step she'd fall to her death but the beast would have her.

She felt her heart beating, so impossibly rapid, so wildly she couldn't catch her breath.

The beast rose up on its hind legs, towering over her now, a loud howl shrieking from its throat.

"Richard!" Richard was on the thing, on its back, beating at its head with his fists, the creature's back arching, the muscles in its shoulders rippling powerfully. Richard's right thumb gouged into the beast's right eye. As if in human anger, the werewolf snapped its body forward, pawing at this thing tormenting it, clinging to it. Richard held on.

Dannie stood there, frozen in that spot, powerless to make her legs respond to her mind.

David.

He rolled over the edge of the roof on the far right of her peripheral vision, on one knee, his pistol in both hands. There was the crack of the shot. Dannie snapped her head away, her eyes closing involuntarily as David's bullet struck the werewolf in the side of its throat and blood sprayed everywhere.

Dannie felt herself starting to fall, threw herself forward onto her knees, burying her face in her hands.

A hand on her shoulder.

The dull echo of a human voice. "Dannie. Come on. Mallory says we need to try and use the rooftops to escape. Come on. We're all all right."

She looked up into Richard's face. His face was dirty and battered and bleeding and she wanted to kiss him and tell him she loved him. Because she knew he loved her, jumping on the back of one of the beasts like that, fighting it with his bare hands in order to try to save her. She let him help her stand. Her right arm throbbed where the beast had grabbed her, raised her up by it, ached from from wrist to shoulder.

David was already moving across the rooftop, skirting the fires which were burning everywhere, running toward the far edge on the river side, one of the little shotguns in his hands. Naked bodies with ragged, bloody gunshot wounds, some of the bodies burning, lay all about her. The stench of their burning flesh was more overpowering than the smell of smoke.

In high school, she'd first read *The Inferno*. But this truly was hell.

Dannie Hardy made her legs obey this time.

See ran, praying she could leave hell behind her.

Chapter Twenty-three:

Figments Of The Imagination

"I can't believe you're really saying this, Brigadier."

MacTavish looked away from Tarleton, the man who'd identified himself as a "special presidential adviser on intelligence," past Centafari, the CIA man, and the still-unnamed black man who was Centafari's partner, over to Bob Magee. Magee shrugged his eyebrows and lit a cigarette.

MacTavish looked back at John Robert Tarleton. "Mr. Tarleton, I happen to know what you really do for a living, sir."

Tarleton's eyes flickered just slightly. The eyes were so pale a gray as to be almost colorless. He was a big man, but with a soft, fleshy pink face, his bigness soft, too, his slicked-back black hair making the pinkness pinker. "That I'm a lawyer, you mean?"

Hugh MacTavish manufactured a smile and hung it on his face. "That you're the personal deputy to one of the three most powerful men in the U.S. Intelligence community, that you carry a title as deputy director of the National Security Agency, charged with intergovernmental operations—whatever the bloody hell that stands for—and that the only reason you're sitting in this office right now is because after I called Sir Phillip Denton at Century House and he agreed to call your people at CIA, something he repeated from our conversation must have struck a tiny nerve somewhere, didn't it? Otherwise, why you, Mr. Tarleton? Why not some flunky? Or did you

263

forget that the Special Air Service has the same sort of relationship to the Secret Intelligence Service in Her Majesty's Government as your Green Berets have to the CIA in your government?"

Tarleton looked down at his hands, his fingers tented over the immaculate blotter at the precise center of the spotless desk. "Why should a friendly call from M6 about a visiting fireman wanting to talk some shop upset us, Brigadier MacTavish? I'll tell you, though, having a retired SAS officer and a former case officer in British Intelligence running around the United States playing spy isn't exactly something I'm fond of. And once I find out who's been helping you out of Langley and got Centafari and Brown here to play delivery boys, their ass—"

"Ohh, shut up," MacTavish groaned.

From the far side of the room, MacTavish heard Magee murmur, "Ohh, boy."

Tarleton thumped both hands down on the desk. "What the hell did you say, man?!" Tarleton started out of his chair.

"I told you to shut up, Mr. Tarleton, because you're wasting time you'll soon wish you had to spare, you're making idle threats because you're pissed off that someone under you did something that seemed to make sense at the time without telling you, and you're wondering if somehow there's a grain of truth in what I said when I spoke about some Nazis at Sutton College about to launch a conspiracy that could cost your nation untold lives.

"And you probably have information about what happened this afternoon at rush hour outside Grand Central Station in New York City that even the New York police don't have, maybe even that I don't have and I was there, in the thick of it," MacTavish told him. "So, I'll tell you this. Either hear me out, Mr. Tarleton, or I'll get on the telephone again and wake up Sir Phillip Denton—which really pisses him off—and have him call the prime minister and the prime minister will be pretty upset, too. Then the PM will call the President. And the President will get really angry that you couldn't make an important decision and the President will call your superior and he'll call you. Then you'll listen. So, what is it? Do we do this the direct way or the indirect way? Time is on the side of the Nazis."

Tarleton looked at Centafari and his black partner, evidently named Brown. "Get out of here. You, too, Magee."

Centafari started to get up.

So did Brown.

Magee said, "No, I don't think so. No reason to; Mac told me his crazy story while you made us wait in the lobby for a half hour because you were running late. No, I think I'll listen to Mac's crazy story all over again. And that way, he's got a witness just in case you don't decide to do anything and it turns out that even though the story sounds crazy, it's true. I'll hang in with you guys."

"I'd rethink that, Magee," Tarleton veritably hissed.

"Why's that? Are you about to threaten me, Mr. Tarleton? Because if you are, before you do, you might want to think about the fact that I'm an old friend of the man you work for. He's the one who called me to pick up Mac at Dulles and bring him over here. And he's an old friend of Sir Phillip Denton. As near as I can figure it, if you don't listen to Mac, Mr. Tarleton, you're the one who's in hot water. But hey, suit yourself. If you really want me to leave . . ." And Magee started to stand.

Tarleton, a look of disgust in those washed-out gray eyes, waved Magee down, looking only at the desk as he said to MacTavish, "What were those naked dead men at the train station in New York, Brigadier MacTavish?"

"Werewolves," MacTavish said quietly.

Magee said, "You'll love the next part, Tarleton. Trust me."

Chapter Twenty-four:

A Fine A Man As Made

What she'd realized would happen happened. They ran out of rooftops.

David would get a running start and bound across from one building to the next, Richard doing pretty much the same but always waiting for her. When she jumped, as soon as she jumped, she closed her eyes.

But now they had reached the end of the block, and behind them, she could hear the sounds of more of the creatures as they howled to one another in the firelit night, in pursuit.

"This way," David ordered. By now Dannie Hardy was so used to obeying that she didn't even think about it, just picked up her feet and ran But what were they doing now? Running toward the alley that separated the two rows of apartment buildings? Where could they go but back along the way in which they came?

She wanted to ask. She didn't.

David stopped, almost too abruptly, along the alleyside of the roof, Dannie catching her breath, looking behind them again. She couldn't see any of the creatures, but she could hear them as part of the dull roar of background noise that had settled in to replace her normal hearing.

Below them, beasts stalked the street and twice since they'd made their first perilous crossing from one rooftop to another, it had been necessary to shoot down into the mob of creatures to keep them from scaling the walls to reach them.

David was dropped into a crouch beside a powerline, thick and black and dirty-looking. He was taking something from one of the pockets in his big black coat. "Sometimes one learns the standard sort of thing to prepare for in the field, usually the last thing one ever expects. But frequently, the unexpected involves electricity" What he took from his pocket was a pair of gloves. "The one problem is that I have one pair and there are three of us, but there's a handy way around that. These are triple insulated and have reinforced palms for rappeling.

"Rappeling?" Dannie queried.

"Letting yourself down along the side of a building or out of a helicopter to the ground along a rope. The height of this rooftop is, fortunately, several feet greater than that of the building across the street to which this cable is also attached." David was doing something with the gloves as he spoke.

Without thinking, Dannie moved her left hand toward the cable, her right arm still paining her badly. Before she could have touched the cable—did he think she was really that stupid to touch an electrical power cable?—David gripped her left hand like a vise.

"What are you suggesting?" Richard asked, his voice low.

"Simply this, and unless either of you has a better idea pretty quickly, it's not a suggestion, it's an imperative. They'll get us if we stay here." He took a plastic spool from his jacket, another of its many pockets. "Fishing line. Each of us slides across on the cable one at a time, then the next person up hauls the glove back with this fishing line. It'll have to be fast, the slide, or else there's danger of the cable snapping or popping loose from its moorings. Or, worse still, getting stuck out there."

"I can't—" Dannie started.

"You can, and you'll be the first. Because you're the lightest, so that means you'll have the best chance of making it."

"And you'll be next," Richard told David Mallory. "Somebody has to keep us covered." Dannie looked at both men, at their faces, features so hard to discern in the grayness of the light that David and Richard seemed very much alike. "And I'm the heaviest so I should be last anyway."

"I'm the better shot."

"Big fucking deal," Richard announced. "I picked up quickly enough. See, you Brits don't understand. All of us in America are born knowing that axiom about not shooting until you see the whites of their eyes. That's how we whipped your asses two hundred years ago."

Dannie Hardy shivered: They were bargaining lives, but her life wasn't a part of it. "No . . . I—"

Both men ignored her. It was as if, suddenly, they were brothers as they clasped hands there for an instant on the rooftop, the beasts howling and snapping beneath them on the street, the sounds of the werewolves behind them all the closer. She hated when men did that, like a woman's ideas didn't count, but her safety was everything.

"You can't . . ." She touched at Richard's arm.

He looked down at her and smiled. "Hey, don't you get any wrong ideas, honey, I'll be right behind you."

Honey?

Why did men start talking like John Wayne or Humphrey Bogart when things got dangerous? It wasn't a damned movie!

"Hold the glove like this . . ." David began.

But she ignored David, and even though her right arm hurt very bad, threw both arms around Richard's neck. "I love you, Richard."

He held her tightly, but only for an instant. She felt his lips brush against her hair, touch at her cheek. She found his mouth and kissed it hard, molding her body against his. "I love you," Richard said, his voice so

268

hoarse, so whispered—was he crying? She tasted salt on her lips. And she was crying, too.

Richard was gone, the shotgun in both his hands like a soldier storming an enemy hilltop in a war movie as he ran back along the roof. He settled into a crouch behind some sort of heating/air-conditioning unit.

David was talking to her. "Lock your hands on both sides of the glove. Release one side and you fall so you need to hold on tightly with both hands. It won't be more than a few seconds for you to cross to the other side."

"Don't say it that way," she managed. The way he phrased it, he made it sound as if she was going to die.

"I meant the other side of the street. Use your feet to stop yourself so your face doesn't slam into the wall, then grab on with both hands."

"Why don't you go first?" Dannie demanded.

"Because this cable is old and the fittings holding it are old and whoever doesn't make it across is going to be dead, Dannie. And it would be better to fall into the street and break your neck than—"

Dannie gripped the glove in both hands as he played out fishing line. "If I fall, you waste a bullet on me. Please?"

"Obviously," David told her.

Her right hand even hurt as she clenched her fist around the insulated glove. She knew she probably wouldn't be able to hold on but told herself she had to. "Make sure Richard doesn't—" She was perched in a crouch on the edge of the roof, ready to jump.

"If someone's going to tell you he loves you, do you really have to slap him in the face? Hold tight!" And he pushed her off.

The weight on her right shoulder made her suck in her breath with pain. She was at once terrified and giddy with the danger. She looked down, the beasts below her snapping at her. The cable vibrated.

Dannie looked up and ahead.

The wall of the building on the opposite side of the street was racing toward her. If she blocked too forcefully with her feet, mightn't she throw herself off the cable?

Dannie Hardy turned her face away, scrinching her eyes almost shut, her head back, neck arched, her left foot and left thigh taking the impact as she slammed against the wall. She hung there, afraid to move, knowing she had to let go and reach.

A toehold for her right boot in a mortarless gap between the bricks.

She wedged her foot there as best she could, looked to the roofline trying to figure out just what to reach for.

"Do it, Dannie!" It was David Mallory shouting from on the other side of the street.

She let go of the glove and grabbed for the edge of the roof, her nails gouging into it, at least one of them breaking, some of the roofing material crumbling away in her left hand. She started to slip, her right hand holding to the edge of the roof, her left hand groping. She almost touched the power cable.

At least then she'd be dead. All of this would be over.

Her left hand found something unyielding and held to it and she just hung there, breathing, her right foot still wedged in the niche between the bricks.

When she was a little girl, she'd climbed her share of trees, climbed her share of rocks on the seashore. She told herself this was a rock, a very tall rock, and that the growling and snapping of jaws below her wasn't what it was, but the sounds of the sea and that if she fell she'd—Dannie bit her lower lip, moved her right hand, lost her toehold for one terrifying split second, regained it and her right arm which ached like a sore tooth now was over the edge of the roof from the elbow downward.

She dragged herself up a little, pulling her butt in close to the building; she remembered that from her tree climbing, that your own weight could drag you back and down. She edged her right hand farther along the roof, her entire right arm over the edge now, flat along the roof's surface. She pushed with her right foot and pulled with her left hand and got her upper body mostly over the edge of the roof.

She sagged there, too exhausted to move anymore, knowing she was safe for the moment, her eyes closed, her breathing heavy.

Dannie opened her eyes, looked back as she heard shotgun fire from the roof on the opposite side of the street. And, from her perspective here, she could see the fires for the first time in their full magnitude. Behind her, as far as she could see, block after block of buildings was in flames, the sky on the side of Highcliffe away from the river yellow-orange and nearly as bright as day.

Beneath her parka, she was sweating. She saw David, the glove reeled in, but he wasn't attempting to cross. He was running back along the rooftop, joining Richard, she realized.

Richard was besieged by a half dozen of the creatures, the man -ide of their nature revealed clearly as they hunkered back in shelter when Richard fired at them. David seemed to be arguing with Richard. David fired his handgun and sparks flickered over the metal at the edge of the roofline as one of the creatures drew down behind it. But the bullet, even though it struck the roof, evidently struck the creature, because it fell away over the side and there was a sickening howl.

Richard was up, edging back along the roofline, as if covering David, David at the cable now, grabbing onto the glove.

Dannie was up, to her knees now at the roof's edge. David was shouting to Richard, "You go first!"

"Dammit, I won't."

David called back to him. "Then I'll cover you from the other side!" And David put the little shotgun down through his pants and, holding to the insulated glove, pushed himself off the roof's edge.

He sailed toward her over the cable much more rapidly than she had envisioned herself moving, because it had seemed like forever until abruptly she crashed against the wall. As David crashed against it, he somehow seemed to leap. She reached out to help him, but his hands were already locked over the edge of the roof. She grabbed on to his wrist, unnecessarily she realized, helping him over beside her. "All in knowing how." David smiled.

Damn him!

"Get over there and be ready to help Richard." David drew his handgun. Richard crouched at the edge of the roof on the far side of the street, the shotgun to his shoulder. Richard fired, killing one of the werewolves as it raced along the edge of the roof on all fours and lunged for his throat. The creature's body was suddenly airborne, crashing down toward the street. "Come on, Richard!"

Richard grabbed up the fishing line, reeling back the insulated glove.

Three of the werewolves bounded across the roofline after Richard. David held his pistol in both hands, dropping to one knee as he said to her, "Just be ready to help Richard!" The gun—it wasn't as big as the one Mac had used and, instead of black, it gleamed like natural steel like the blade of a knife. There was the thunder of the shot and a long, ragged, elongated bubble of flame.

Her eyes followed toward the far side of the street. All three of the werewolves were still closing with Richard. David cursed. He fired again. The werewolf closest to Richard was hit, fell back on the roof dead, the two behind it pulling back, as if hesitating.

"Do it now, Richard!" Richard was trying to do something with the shotgun because both his hands would be holding on to the glove. "Forget the bloody gun! Come on!"

Richard got the shotgun through his belt, alongside his

left leg. He looked to be having difficulty bending down to grab the glove, but at last he had it, the glove in both hands.

Dannie screamed, "Richard!"

As Richard pushed himself off the edge of the roof and onto the cable, one of the beasts launched itself through the air toward him.

Onto Richard's back.

They stalled on the cable, the creature clinging to Richard with all fours, Richard shouting, "Shoot it!"

David was on his feet now, edging along the roof. He fired his handgun.

A miss.

Four things happened almost within the same instant of time.

The werewolf bit Richard on the right side of the neck, but it wasn't a killing bite. It was the kind of bite that she had witnessed from the apartment when she'd first seen the creatures coming along the street, the kind that would turn the victim into a creature like itself.

David fired and hit the werewolf. It fell from Richard's back, into the street, already starting to transform.

Richard shouted, "Dannie! I love you!" Richard's hands moved and he let loose of the glove but grabbed the electrical cable.

Dannie screamed, "Richard! Don't . . . I—!"

David grabbed her, pulling her against him. She tried wrenching away from him, couldn't, but was able to turn her head and for an instant saw Richard, electricity arcing along his body, his clothing, his flesh smoldering. She buried her face against David's chest as Richard's body fell away into the street, dead.

The crying that welled up inside her, her body shaking uncontrollably, her throat gagging, was nothing she'd ever known in her life except for the morning she watched as her father's coffin was lowered into the grave.

David was holding her. She heard his voice, could say

nothing in response. "I've never met a braver man than your Richard. I didn't like him, and he didn't like me. But he was as fine a man as made, Dannie, as fine a man as made."

She bit her lower lip, forced herself to nod, couldn't speak.

David whispered beside her ear, "We have to run, or else we'll be saying Richard died for nothing. We have to run."

She wanted to tell David that she was tired, that she didn't care at all what happened to her now because the werewolves would get her and kill her anyway, or worse, turn her into one of them. She wanted to—

David shook her, held her at arm's length. "We have to go. Now!" And he was moving her along the roof, an arm fully around her waist, propelling her forward.

Dannie Hardy was too numb to resist or care.

Chapter Twenty-five:

The Truth

There was no knock, no advance warning at all. The door leading into the office they used just opened, two men in overcoats with three-piece suits underneath coming through the doorway, Uzi submachine guns in their hands.

Hugh MacTavish started to move, thinking Tarleton was up to something and determined to get his fingers around Tarleton's pudgy throat before the men with the Uzis could nail him.

But he heard a voice from the doorway, a voice he'd heard before. "Tarleton, what's going on?" But where? Television?

Bob Magee said, "Mr. President?"

Hugh MacTavish froze, half the distance to Tarleton's desk already crossed.

The voice again. "All hell is breaking loose in the Northeast."

This time MacTavish turned around, immediately straightening to attention, saying, "Sir!" Force of habit kicking in, he knew. But it wasn't every day that the President of the United States walked in unannounced behind two bodyguards armed with automatic weapons. And there was no way the President could have known about—

The President—he was younger looking in person than he seemed on the telly—interrupted MacTavish's ruminations. "There is something very close to rebellion going

275

on in upstate New York and north along the eastern seaboard and spilling over into Canada." The President crossed to the center of the room in two easy strides. "Five minutes ago, I received a phone call that sounded like something out of a late show monster movie, about beasts of some kind killing and maiming and burning. The person who called me was the Canadian prime minister. I called the FBI director and he didn't know anything. I called the CIA director and he gave me some additional details about that thing in New York around rush hour tonight. And he reassured me that it was already being investigated by your office, Tarleton."

"Mr. President, I—"

"Then I called the National Security Agency director, Tarleton. And that's why I'm here." The President turned toward MacTavish. "I take it, sir, that you are Brigadier Hugh MacTavish?"

"Yes, sir."

"What is going on?"

Magee groaned.

Tarleton began, "Brigadier MacTavish has some intriguing information concerning a possible neo-Nazi conspiracy which we're in the process of—"

"I asked the Brigadier." The President looked Mac straight in the eye. "Well?"

"In a nutshell, Mr. President?"

"Whatever's more to the point."

"In 1939, Hitler's SS found a real, genuine werewolf. Over the years between 1939 and 1943, scientists working for the Nazis developed the means by which volunteers from the SS Panzer Division Liebstandarte Adolf Hitler could be injected with the blood of a werewolf and control when they would transform into the beast or return to human form. An unsuspected side effect was that the creatures either never die or age so slowly that aging in the normal sense is imperceptible. They attacked a unit of which I was a part in Germany in the spring of 1945.

276

Along with a young American officer, I survived. That officer died just a few weeks ago under mysterious circumstances after encountering the leader of the SS unit all but unchanged in forty-five years. That officer's daughter, a professor of history at Highcliffe, was able to locate me in semi-retirement in England. While she was visiting with me, the house was attacked by nine creatures the size of tall men, stronger than ordinary men, their bodies covered with hair, fangs in excess of three inches. They only could be killed by firing a silver-impregnated bullet into the body or severing the head or spine with a sword. Creatures identical to this wiped out the unit of which I was a part forty-five years ago. The leader of the unit, then and now, goes under the name of Dr. William Stein, also a professor of history, but at Sutton College. He was born in 1910. He looks to be thirty-five years old or less."

Several other men and a rather severely dressed woman had entered the room in the President's entourage. It was the woman who cleared her throat now. The President, not looking away from MacTavish, said, "Helen?"

"Mr. President. From what little we've been able to put together so far, the center of this activity seems to be somewhere around the Sutton/Highcliffe area. And many of the preliminary reports indicate that the—"

"Creatures?" MacTavish suggested.

The woman named Helen—MacTavish imagined she would have been pretty with a softer arrangement for her hair and different clothes, or none—cleared her throat again. "The creatures in many of the preliminary reports seem to bear some marked similarities to those described by the Brigadier, Mr. President."

The President looked at Tarleton, then back at MacTavish. "Everyone in this room be advised: What is said here, stays here. Brigadier?"

"Yes, Mr. President?"

277

"Are you telling me that a group of more or less immortal Nazi stormtroopers from World War II, who can change into werewolves at will, are attacking the eastern seaboard of the United States on the night before Christmas Eve?"

"No, sir. I would be more inclined to suggest that what you describe as happening is merely the first thrust of a major offensive, at the minimum, the objective the entire northeastern quadrant of the United States as well as Ontario, Quebec, Newfoundland, and Nova Scotia, perhaps the scope even greater still. There is no reason to suppose Dr. Stein's plans for his movement are limited by anything other than the time necessary to overrun the entire planet."

Tarleton forced laughter.

MacTavish looked at him. "Tarleton, you twit. You bloody twit. Think about it, man! You can't kill them! What's to stop them? Nuclear bombs and missiles? On your own cities? How many silver bullets can this government lay its hands on at this second?" And MacTavish looked at the President, saying, "This is worse than I had feared, sir. Stein has apparently accelerated his timetable by a considerable degree. If we fail to act decisively and effectively, we are lost."

The President sat down in the chair MacTavish had moments ago vacated. There was no air of defeat about the man but rather a sense of determination that he seemed to exude. "Let me get this straight. You can shoot these, whatever they are, all you want and nothing happens?"

"I've witnessed the werewolves shot with all types of smal larms fire. The heavier calibers will perhaps knock them down. But they are back up, moving, unaffected, it seems, and as powerful as before an instant later. The most severe wounds heal within hours, tissue and organ regenerating."

"A blessing and curse in one," the President remarked.

278

"Yes, Mr. President," MacTavish said. "But to Stein and his men, it is not a curse, but an opportunity to fulfill the mission with which they were charged almost a half-century ago."

The President looked at him.

MacTavish said, "To destroy the allied enemies of the Reich and restore the fatherland so that Hitler's dream of an empire that would last one thousand years will become reality, but Stein himself would be the new Führer. And the means then and the means now was terror, striking where the enemy was most vulnerable and least suspecting, striking mercilessly to instill fear and panic and disorder among the ranks and within the civilian support population."

The President stood up. He clasped his hands behind his back, more like a British admiral than an American President, MacTavish thought. "Helen."

"Yes, Mr. President."

"I understand that in the affected areas, National Guard units are already being called out. I want to nationalize them under central control for a coordinated effort. Contact the Joint Chiefs for a meeting in my office in ten minutes. Better have a helicopter meet us at the closest available point to land me on the White House lawn. Contact the Treasury. Find out the exact quantity of silver available, as coinage or otherwise." He looked at Magee. "I've seen you around Washington and Alexandria, Mr. Magee. With your contacts, how rapidly could some of this silver be remanufactured into bullets to arm a small unit?"

Magee was already standing, dug his hands into the pockets of his slacks. "As soon as the silver's available, with a lot of telephone work, police departments in the area and the military marksmanship units, without time for dissemination or collection, of course, which has to be worked out, we could have as much ammunition as you might need within three hours' time."

279

"Half that, Mr. Magee."

"There are gun clubs in the area; through the various firearms rights organizations, like the NRA and the Citizens Committee For the Right to Keep and Bear Arms, I should be able to get names of the club officers and there should be quite a number of reloaders among the rank-and-file membership. If we can get their cooperation, we could do it in that amount of time, a large number of individuals each fabricating a small number of projectiles. Maybe."

"You're in charge of that, Mr. Magee. As soon as you've gotten it going—Helen will give you whatever assistance you need in personnel, equipment, what-have-you—contact the major ammunition manufacturers. You know them, I understand."

"Yes, Mr. President."

"Arrange for silver to be gotten to them by the most expeditious means possible. By the time you've got it organized, we should know whether or not to order them into production."

"Yes, Mr. President."

The President looked at MacTavish. "Give Mr. Magee the specifications, if you know them, for the silver bullets, whatever other information that would be useful to him which you can supply. One of my Secret Service personnel will remain with you. He'll get you to a pick-up point and I'll expect you in my office in fifteen minutes or less, Brigadier. As you are not an American citizen, I cannot give you control of this unit I'm sending in, but I can request that you accompany it as an observer. Your experience could prove invaluable under the circumstances."

"May I suggest the SEAL teams stationed in the Washington area, sir?" MacTavish said.

"Is there anything else you'd like to suggest?"

"We're hitting Sutton College, of course?"

"Of course. And . . . one thing. You'd better be right,

280

Brigadier, or I'm not going to be the only one upset with you."

The President started out of the room.

Hugh MacTavish watched, waited until the door closed. Then he turned to Bob Magee. "About the composition of those silver bullets, Bob . . ." MacTavish began.

Chapter Twenty-six:

Flight

Werewolves had made their way onto the rooftops of the block where David had taken her across the rooftops again, and through her tears for Richard she'd heard clearly as David told her, "I'm down to three slug loads for the shotgun and two rounds left in my revolver. We can't fight them off."

So they moved with painful slowness, the only acceleration of their pace when they would actually make the jump from one roof to another. She was actually getting quite good at it. And then they would hide for what seemed like the longest time imaginable, after that to creep along in the darkness and dirt while the fires burned closer and small packs of the werewolves prowled about in the streets below, hungry for them.

She knew how it felt to be a hunted animal, some vastly superior creature stalking you, out there in the silent darkness, the eyes watching you with flesh hunger.

The snow was falling again. She'd hardly missed it when it had stopped, only noticed its absence, really, when it returned again.

They lay huddled within a small building, a tool shed without any real door anymore, abandoned years ago and the roof nearly gone. But it cut the wind which blew alternately with scorching heat from the fires or, when it shifted and came at them off the river, bitingly cold. And, if she sat just the right way, she could pull her dress down over her boottops to keep out the chill, she could keep her eyes open and still not see the fires or the beasts.

David's right hand was beneath her coat. At first, when he'd first begun to touch her, she'd thought that he wanted something sexual. But women grew up conditioned to that. It was nothing more than his rubbing her shoulder, kneading at the muscles there. Sometimes the pain from his fingers was intense, but always the pain in her arm was better when he had done it.

"Where did you learn to do that?" And she sniffed.

"Martial arts."

"Kung fu?"

David laughed. "It's gung fu, really, and no, I'm more or less eclectic in my tastes. I learned a great deal from the Brigadier."

"Do you think he'll come for us?"

"He needs to get things set in Washington, but I daresay that what's been happening around here tonight can't have escaped the attention of your government, so actually the Brigadier's chances of arriving in the nick of time with the cavalry to save us from the hostiles are somewhat improved, I'd say."

She hated to ask, to bring it up, because she was safe here and too tired to go on. "What are we going to do now, David?"

"After a bit, what we're going to do is dash along this roof and either shinny down the downspout or, with any luck, find ourselves a fire escape stairway. All that's dependent, of course, upon none of our friends being in the immediate vicinity—"

"Don't . . . don't call them 'friends,' David. Call them anything else."

"The Nazis? Werewolves?"

"Anything."

David smiled at her. She could barely see his eyes or the rest of his face, but knew that it was a smile. "The opposition, all right?"

"Yes. If we can get down, where will we go?"

"A direct dash for the river. With any luck, we'll find the

283

Brigadier's automobile intact and we'll bowl over a few of the beasties, perhaps, and be on our way."

She leaned her head against his chest. "You're sweet."

"I'm what?"

"You're lying to me, aren't you? I mean—"

"I only lie professionally. This is a job I'm doing for personal reasons. So I can't lie."

"Bullshit, David."

"A girl shouldn't talk that way."

"And you don't call a woman with a Ph.D. a girl, David."

"Sorry, Doctor Hardy." His other hand was on her neck, rubbing it gently. "But we have a really good chance now. You see, once they've wasted a lot of time looking for us, they'll get bored and go on. Anyway, this building should be burning in another ten or twenty minutes. Where you're sitting, you can't see, but some of the sparks blowing in on the wind are enormous, red-hot and glowing. The werewolves may be able to be killed by fire. At least, I'd think so. Anyway, even if they can't, can't be too pleasant for them, burning up and all. So they'll leave us to burn. Once the fire catches here, that's when we make our run for it. And you'll see; it'll be all right."

"Yes, David." She kept her eyes closed . . .

"Wake up, Dannie."

She almost screamed. But apparently David Mallory had awakened women before from the sleep of exhaustion while there was danger about them because his hand covered her mouth and she couldn't have screamed if she'd tried. She didn't know if he could see her eyes, but she blinked them several times. Either he saw, or he sensed she would not scream because his hand left her mouth.

"I didn't know—"

"You were only asleep for a little while, but you need the rest. It's time for us to get out of here." The crackling noises she'd been hearing since the fires had started were louder than she remembered them. "The opposition—remember, that's our agreed-upon word?—can't smell us with the fires so close. But we'll have to be quick about it if we're to escape. There's a fire escape. I checked while you were asleep, but I was always able to keep the shed here in sight to make certain you were safe."

"What if the car isn't there? I mean, when we get to the river, David?"

"Then we'll just steal another one; under circumstances like this, that's perfectly all right."

Dannie nodded. When she moved, her right arm hurt so bad she winced, but it was stiffness from not moving it for a time, she thought. "I'm ready when you are, David."

David started to help her to her feet, but didn't. He knelt beside her in the darkness there for a moment instead. "Look, Dannie, whatever happens, well—"

"Yes?"

His voice changed, hardened. "Never mind. Come on." And David started her to her feet. She grabbed up her purse and the athletic bag, slinging them to her body.

They waited by the broken-down doorway of the shed, David looking to all sides, Dannie behind. At last, he grabbed her hand and they started running.

For the first time since they'd taken shelter in the dilapidated shed—how long ago?—she could see clearly what surrounded them. There was fire on three sides, the rooftop so bright she could have read in the light, hot winds whipping back and forth, tugging at her hair and her dress. As she ran, she forced herself to work her right hand into a fist, then open and close it, to fight the stiffness.

Snow was no longer in evidence anywhere on the roof, melted away she realized, not even the puddles left.

The building on whose roof they'd taken shelter from the beasts was a warehouse, David had said. And it was enormous, covering half a square block at least. At the center of the roof, there was an abrupt, high peak, skylights set into the slopes on either side. They passed this

285

section of the roof and David steered them right. She kept up with him, not because she was afraid to let go of his hand (which she was), but because he was holding her hand so tightly, if she'd fallen behind she might have been dragged.

They were running toward the edge of the roof on the river side and she could see the iced-over surface clearly because it caught the light from the fires, reflecting it.

At last they reached the edge. David kept back slightly, pulling her down into a crouch, both of them low to the rooftop as David peered over the side. She edged up after him, looking over. The fire escape was a ladder affair, smallish landings spaced along it at regular intervals, two landings in all. Smoke curled through the walls in spots and, as she touched her bare hand to the roof surface, she drew her hand back. The roof was warm, almost hot. The warehouse itself was on fire.

None of the werewolves were in evidence anywhere below them as far as she could discern. She remarked about this to David. "No, I think they've given up on us, may think we've been killed in the fires. Most of the buildings behind us are infernos now, anyway. I'll take to the ladders first; you follow. If we get surprised down there, run for the river. It would be your only chance."

"I understand."

David looked again in all directions, then slid the little shotgun through his wide black belt. He scrambled over the raised ledge at the edge of the roof and started onto the fire escape.

It trembled, rattled under his weight. He called up to her, saying, "Wait until I'm past the first landing. We'll distribute the weight more evenly that way."

"All right."

She watched him, learning the difficult way earlier when she'd crossed the cable that climbing around on things was more technique than muscle. She watched him for technique.

He reached the first landing.

286

Dannie looked around her on the roof. Columns of smoke were rising from the roof itself now. She slung the athletic bag and her purse well back. As she did, she noticed her clothes. Dirt stained beyond repair with tar and everything, smudged from smoke. "Hell with it," she commented to herself, bunching her dress into her weakened right hand in front of her, then climbing over the ledge and putting a foot tentatively out onto the ladder, holding to the side support with her stronger left hand.

As she got fully onto the ladder, the athletic bag and her purse swung away from her and for a second her balance was off, but she regained it quickly enough, looking past the hem of her dress as she picked her way down carefully with her feet.

She was on the first of the two landings, caught her breath, looked below her, David already on his way down from the landing below her, almost to the alleyway surface.

She started descending again.

There was a sound of the groaning of the fire-escape ladder, over the crackling and hiss of the flames: the howl of a werewolf, and then another, and still another.

She quickened her pace, seeing David already on the ground, the shotgun back in his hand. He was waving her down more rapidly. She tried to oblige.

More of the howling.

She slipped, caught herself, a spasm of pain through her right arm and shoulder. She kept going.

The lower landing. Dannie didn't pause to rest, just continued downward.

"I know you're hurrying, but hurry faster!"

The heel of her right boot caught in the hem of her dress; she shook it free, hearing the fabric tear. She kept descending.

More of the howling.

And, as she looked up and down the alley, she could see them, three of them, bounding past the buildings, already totally consumed in the firestorm, one of them tawny-colored, the other two darker brown, sprinting toward the base of the fire escape with frightening speed.

"Come on!"

Two more rungs. She jumped the last two, David catching her. She wanted to sag against him, tremendously tired, but instead she pushed away from the wall. "Which way?"

"The river. Only option, Dannie!"

And they ran.

Dannie looked behind them. The three werewolves were less than a half block back. She quickened her pace, imagining she could hear the padding sounds of their feet thrumming against the alley surface, getting louder and more distinct by the second.

David grabbed for her hand. She let him fold his hand around hers, quickened her pace still more.

"Where's . . . where's—the car?"

David shouted to her, "About a block or so from here. We'll never reach it. We'll have to get out on the ice and try to kill these three before their howling brings the rest of them."

Dannie started shaking her head. David didn't understand. "The river, it's the ice, it's not thick enough yet!"

"No other choice!"

There was a chain-link fence just directly ahead of them, David letting go of her hand suddenly and shoving the shotgun toward her, then outdistancing her, jumping onto the fence with a loud clattering sound. And he was climbing as she stopped just beneath it. She didn't want to look back. The beasts had to be very close.

He was at the top of the fence, perhaps ten feet tall and he shouted down to her, "Throw me the shotgun!"

She threw the gun toward him, but not high enough. He missed it, but she caught it. She tried again.

David caught it.

He rolled over the fence with the grace of a cat, landing in a crouch on the other side. "They're right behind you. Get a running start and jump, then climb; I'll catch you on this side."

Wasn't there another way?

She looked behind her.

She'd never been all that good at judging distances, but the werewolves were so close she could see their fangs.

She ran a few steps back, then ran toward the fence, jumping as David shouted, "Easier for you! You've got smaller feet! Dig in!"

Her fingers grasped for the chain-link and her right arm screamed with pain and her right foot slipped and she hung there for an instant.

"They're right after you! Get your feet in there and climb, Dannie!"

Damn him!

"I'm coming!"

She brought her right foot up, the toe of her boot gouging into the gap in the chain link, her hands moving, her feet moving now.

At the top of the fence, she threw one leg over, found a toehold.

The fence rattled and she looked down and screamed, one of the werewolves just falling away, inches below her other foot. She hauled the other leg over, her dress catching on the exposed wires at the top of the fence.

She tore it free.

David fired the shotgun through a niche in the fence, and as she looked down, one of the werewolves was hit, starting to change back into human shape. She wanted to vomit.

"Jump, dammit!"

Dannie jumped, David catching her against him, both of them falling back, sprawling into the snow on the other side of the fence.

She looked through the fence. Three more of the werewolves were coming. "River's our only chance; otherwise, the others will follow our scent. Come on!" And David was hauling her to her feet.

The two werewolves closest to the fence jumped against it again, one of them clambering to the top, vaulting over.

"David!"

David fired his shotgun, killed it.

They ran.

And she remembered now how many silver bullets David had left: just one for the shotgun and two for his handgun and there were at least four of the werewolves.

She bunched her dress into her right hand, her fingers torn and bloody from the fence, stiff from pain. She ran as fast as she could.

The river was just a little distance ahead, the ice gray-looking except toward the riverbanks on both sides where it was whiter, maybe from snowfall. And, toward the center, it was darker, almost black— Open water? or shadow?

They ran.

The ground began sloping off below them, Dannie skidding on her bootheels, slipping on a patch of ice, catching herself, running. She looked back. One of the werewolves was over the fence.

The ground fell away sharply now, David just ahead of her, running for the ice. "What if it won't hold us?"

"Don't worry!"

Don't worry?

Running.

She reached the ice, slipped, fell on her face, looked behind her.

"David!" The werewolf that had gotten over the fence was coming up fast and she heard the blast from David's shotgun. He killed the thing. She was already on her feet, running after him on the ice.

Seconds, maybe, until the other three creatures were over the fence, after them, at their heels.

David slowed down, waited for her, grabbed for her, shoved her ahead of him. She almost fell again, but kept running. As she looked back, she saw the other three werewolves, on this side of the fence, sprinting toward them. She shouted to David, "What'll we do?"

"Run toward the center."

"If it cracks?"

"Good!"

The strain, she realized, the calm, damnably macho front he put on had to be just that, a front. The strain was too much on him. If they went through the ice, they'd drown, be dead.

As she ran now, she could hear the ice cracking beneath her feet, feel it giving slightly more with each step. This was insane. "David?"

"Keep going, Dannie; right behind you!"

She looked back. The three creatures followed them onto the ice, running more rapidly, more easily it seemed. Beneath Dannie's feet, she could feel the ice starting to break.

And then David was beside her. "Stop here! Remember. Get a good, deep breath. Forget about your bags. And don't let go of my hand!"

Around them the night was bright as noon, the fires from Highcliffe burning on. She could see where the ice wasn't ice, merely a blue-black glaze over the water, paper thin.

He locked the fingers of his left hand through the fingers of her right hand, dragged her along beside him, running for the center of the river. "David? This is . . ." She glanced over her shoulder. The three werewolves were just behind them.

The surface of the ice beneath her feet shifted violently. Cracking sounds were everywhere around her. David kept dragging her on, toward the darker surface.

There was a sudden shift beneath her feet. As she tried to keep her balance, she looked back. The werewolves were only a few yards back, now. She could hear the panting of their breath.

David jumped, shouting to her, "Jump up and down! Come on! Only chance! Jump!"

He wanted to make the ice crack around them, take them down into the riverwater— "Are you sure?"

She wasn't. But she was jumping, in unison with him, once, twice. She saw the werewolves, so close that— And the ice beneath her and beneath David collapsed and David was holding so tightly to her hand that she thought he'd break it.

They went under, Dannie remembering to suck in the deepest breath she could.

Below the ice, so dark she could only make out David as a darker shadow against the blackness. He was swimming back, under the deeper ice, pulling her with him. Her clothing felt impossibly heavy, her bags— She shrugged out of the athletic bag, determined to hold onto her purse if she could.

There was a disturbance on the ice above. She could feel it and where there was the break in the surface through which they'd fallen, she saw one of the werewolves, diving in, then scrambling back out to disappear on the surface. The same one or another one tried again; then again vanished to the surface.

Dannie's throat was beginning to burn, her lungs beginning to ache.

Still, David towed her after him.

She tugged at his hand. He only pulled harder.

They swam on, the time like an eternity, her lungs feeling ready to burst. He hadn't even asked her if she could swim. Just dragged her— David stopped, treading water now, moving her hand to his belt, closing her fingers around it. She held to him. In the darkness she could barely make out that he was doing something with the little shotgun. What? It was empty, useless.

He was taking it apart.

He threw part of it away, then hammered up at the ice with the other part, the barrel. He smashed it into the ice again and again and— He punched it through, pulled the barrel out, punched it through again, pulled her to it, touched at her face, his fingers against her mouth.

She understood, putting her lips against the shotgun barrel, breathing.

She took so deep a breath she almost started to gag, then pulled away, let David take air. It was her turn again.

Then his.

Above them, she realized, the werewolves hunted them.
But they no longer could smell them.

She was cold, weary beyond endurance.

But she was alive.

Chapter Twenty-seven:

Counter-Attack

Smoke hung in the dawn air like fog, and fires still burned everywhere, not a building standing. Charred and mutilated human corpses littered the streets and, as the huge transport helicopter's black shadow would move over the streets, the feral dogs and the birds which fed on the corpses would flee, perhaps afraid that this creature bigger than themselves had somehow come to feed on them.

"Set her down here!" MacTavish ordered the helicopter's pilot. Mac began folding away the map of Highcliffe on which he'd plotted the location of the apartment building where Dannie Hardy, David Mallory, and Dannie's young man, Richard, were to have taken hiding. Like the other structures throughout Highcliffe, the building looming up beneath them was a blackened, fire-gutted shell.

MacTavish had seen devastation like this in Africa, in Europe, of course, during and after the war, but his past experiences didn't make the sight any easier to handle.

Light snow fell.

Although there was little likelihood any of the beasts had stayed in the area (there was no evidence of them from the air, only the occasional human survivors wandering about the rubble), MacTavish racked the bolt of the Heckler & Koch MP5 submachine gun which he carried anyway, the thirty Navy SEAL Team members and their leader doing the same at his cue. MacTavish continued moving back through the fuselage of the chopper, the slight sway of the machine as it dropped making MacTavish take hold of a grab strap.

Although a heavier caliber than 9mm—like .44 Magnum—would have been more to Mac's liking, the matter of logistics for the shock force being sent in against Stein at Sutton College could not be ignored. Consequently, they had settled on 9mm Parabellum because of its interchangeability between the submachine guns and handguns. The other choice would have been the United States Army's M-16, a weapon MacTavish personally disliked. Be that as it may, there was no handgun available in the 5.56mm caliber at any event. At his hip, MacTavish carried a Walther P-88 in the same caliber as his submachine gun, loaned him by Magee. Walther pistols were something Bob Magee believed in as much as apple pie and motherhood, and MacTavish had always liked Walthers, too.

The SEAL personnel carried 9mm handguns as well, military-issue Berettas.

Nine-mm ammunition was what they had in the greatest abundance, remanufactured by Herculean effort to have silver tipped bullets. But there was also a fair amount of shotgun slugs in 12-gauge, and each of the men in the team as well as MacTavish himself carried a full-stocked Remington 870 pump shotgun, each weapon fitted with swivels, sling and extension magazine.

The helicopter—a big Sikorsky CH-53D Sea Stallion on loan from the Marine Corps—hovered well above the street, men in the open rear fuselage doorway in teams of two. At a signal from the team leader, exactly half of these men—eight in all—flung ropes from the doorway opening and jumped, rappeling down into the street below.

As the men reached the street, MacTavish watched while they dispersed to positions from which they could cover the helicopter's descent.

The helicopter began again to move and touched down in the snowed-over street, a storm of snow rising around the machine as the snow became caught in the main rotor's powerful downdraft. The remaining SEAL team personnel jumped out before the craft landed, taking up defensive positions on both sides of the aircraft and covering the three-way intersection completely.

The team leader, a tall, strappingly fit naval commander in his early forties with the odd-sounding name of Ivan Tailor, asked MacTavish, "Do we search the ruins for the bodies of the two missing personnel, Brigadier?"

"No. Stick with me." And MacTavish jumped down into the street, Tailor beside him. "If they're dead, finding their bodies might make us feel a good bit better, but won't make any difference to them. I'm banking on my friend David Mallory's resourcefulness. Tell me, Commander, what would you do, considering the terrain, if these implacable creatures were after you, the entire area were in flames around you and no help seemed forthcoming? And you had a woman with you, a plucky woman, granted, but someone whose experience couldn't be counted on and whom you wished to protect?"

Tailor looked from side to side up and down the street in which they stood. "I'd try to make it to the river. As you indicated during the briefing, sir, these creatures can smell their prey, just like real wolves. In that respect, the fires might be an advantage, masking human scent. But reaching the river would provide some measure of safety against the firestorm and make it harder for these things to easily pursue."

"My sentiments as well, Commander. Shall we?" And MacTavish, his weapon at the ready, began to walk along the street. At ground level, the loss of human life was more profound-seeming, but as he walked, a phalanx of the SEAL personnel behind and on either side of him, MacTavish would notice an occasional whole or partial corpse that was without clothing and/or showed evidence of a gunshot wound. David's work, he thought.

As they walked along the center of the street, some of the SEAL personnel moving along the sidewalks, flanking them, Commander Tailor said, "Brigadier—"

"Yes, I see her." MacTavish stopped, his eyes following a young woman about a half a block down the next street. She wore no coat, only a thin-looking dress, but didn't seem to be showing any ill effects of the cold. And the left side of her dress, near the shoulder, was covered with a dark stain. "Come on, Commander."

The SEAL team leader called to six of his men, falling in at double time on either side of Hugh MacTavish, running toward the woman. The closer they got to her, the more evident it was she seemed to be in some sort of daze. And there was caked blood on the left side of her neck and on her left cheek, even in her hair.

"Miss?" Commander Tailor called out to her, running past MacTavish. It was as if she didn't hear, because she did not respond.

"Miss. We can help you." Commander Tailor volunteered, reaching out for the woman as he closed with her.

The woman wheeled away from him, took a step back, hissed at him.

"Tailor!" MacTavish shouted. "Stand back!"

"She's one of them now," Tailor said.

A young sailor beside MacTavish whistled under his breath, said, "Holy shit."

"Exactly, Son," MacTavish said through his teeth. Slowly, MacTavish approached Tailor, the woman about a yard from them both now. "You were bitten last night, weren't you, ma'am?"

The woman—not more than a girl of eighteen or twenty—touched at her shoulder where the bloodstains were greatest. She said nothing in reply.

"There is no facility to get you to hospital, ma'am. Even if there were, there's nothing that could be done now; I don't think sedation would prevent what would happen. Do you understand? Now you'll be one of them." Her eyes—pretty, hazel-colored, and big—just stared at him.

"What are you telling, sir?" Commander Tailor asked

suddenly.

"The truth, Tailor." And MacTavish looked at the woman. "I can leave you here unmolested, ma'am, in which case you'll become one of the beasts tonight. Or . . ." MacTavish slapped the palm of his hand against the action of his weapon.

"Brigadier!"

"No, dammit!" And MacTavish looked at the girl.

As he did, MacTavish's eyes filled with tears. The girl, like an animal instead of a woman, approached him, her steps hesitant, edging back, then coming forward. Then, quickly she threw herself on her knees at his feet, lowering her head.

"Aww, Jesus," Tailor whispered.

Hugh MacTavish set the submachine gun's selector to semi-automatic, placing the muzzle close against the nape of her neck. "This bullet is silver. You'll rest in peace, I promise you."

Hugh MacTavish touched the trigger, turned away as she fell and he wept . . .

At the river, MacTavish found the car the United States government had loaned to him. Although he'd enjoyed driving it, he was glad at the moment it didn't belong to him. It was gutted from the fires, a blackened, amorphous hulk.

MacTavish closed his eyes for an instant, saw the girl's eyes, shook his head to clear it. Tailor had been silent since they'd left her body, continued toward the river. But now he spoke. "I've been thinking about what you did, Brigadier."

"I had no choice, and she wanted me to; I didn't want to."

"I know that. All of these people we've seen in the streets as we flew in here, they'll—"

"Not all, only the ones who were bitten and didn't die;

298

tonight, they'll be part of it. However many hundred there were last night, there'll be at least twice that number in the area around Highcliffe and Sutton tonight, all around upstate New York, into Canada. Every one which was bitten will become one of the creatures. Those we don't kill during the daylight will be trying to kill us tonight."

MacTavish let it alone, then, starting up along the riverbank, looking for some sign of Dannie and David. Finding the car burned wasn't a good sign that they had survived; and one side of himself danced with the question of what he would do if he found Dannie had been bitten, or David. Dannie—daughter of the man who had been his best friend. David—like the son he'd lost when his wife died.

Could he kill them, like he'd killed that poor young girl? The corners of his mouth turned down, the muscles in his neck tensing. If he didn't, he'd be sentencing them to something far worse than death, to join these beasts, be one with them as they hunted the innocent.

"Over here, sir! Over here!" It was one of the SEAL team personnel, down by the riverbank on the other side of a high chain-link fence.

MacTavish started for the fence. Tailor shouted, "Get me cutters!"

MacTavish let the submachine gun fall to his side on its sling as he quickened his pace for the last few yards, then jumped, grabbing hold of the chain link in his leather-gloved fingers, the fence rattling under his weight. He climbed, up, over, let himself half the way down, and jumped.

On the alleyway side of the fence, there was a naked body, partially devoured by something, but here there was another body that was untouched, a gunshot wound—likely a shotgun—clearly evident. "That a lad, David!"

MacTavish heard the fence ringing behind him, Tailor and some of the SEAL personnel making the crossing.

"Over here, sir!"

299

Macavish ran toward the ice at the riverbank, another body visible, another fatal gunshot wound. The SEAL was crouched over a portion of ice about thirty feet into the river, MacTavish slowing his pace slightly because of the slippery surface. "What did you find?"

"It looks like a shotgun barrel, sir."

"A shotgun barrel?"

"Only awful short, sir."

MacTavish reached the man, dropped to one knee. "Indeed, it is a shotgun barrel. Use your knife, hammer out around it. I want it freed. I'll hold onto it so we don't lose it. Watch my fingers, lad."

"Yes, sir."

The sailor got started hammering, chopping at the ice, MacTavish holding to the inch or so of the barrel which protruded above the surface. After a moment, by then Tailor and several of his men around them, the section of ice into which the shotgun barrel was locked was broken away from the rest.

MacTavish inspected the shotgun barrel, smiled. "You know, Commander, my young friend David Mallory is even smarter than I thought he was. He used the barrel from his shotgun, which was presumably out of ammunition, as a bloody snorkel so he and whoever was with him could breathe under the ice while the bloody werewolves prowled over the ice searching for them. If we'd had more like him two hundred years ago, you and your lads, Tailor, would be British Navy!" And MacTavish stood, looked at the men around him. "They made it this far, at least one of them, maybe all of them. Fan out in both directions, up river and down, and find them!"

"You heard the Brigadier—let's show him the Brits aren't the only ones who can get the job done! Move it!" Tailor ordered . . .

David Mallory's left arm had to be asleep, Dannie realized. It had been around her through the night.

When they had finally dared to leave the water, she had barely been able to move, and once out of the water and into the cold air over the river, her clothes freezing to her body, she'd honestly thought she would certainly die, her body wracked with chills.

David found a storm drain, the smell of it mildly disgusting, but nothing too obvious living in it, and using waterproof matches—"The kind they use on British lifeboats, Dannie; of course, that means they never fail."—he'd built a small fire from scraps, drying her coat over the fire, not perfectly, to the point at least where it provided some minor degree of warmth. Then he'd made her take off her dress and top, sitting there with his wet coat over her legs while he shivered and her dry coat covering her on top, drying her dress over the fire, too. She stripped off her underwear and changed into the dry clothes, now asserting herself with David, ordering that he warm his clothes, too, before he succumbed to pneumonia or whatever. "A hell of a protector you'll be dead. Come on!"

Once most of their clothing was dry, they'd fallen asleep, but not before David had told her, "Don't worry. These last cartridges in my revolver should still be serviceable. So we've got some protection."

If the werewolves found them here in the storm drain, she knew that she and David would die, but she didn't tell David she knew that. Instead, she rested her head against his left shoulder.

When she awakened, the smell of smoke from their little fire heavy in the cold air, sunlight of a sort visible at the end of the drain, his arm was still around her, and his fingers had somehow trailed to her left breast, held her.

For a long while, Dannie didn't move his hand.

But there was sound now. Men, shouting. But what they said, she could not be sure, the drain pipe distorting sound, making it echo and reecho against itself. "David?"

"What?" He was instantly awake. He started to move his

301

left arm. He looked at her. She looked at him. "I think someone's outside. I don't know who, but it sounds like men, not animals."

"I'll . . . ahh—I'll go have a look."

"Hey?"

"What?"

"This," she told him, and she leaned up and kissed him on the left cheek.

"And what was that for?"

"Because I wanted to, all right?"

David looked down at her and smiled. "All right." He got up into a crouch, almost banging his head against the overhead arc of the storm drain, moving toward the light now. She grabbed up her filthy but reasonably dry coat and went after him, her right arm stiff but not hurting her as badly as it had.

And when she heard David's voice shout from the end of the tunnel, "Brigadier!" she wanted to cry.

David spun back toward her, took her in his arms, again narrowly missed banging his head, and he kissed her hard on the mouth. "It's the Brigadier!"

For a moment, that didn't matter. She looked at David Mallory differently than she'd ever looked at him, and liked it. After a long few moments, she heard Mac's voice from the mouth of the storm drain . . .

"I'm sorry about your young man, Richard, Danielle, but—"

"Why did you call me that?" Dannie Hardy asked him.

And Mac smiled that smile of his that, despite his age, made her want to melt. "I guess, for some reason, you remind me of your mother, don't ask me why. But, I think she had a lot of courage, too."

David said, "I'll go with you; Dannie will be safe if we send her back—"

"No," MacTavish told him. "Dannie will be safer with

302

you than with anyone. And you, David, you're a bit the worse for wear. At least until we know what Sutton's going to be like, you're out of it. Take the rest; you need it and deserve it."

Dannie pulled the blanket tighter around her. "I can fight, too."

Mac turned around and smiled at her, then kissed her on the forehead. "Of course you can, Dannie."

Men.

Chapter Twenty-eight:

Waylaid

The helicopter—it was as big as a school bus—dropped them in the town of Bankhead, by sharp contrast to Highcliffe, untouched by fire, untouched by death. It was on the outskirts of Bankhead where the National Guard had set up its headquarters in the field, the National Guard commander a man Dannie Hardy recognized because she had gone to college with his son. P. Arthur Hempstead the fourth, when a civilian, was the heir to a family fortune derived from an industrial empire which at one time had employed nearly a tenth of the state's workforce through its diversity; but that was a century ago. Today, as well as Dannie Hardy understood it, his family's greatest industry was pleasure and most of the money his family enjoyed was inherited from the past rather than earned in the present.

She guessed it was the natural snobbishness against the rich—were people going to feel that way about her now, now that she had inherited her father's estate?

P. Arthur Hempstead the fifth, the boy she'd gone to school with, had been overbred, overbearing, and over-sexed. She told herself not to judge Lieutenant General P. Arthur Hempstead the fourth by his son, although he reminded her of the boy the instant she saw him—that rare combination of trim physique and slack features, a uniform that was too perfect, boots too shiny, a voice too old school and Back Bay to be genuine in any man.

As the helicopter with Mac and the others aboard took

off, she found herself standing between Lieutenant General P. Arthur Hempstead and David Mallory, just watching. She was still wrapped in the heavy blanket the young Navy man dressed in camouflage had given her when she and David had come out of the storm drain; but despite the blanket, she was cold.

As she looked up at David, the look in his face almost seemed to be disappointment at having been left behind. Her feelings might have been hurt, had she not understood both David and Mac better than either man thought. David felt it his obligation to be out there in the trenches with Mac, fighting the creatures. And Mac, although ostensibly leaving David behind to guard her and to rest after the previous night's ordeal, was actually trying to protect David, keep him from harm.

The love of friendship between two men was at once very awkward and very sweet, she thought.

Having said nothing when he joined them at the drop point, at last P. Arthur Hempstead announced, "You people have no need to fear now; this quadrant is secure against these godless creatures no matter what they try. Let's see them try for us."

"I'm happy to know that, General," Dannie told him, feeling that either she or David should say something and figuring that David wouldn't.

Hempstead might have believed what he said, but there was no reason for anyone else to. As they'd flown in the gigantic helicopter over the ruins of Highcliffe, most of the college buildings even destroyed, tears in her eyes seeing that, Mac had been briefing them. "Silver-bullet production is going apace, but not fast enough. The 82nd Airborne will be equipped with eighty rounds per man by late this evening, them coming into the area to start a search and destroy mission for every werewolf out there. This Lietenant General Hempstead has considerable manpower and equipment, so if the werewolves attack via hit-and-run he may be able to hold his position. But if the werewolves attack in force, he's history. You'll be safer there than on your own, but not that much safer. I've organized an evacuation flight that will bring you both out of the affected area; you'll eventually get to Washington. But the evac flight won't be until this afternoon." And then he'd given David a pistol, taken it from under the black uniform he wore.

She thought she'd seen one like it in a movie once. She asked what it was, but the name—a Walther P-5—wasn't something she recognized. Mac gave David several things called "magazines"; they were black, skinny, and she recognized them as the things that were put into the handle of a gun to resupply it with bullets. "Are there silver bullets in them?"

"Yes," Mac told her, smiling. "A personal supply for you and David. Don't tell your host, Hempstead, that you've got them."

She didn't know why, but she agreed that she wouldn't.

After the voicing of P. Arthur Hempstead's utter, total confidence, she at last understood. It was always possible, she supposed, that the general was attempting to give them confidence, build their morale, but she didn't think so; he actually believed his position was all but invulnerable to attack by the werewolves.

She felt it would have been instructive for him to have flown over Highcliffe, as she and David had done, or the farm country between Highcliffe and Bankhead, houses burned, farm animals and people alike lying slaughtered.

They went with Hempstead toward his car, a civilian Cadillac Brougham, black with black interior, David riding with the driver, Dannie in the backseat with the general. "I've taken over the bed and breakfast as my headquarters. There'll be a room available for you to use, with shower facilities, of course. Dr. Hardy, I'll have one of the women in my command check with you and she can secure proper attire for you from the town. No need to pay for it. We'll worry about that later."

"I could use some things," Dannie told him. She'd never been so dirty or bedraggled-feeling in her whole life as now. "Do you have hot water?"

Hempstead smiled as the door was closed and the Cadillac started moving off . . .

Aboard the helicopter, after giving David the handgun, Mac had spoken to them with considerable urgency. "I'm carrying the counterattack to Sutton College and Stein himself. Several things are clear from what occurred last evening. There are vastly greater numbers of the werewolves than there were in 1945, which means he's been making more of them, perhaps ever since then, perhaps only recently in preparation for his coup or whatever it is.

"There seem to have been two distinct behavior patterns evidenced in the beasts. Did either of you observe behavior differences?"

Dannie spoke. "When the werewolves first started filling the streets near the apartment building, some of them were more or less just there, more bestial, somehow, less like sentient beings, while some of the others were actively seeking out prey. And some of the creatures seemed very skilled at climbing, accomplishing humanlike tasks, like when they knocked down the chimney over the hearth as a means of gaining entrance to the apartment—"

"Or even going against the apartment door itself," David added. "She's right, like two classes of the same creature. And some of them had to have remained in human form to start the fires, so they didn't all transmute at once."

Mac nodded then, telling them, "Your observations confirm other eyewitness reports. The only logical thing to infer is that some of last night's creatures had never been activated before while others were experienced hands at it, could change at will and easily."

"Activated?" Dannie repeated.

Mac took something from his pocket. It was an ordinary solar calculator. Or, at least, that was what it looked like. "Remember seeing one of these in one of the cars the werewolves left behind near my house?"

David took it from Mac, turned it over in his hand, offered it to Dannie. She wouldn't touch it.

Mac went on, saying, "When I reached New York, I

307

was attacked. Conventional sort of thing at first, two men a little too obvious with suppressor-fitted pistols coming at me in the crowd just outside Grand Central Station. When the guns didn't do the job, first one and then the other used these. Stein told me that sound waves were utilized to control the transformation from human to werewolf, bragging, as it were. The frequency on this little device is in the ultra-high end, something no human ear could pick up. But, evidently, an infected person can pick it up and it begins the metamorphosis—sort like the full-moon-rising shots in the Lon Chaney, Jr., films—and the man becomes the beast."

"But how would Stein infect that many people, if you're implying they were unwilling, weren't volunteers? Not by biting them nonlethally," David mused.

"When I observed this in use," Mac said, "it was held to the ear and actuated. When you were planning on matriculating at Sutton College, you studied the campus, didn't you, David?"

"Maps and like that, brochures."

Mac nodded. "There's an observatory on the campus, only built within the last ten years. And it's fitted with a satellite dish, a powerful-looking one. I passed the observatory when I paid my call on Stein. Somehow, our man Stein has infected large numbers of persons, and I'd bet most or all of them had no idea they were infected until last night. And he utilizes that satellite dish to broadcast the frequency which can activate them. The high-frequency sound triggers the release of some chemical in the brain, probably the pituitary gland, and the chemical begins the metamorphosis. The sound takes the place of the moonlight of fiction, and perhaps fact in the case of werewolves occurring naturally, turning man into beast. Perhaps the sound can also be used to trigger the change back into the human state. Maybe we'll discover more about that when we invade Sutton College, about the sound waves, about everything—I hope." Mac put the calculator beside his ear. "A wolf would hear it, or a man who could become one," Mac declared.

General Hempstead gave them the option of one room or two. She didn't think twice when she asked for one room only.

She and David were not settled in for more than five minutes, David already gallantly offering her the first shower, when a knock came at the door. David held his silver-bullet-loaded handgun behind his back, telling her, "Answer it and step back and away."

Statements like that would have been strange, almost offensive to her a few days ago. Now, thinking that way was just an ordinary thing that was a part of staying alive. She opened the door, stepped back and away quickly.

A woman in a green army uniform, about Dannie's own age, with blond hair and blue eyes behind wire-rimmed glasses, stood there. "Dr. Hardy?"

"Yes?"

"I'm Corporal Mays, ma'am. I've been instructed to find out what you need from town and bring it back for you."

Before she could answer, David said, "Then I'll take the first shower," and walked into the bathroom. There were already clothes en route for him. He'd simply given his sizes to General Hempstead's driver.

Dannie let Corporal Mays in and closed the door behind her.

Sunlight filled the room through the window opposite the doorway, Corporal Mays going over to stand beside the smallish dresser, a notepad and pen already in hand.

From the other side of the closed bathroom door, Dannie could hear the shower running.

Corporal Mays asked Dannie's sizes, Dannie running the list from shoe to bra. "How about slippers and sleepwear, ma'am?"

"Slippers—good. You're sure this won't be too much trouble?"

Corporal Mays smiled. "No, ma'am. It's just fine. Pajamas or a gown, ma'am?"

"A gown. I hate pajamas."

"Long or short, ma'am?"

"Long, please."

"All right, ma'am, let me just check something," Corporal Mays said, smiling. She turned over the notepad, and in a pocket on the inside front cover there was a calculator. Dannie Hardy just stared.

Corporal Mays took the calculator into her hand.

"You're one of them!"

Corporal Mays smiled and said, "Yes, ma'am." She brought the calculator to her right ear and Dannie saw one of the corporal's fingers touch at the buttons in some kind of series.

Dannie started to shout for David.

Corporal Mays was already beginning to transform as she spoke, her voice slowing down, deepening, like a record player suddenly but slowly losing its power and the sound starting to die. "If . . . you . . . call . . . him . . . then . . . he . . . will . . . die . . . too . . ."

Dannie stood there, her mouth open.

And she realized, as Corporal Mays transformed, that she valued David Mallory's life more than her own. She didn't scream.

She told her eyes to move, to stop staring at Corporal Mays, but they wouldn't move, to move, to look for David1s gun, his Walther something that Mac had given to him for their protection, his gun with the silver bullets in it.

The sounds of bone and skin crackling made Dannie want to retch, made her skin crawl.

Corporal Mays's face was almost completely through the transformation now, the muzzle of the wolf distending from the front of her skull, her cheekbones seeming to swell, stretch, her mouth tearing at the corners, and the lips widening out of the flesh of the cheeks, the lips drawing back over gums which grew deeper and thicker, fangs bursting from them in a spray of blood. Her neck stretched, thickened, her shoulders drawing inward, but muscles rippling up and tearing open the seams of her uniform, the top and the bra beneath it falling away, her

310

breasts flattening away, hair growing in clumps, the clumps joining, the hair a soft honey-gold.

Her trousers fell away as her upper body stretched higher and her hips pulled together, hair in huge, thick clumps on her thighs, the legs themselves disjointing, twisting, the knees bending back against themselves, a bushy tail growing downward from the base of her spine.

Dannie was edging toward the window, near which David had been sitting. Had he left the gun there?

Corporal Mays's muzzle opened wide.

"Don't—" she started to say, "Don't kill me," but wouldn't let herself. She couldn't find the gun. She picked up the dresser-top lamp, tearing the cord out of the wall socket. She'd die, but she'd cause the beast some pain.

Corporal Mays hunched forward, a motion Dannie knew too well, ready to lunge for her throat.

Dannie readied the lamp to beat at the beast with.

As Corporal Mays's hind legs tensed to spring, the bathroom door was flung open and David stepped through, still dirty, still in his clothes, the gun Mac had given him in his hand. "You are dismissed, Corporal!" He pulled, the trigger once and Corporal Mays, already starting her leap, seemed to hesitate for a split second, Dannie Hardy throwing herself out of the way, onto the bed, Corporal Mays's body vaulting past her, into the window, through it, already starting the transformation back to human form.

David crossed the room in three strides, stopped beside the shattered window, looked down, then looked back toward the bed. "I'd worried General Hempstead might be so cocksure of himself that he was infiltrated already. Why didn't you call out?"

Before she could think of a better answer, the truth blurted out. "She said she'd kill you and I didn't want that."

"You were willing to give up your life for mine."

Dannie didn't say anything to that.

"That was foolish; you're much more important than I am. Don't do that again."

Damn him . . .

Dannie Hardy realized there could be no other motive behind it than personal revenge, against her father and Mac, through her. She was still shaking, rage and fear together, as, running beside David, she reached the ground floor of the old three-story inn that had been converted to a bed-and-breakfast and was now General Hempstead's field headquarters.

On the second floor there was no sign that anything was wrong, but on the ground floor, as they'd come down the stairs, she could hear the sounds of the beasts on the grounds outside. And here on the first floor, she saw no dead, either, no bodies partially dismemembered with pieces missing. "Stay close," David told her.

If the shot had gone unheard or the crash of Corporal Mays's body through the window unnoticed, Dannie couldn't understand how. And there was another thing. Her voice a low whisper, she asked, "How could they do this in daylight?"

"Remember? The calculator, the high-frequency sound. They don't need moonlight." Dannie and David crossed the floor through the reception area, two dead military police there, David making her stay back as he went to examine the bodies. He returned after a moment, carrying their rifles. "Some spray and pray might help," he told her.

Outside in the driveway beyond the yard was Hempstead's Cadillac, but there was no sign of Hempstead. Along the road, werewolves passed, most of them looking as if they were drugged, some, packed together, looking more in control, like leaders.

"We run to the car, then drive like hell."

"Shouldn't we alert General Hempstead? What if the keys aren't—"

"I wasn't an agent for Her Majesty's Government as long as I was without learning how to wire up a car so it'll start without keys."

She looked at David. "How long?"

"What?"

312

"I mean, how old are you?"

"That's—"

"How old are you, David?"

"I'll be thirty next month, if we live to next month."

That was perfect, just like in a book, because he was only a little bit older than she was and a man— She breathed, looked away. Richard, my God, dead, less than a day past.

Then David said something to her. "In case we don't get past our—the opposition, I mean."

"In case?"

"Why were you willing to die to save my life?"

"Beats hell out of me," she told him, looking him square in the eye.

David leaned the two rifles against the wall and pulled her tight against his chest, his arms encircling her, her back arching. She bent her head back, just to see his face, not to let him— His mouth came down toward hers and she didn't turn her face away, didn't try to pull away from him.

And she kept her eyes wide open . . .

Sporadic gunfire was everywhere around the bed-and-breakfast inn now, and as she crawled alongside the hedgerow behind David, Dannie Hardy realized that Hempstead's entire army was being taken not from without, but from within.

There were men and women like Corporal Mays, obviously well experienced at making the transformation from human to beast, and the others like those wandering about in a cloud of stupefaction for whom this had to be a first transformation. And Dannie realized something, now, that if Stein did use that observatory satellite dish Mac had spoken of as a means of controlling, or "activating" the creatures, he could use it with considerable precision. Otherwise, all of the first-time werewolves would have had their first transformation the previous night.

David handed off the two ugly-looking black rifles to her

and she held on to them, waiting as he edged forward, the handgun with the silver bullets in it in his right fist.

David reached the car, pulled open the door, and Dannie almost screamed. P. Arthur Hempstead's driver collapsed from behind the wheel, eyes staring wide open in death. David—he was brave, she thought—pulled the dead man out from behind the wheel, dragged the body into the hedges, then went back to the car.

There was no reassuring instantaneous hum of an eight-cylinder engine coming to life, rather, David's muted whisper as he hissed, "Damned steering column lockouts!"

She looked at her wristwatch, remarkably still running, but maybe not that remarkably because it was very good and very expensive. It was nearly one o'clock in the afternoon. And, oddly, she realized that she was starving.

The Cadillac's engine coughed, then purred. "Dannie!"

Dannie Hardy got up from her knees into a crouch and ran, her water-logged purse on her shoulder, one of the rifles in each hand.

There was a gap of six or seven feet between where the hedge ended and the Cadillac was parked. Dannie started to cross it in a run, but stopped dead in her tracks. Coming along the driveway at a run were a dozen men, soldiers, carrying rifles, "David! Look! Help is coming!"

"Into the car, Dannie. Hurry!"

She couldn't understand that. And now she could see even more clearly At the lead of the group of men, looking proud and fit, a pistol in his hand, was P. Arthur Hempstead himself. "We've got to tell—"

David was out of the car, reached for her, grabbing her by the front of her clothes and dragging her to the car. David pushed her in, jumping down behind the wheel.

"What about Hempstead?"

David threw the transmission into drive and the Cadillac began pealing out along the gravel driveway, a spray of the stuff rising in a wake behind them. The driveway was a horseshoe, and David was taking the opposite leg of it from General Hempstead and his troops. They broke off, starting to cross the snowy area in between, as if trying to cut them off.

"David!"

"Dannie, the two MP's on the first floor and Hempstead's driver—they weren't bitten to death or torn apart; they were shot to death."

"Ohh no—"

She looked past David, toward General Hempstead and his men. Three of the men threw themselves down into the snow, and in the next instant they were firing their rifles, bullets hitting the hood of the Cadillac, zipping across it in a shower of sparks. The windshield seemed to vibrate, a spiderweb pattern suddenly appearing in its upper left corner as David swerved. "We're all right! Stay down!" More gunfire now. She dropped as low as she could on the seat but peered over the dashboard to look ahead of them. There was an army truck coming, to block them, cut them off.

She looked at David. He had one of the two rifles they'd taken from the dead military policemen. He was firing it through the open driver's side window, the gun resting in the crook of his left elbow between his chest and the steering wheel, his right hand on the gun, his left hand on the wheel. "But those aren't silver!"

"They can't be certain, so they won't go out of their way to find out! Hold on to something so you don't go bouncing around."

She knew she should get down further for her own safety, but she had to see. The army truck was narly fully across the end of the driveway. The Cadillac's engine was roaring loudly now, the sound of gravel continuously pelting at the car's underside almost as loud as the gunfire.

Men were piling out of the back of the army truck while it was still moving, with rifles in their hands.

David threw one of the two rifles down across the seat, just missing her head. He took up the second one, holding it in his left hand now, pointed out the window and ahead of them, firing it as they narrowed the distance between themselves and the army truck.

The men were opening fire.

The truck had the end of the driveway nearly blocked.

David threw the rifle away out the window and warned her, "Hold on, remember!"

His right foot went all the way to the floor, the Cadillac seeming to lurch, then rocket forweard, the sound of the gravel and the gunfire now all but lost under the sound of the slipstream of air around them. She wanted to close her eyes, couldn't, braced herself.

David didn't cut his speed, but he stomped on the parking brake with his right foot, cutting the wheel into a full right, the Cadillac swerving, a sick feeling filling her stomach, David's left hand tugging back on the brake release, then grasping the wheel as, with both hands, he started fighting the wheel back.

There was the sound of metal tearing against metal, a shower of sparks arching up on the left side of the car as it slammed into the front of the truck, the Cadillac hesitating, then pulling away. The engine sounds had softened for a split second, but now were louder than before.

Gunfire all around them.

The rear window shattered inward. She screamed in spite of herself.

Another spiderweb shape in the windshield.

The passenger-side window disintegrated, glass spraying all over her as she scrunched her eyes shut. But she held on, the Cadillac bouncing, trying to drag her upward to smash her downward, swaying side to side.

The gunfire was quieter now.

David told her, "Don't move around much; you're covered with glass. But we're away from them for now."

She just lay there, huddled up, eyes closed, reminding herself to breathe.

Chapter Twenty-nine:

Talking With Yankee Doodle

They had taken the Sikorsky Sea Stallion as close in to Sutton College as they dared, MacTavish directing the Marine Corps pilot to find a place to put down. Bringing the helicopter in low over a strip of woods, circling, they landed in a clearing a half mile inside a barrier of dense conifers.

Commander Tailor moved his men out quickly in the event that there was enemy activity still undetected from the air, MacTavish not interfering with this, instead working with Tailor's radio man. MacTavish wanted confirmation that, ten minutes ago at four P.M., EDT, a helicopter dispatched at MacTavish's request to pick up Dannie Hardy and David Mallory had them.

"This is Brit calling Yankee Doodle Three, Brit calling Yankee Doodle Three. Over."

Static.

Behind MacTavish as he sat beside the radio, Tailor re-entered the craft. "LZ's secure, Brigadier. Any luck reaching General Hempstead's command?"

"Not yet, Commander." MacTavish tried again. "This is Brit calling Yankee Doodle Three, Brit calling Yankee Doodle Three. Do you read me? Over."

Static.

MacTavish lit a cigarette, telling the man at the radio, "Try reaching Yankee Doodle One near Hartford. It was their aircraft."

"Aye, sir." The operator changed frequencies, began

317

sending. "This is Brit calling Yankee Doodle One, Over."

Yankee Doodle One came on. "Brit, this is Yankee Doodle One. Reading you Loud and Clear, Over."

MacTavish took the microphone. 'Yankee Doodle One, this is Brit Leader. Cannot establish contact with Yankee Doodle Three. Advise on aircraft sent for personnel pickup per my request at 1600 Hours this date, Over."

"Brit Leader, this is Yankee Doodle Leader." MacTavish recognized the voice of General Abner Black, Army Chief of Staff, given overall direction of the operation by the President just last night, also on the ground commander of Yankee Doodle One, charged with sealing the lower quadrant of the circle formed around Highcliffe and Sutton, Yankee Doodle One personnel all regular Army, including the 82 Airborne who were scheduled to drop on Sutton tonight. "Have lost all radio contact with Yankee Doodle Three, Brit Leader. Over."

MacTavish said to General Black, "Yankee Doodle Leader, what of aircraft dispatched for 1600 Hours pickup, Over."

"Aircraft reports fires in Bankhead and evidence of conflict on the ground. Looks like Hempstead's forces may have been infiltrated. Cannot spare personnel to investigate at this time. Is Operation Wolfbane proceeding as scheduled, Over?"

MacTavish looked at the Rolex on his left wrist. "Yankee Doodle Leader. I must know whereabouts of subject personnel to have been picked up. Operation Wolfbane proceeding as planned. Advise condition of my colleagues A.S.A.P. Over."

"I Roger that, Brit Leader, and Wilco A.S.A.P. but nothing seems promising. Over."

"Status on Yankee Doodle's Surprise, please. Over."

That was the 82nd. Was it ready to go in as had been planned when he gave the signal? Was it equipped with eighty rounds, silver-bulleted ball per man?

"Brit Leader, status on Yankee Doodle's Surprise Af-

318

firmative, I say again, Affirmative, Over."

"Don't forget to advise on status of my colleagues. This is Brit Leader Out." MacTavish racked the microphone, looked at Tailor. "Hempstead's command may be neutralized, and Dr. Hardy and Mallory didn't get picked up."

Commander Tailor said nothing.

MacTavish cupped the palm of his hand, flicked ashes into it. "If I'm reading the map correctly, we should be in position on the outskirts of the Sutton College campus by nightfall. Then we hit that observatory. If we haven't heard any word on Dannie and David . . ." *What?* MacTavish asked himself. Save Stein for him? For his own personal vengeance? That was poor tactics, and he wanted Stein for himself already. "If we haven't, I'll content myself with hoping they made it out alive, somehow. But, regardless, we can't count on any fast back-up from Hempstead Yankee Doodle Three, and I won't call in the 82nd Airborne Division until we know for certain that Sutton is the center for the thing, that he's controlling the transformations from there. Because they have to stay on alert in the event Yankee Doodle One can't contain the werewolves tonight and New York City is targeted. That would mean a slaughter of unprecedented proportions."

MacTavish looked at Commander Tailor and smiled. "Which means, Commander, it's us against all of them."

When Tailor said nothing, merely nodded grimly, MacTavish felt a moment's pride working with the man and his elite unit. Because, if Tailor had said something like, "We can handle it, Brigadier," MacTavish would have known, instead, he was working with a liar or a fool.

Chapter Thirty:

The Road To Knowledge

David had tried, tried turning back the first party of refugees they had encountered moving toward Bankhead, but no one would listen to the man in the stained and dirty black clothes with the wild blond hair and a pistol shoved into his belt.

One or maybe several of the bullets fired on the Cadillac had hit something which caused the car's gas tank to be drained to empty by the time they had been on the road for twenty minutes, and she and David had been walking ever since. And she agreed with his reason as to the only direction in which they could travel, toward Sutton in the hope, however slim, of "linking up," as David termed it, with Mac's SEAL team force.

The refugees were to be pitied, whatever their fate when they reached Bankhead. If elements of General Hempstead's force were still holding their perimeter (as were their orders), no one was to be allowed out of the enclosed area, lest the werewolves should use the flow of refugees from the farms and smaller hamlets dotting the area as a cover for what David called "exfiltration." If all of Hempstead's force were either werewolf or dead by now, on the other hand, the refugees were walking into death or worse, transformation.

So, as Dannie and David walked now, they avoided the bands of refugees by leaving the roads for the woods whenever a group came in sight. And there was another, practical reason for that; there was always someone who was armed and — she couldn't blame them — the possibility of being shot at was very real.

She was reminded of the Orson Welles broadcast in 1938, about the invasion from Mars, and how people in this very area had taken to the roads, evacuating, fleeing the dreaded Martian machines of destruction.

She wished this were a Halloween night hoax . . .

They moved along both sides of the road with a brisk, long-strided commando walk, every man alternating a shotgun or a submachine gun at the ready, to be as prepared as possible, whatever the deepening shadows on either side of the road might hold for them.

They followed the road for the sake of time only, MacTavish feeling a heightened sense of urgency since learning that instead of leaving Dannie Hardy and David Mallory in relative safety, he had delivered them into unknown danger instead. Several times, Mac reminded himself how he had given David the Walther P-5 and several spare loaded magazines, as well as a box of shells. David was a good shot, had a cool head. With almost a hundred rounds of ammunition, David could be expected to fare well.

And, from his hopeful optimism, MacTavish drew his heightened urgency. If Dannie and David were out there in the coming night, fighting to stay alive, the sooner he neutralized Stein's base of operations and Stein's means of controlling the metamorphosis, the better chance Dannie and David would have of making it through.

The road split, the advance guard returning to be replaced, MacTavish suggesting to Commander Tailor, "If we cut through those fields to the north, we should save some time, and it'd seem safer than paralleling the road."

"Agreed, sir." Tailor ordered out another three-man advance unit, toward the north.

MacTavish gripped his weapon tighter and pressed on. It wasn't that he was becoming too old for the work, but

321

he was too emotionally involved. This wasn't an operation—name the enemy in the last forty-five years and he'd fought that enemy on some ground somewhere; this was a vendetta. But he'd always heard that a man could better live with his shortcomings once he became aware of them . . .

It was full dark and the moon was all but full and very bright.

The closer they came to Sutton, the greater the flow of refugees and the more certain David seemed that they would encounter not only refugees but wolfpacks.

It was imperative to find a vehicle, because on foot they would be doomed to be run down or fight a holding situation until David ran out of silver bullets for his pistol.

"Over there, those darker shadows," David hissed, parting the pine boughs so she could see.

There was a house, no lights on, of course, and a garage or barn a little behind it. "Do you think there'd be a car?"

"A tractor would do. Come on. Let's see." Holding her hand, he started out of the trees but stayed by the treeline as they walked along the edge of the field, his pistol in his right hand, her right hand in his left. "If anything happens to me, take the gun and the magazines and the loose ammunition and make a run for Sutton. Don't stop for anyone and—"

"Nothing's going to happen to you."

"I appreciate the sentiment, but we don't know that. Just remember what I said."

She wouldn't argue, but she had no intention of leaving David behind. Despite his gruff manner sometimes, despite Richard's recent death, she was in love with him; for the first time in her life, it wasn't something she was uncertain of, had to convince herself to believe in; it was something she knew inside her as sure as she knew her

322

sex, as sure as she believed in Mac's loyalty, as sure as she knew her father had loved her.

She shifted her hand a little so she could hold David's hand more tightly. Her right arm still hurt when she moved it wrong and was a little stiff, too.

At last they were on a line with the garage or barn, and David, looking side to side first, ordered her in a hushed whisper, "Now we run for the building, whatever it is, fast as we can. Watch out for holes so you don't twist an ankle or something. Ready?"

"Maybe there's something to eat in there."

"I doubt it. Let's go!" And, still holding her hand, David took off at a dead run, Dannie beside him, catching up her dress in the fingers of her free left hand so it didn't bind at her calves, running flat out as hard as she could.

As they neared the edge of the field nearest to the buildings, David rasped, "Watch it!" He grabbed at her, her right arm screaming with pain as he dragged her back.

She dropped to her knees in the snow-splotched field, David dropping down beside her. "What is it?"

"Ditch. You'd have broken an ankle for sure. I'll cross first. You jump to me. Let's go." And he was up and moving forward again, slowly for a pace or two, then took a broad jump, and at last she saw the ditch as well. She nodded to herself, telling herself she could make it. She stood, hitched up her dress and ran, jumping, David catching her against him, holding her. She was getting the feeling he liked doing that. She liked it when he did it.

"Come on." He jogged toward the barn—it was clearly that, or once was, too large for a garage. Rubbing at her sore arm, she went after him. He stopped by the double doors. There was no evidence of a lock of any sort, just a long nail or something dropped through the two ends of a hasp to keep them together. He pulled it out, opened the doors, and turned on a little flashlight she

323

hadn't known he had. "Be careful."

"Where'd you get the flashlight? That's cute. It's so little!"

"I always carry it. I'll get you one of your very own once we're out of this." As he shone the narrow but surprisingly bright beam across the interior, her spirits rose. There was a pickup truck. "Why it's been left here may prove interesting, but let's have a look, shall we?" He started forward, telling her, "Keep a lookout at the doors."

"All right."

Dannie stayed by the doors, not wanting to see were-wolves lurking in the darkness, surrounding them. She wanted to somehow find Mac and his unit and be safe. She laughed at that. Safe. How would she be safe joining a commando unit that was about to assault the headquarters of the enemy. Dannie Hardy shook her head.

She'd always thought the girls who'd gone in for ROTC could have done something better with their time. She'd heard the line from ROTC cadets so often, "Fundamental military training that will be of benefit in my future military or civilian career," or something like that. There might have been something to it, after all, learning how to shoot and fight and jump out of airplanes and things, even for a girl. But they didn't teach anything about werewolves, she bet.

She heard the sound of the truck's hood being opened. "How's it look, David?"

"There's a battery. That's always a good start. Tell you in a mo, Dannie."

She wondered how it would be being married to an Englishman? They did talk kind of funny, but not too funny. Married. It was the first time she'd thought about that in a long time. She wondered if David had thought about it? Or maybe he was already married. That was a very sobering thought. She went back to looking for werewolves.

"Fuel pump's beaten up a bit. No wonder the thing's

324

been left here. But I think I can fix it."

"Can I help?"

"No, I'm fine. Can't be too dissimilar to an aircraft."

"Do you fly?"

"Uh-huh, when I get the chance. Fixed wing, singles and twins."

"Are you married?"

That was a dumb thing to ask him! She would have kicked herself if she'd ever figured out how somebody could do that effectively. And he hadn't answered her yet. That was very discouraging.

Then David spoke. "No. Want to discuss correcting that sometime?"

"Say that again?" She could just see him in front of the pickup truck when she turned around. She knew that he was looking at her, too.

"Do you want to discuss correcting that sometime?"

"I mean—"

"Would you have any interest in marrying me?"

"Yes."

"How much interest?"

"A lot, David."

"Good. Now watch for the opposition while I fix this bloody fuel pump."

"Yes."

"Yes?"

"I'll marry you and I'll watch for the werewolves."

"Good. Both times."

Dannie Hardy looked away. This was insanity, because she hadn't known David Mallory for more than a few days and didn't know much of anything about him and it was all the danger they'd shared and her seeing him be heroic and everything and "Yes."

"What?" David called back.

"Just telling you yes again."

"Ohh. Thanks."

She nodded, said nothing, just looked out into the darkness . . .

Animal husbandry, MacTavish deduced. Barns, corrals, pens. There was even a classic American-looking silo like one he saw in a painting. A board fence encircled the farmlike area. "Sutton only began an agriculture department about ten years ago, Brigadier," Tailor advised.

"About the same time the observatory was built," MacTavish noted. Along with a half dozen of Tailor's men, they crouched at the edge of a cultivated woodlot about fifty yards from the fence, the farm area on a rise sloping off into the dish-shaped valley below, the rest of the Sutton campus spreading before them. There was light on the Sutton campus, emergency generators no doubt, because the entire power grid in the surrounding area was down, had been since the previous night's violence.

"Consider . . ." MacTavish started to say to Tailor. "The new volunteers must have to go through a number of metamorphoses to get perfect control, like the original SS personnel. The farm is essential. Can't have werewolves running about the countryside killing women and children, but it's easy enough to lock the first-timer into a cage with a domestic animal and let him have at it, isn't it? To do that, they needed an agricultural department. Clever."

"How many of them do you think there are, sir?"

"Maybe a few hundred, maybe a few thousand, and probably ten or twenty times whatever that number is of ones who don't know they're werewolves, may perhaps transform for the first time tonight."

"How?"

"I don't know that. Probably something simple and obvious, knowing Stein. He's a clever man, and he's convinced of his supreme rectitude, and he's also, of course, totally insane. That's why I'm sure it's some really clever device he's used, nothing mundane, nothing obvious. After all, he's had long enough to work out his plan, and some of the best scientific minds available after the war

326

were German. He could have gotten his hands on the right people, done whatever he liked. And the money would have been there, too. Imagine, a functioning SS unit with the highest security clearances, imagine the wealth they could have availed themselves of. Gold. Diamonds. Works of art, all the plunder of Europe and North Africa. Maybe Stein will tell us. Come on!" And MacTavish drew back from the treeline to rejoin the bulk of the force . . .

The battery hadn't been used for so long, it barely groaned, but David said it would take a charge once they were rolling and he was able to top off the gas tank as well. Shoulder to shoulder—she liked that, too—they pushed the truck along out of the barn and into the yard fronting it. "Right. Dannie. Behind the wheel you go."

"I can push some more!"

"Somebody's got to slip it in gear when it starts, and steer, too; you're elected. Up you go!" And David propelled her toward the cab and up and inside. She pulled her dress over her knees and took hold of the wheel. "When it catches, out of neutral and into gear, all right?"

"All right."

"And don't stop, just go slow and I'll catch up."

"All right."

"Here we go then," and David slammed the door.

He wasn't able to keep the truck moving by himself because the ground was too flat. So, back out of the cab, one hand on the wheel—if it was power steering, she couldn't tell as she fought the wheel with her already stiff right arm—her shoulder against the door panel, pushing with her body weight against the vehicle.

But, between the two of them, they got the truck moving, and it was picking up speed, more and more. "In you go, Dannie!"

She hitched up her dress and half threw herself into the cab, the stick in neutral already, her fingers working

327

the key on and off and on, waiting for the engine to catch. And, at last, as the truck rolled over a little rise and started down toward the house, the engine caught and she shifted into first.

"Hang on!" And then David was running up beside her on the passenger side, jumping up and onto the seat next to her, slamming the door after himself. She remembered to slam her own door. "Down the drive and to the left and don't stop. You can drive a standard transmission?"

She resented that, but she loved him anyway. She made the smoothest shift she'd ever made into second, then double clutched back into first as she took the left, then upshifted into second again, then into third. That would shut him up about her driving . . .

It was the prologue from Richard Wagner's *The Twilight of the Gods* in which three goddesses presiding over human destiny spun their golden rope of fate. When the rope snapped, it was recognized that final doom was at hand. MacTavish followed the music in his mind. Like many an Englishman, even a Scot living among the English, Mac-Tavish had come to detest Wagnerian themes, but he had studied Wagner as part of his study of Nazism, recalling the old aphorism, "Know thine enemy!" Sunlight in the rugged Highlands where Brünnehilde and Siegfried dwelt. And Siegfried gives Brünnehilde a ring as token of his undying love. Soon the music moved to "Seigfried's Rhine Journey." At the end of the "Rhine Journey" the curtain would rise on the first act of the opera and so was Stein's assault for the Third Reich reborn about to begin.

"We move now," MacTavish ordered, and Commander Tailor reechoed the order as elements of his SEAL team moved out toward the main entrance to the Sutton College campus.

The music blared from loudspeakers everywhere, but inside himself, Hugh MacTavish knew its origin — the observatory . . .

Dannie felt almost relaxed, a little sleepy, and she was embarrassed because her stomach had rumbled twice now. "I can see where feeding you won't be the cheapest thing in the world," David remarked, his arm around her as she drove.

"I'm usually not that noisy about it. Anyway, I'll still teach history, so we'll have plenty of money for food. And what my father left me; it means we'll be rich, a little rich anyway."

"Here we are, already arguing about money." David laughed.

"I know you don't smoke, but light me a cigarette?"

"I don't—"

"Mac gave me a pack and some matches. In my purse."

"All right." She could hear the sounds in the darkness of his rummaging around. "My God, the junk—and it's all wet."

"The cigarettes should be dry."

"Got them." She heard the sound of him trying to strike a match. "I think they're damp. Use one of my emergency matches, or—wait, there's a lighter here." He pushed in the dashboard lighter and after a second or so she heard it click. It was slow going, driving by the moonlight alone, because David had advised against the use of headlights. She smelled the smoke as he lit the cigarette. He coughed, offered it to her. "This is terrible for you."

"I don't smoke that much. Do you want me to quit?"

"Only if you want."

"We can talk about it."

"All right," he told her. "We can talk about it."

Dannie imagined she could taste his lips as she took the cigarette to her own lips, inhaled, let the smoke fill her lungs. She knew cigarettes were bad for anyone, and smoking these days was a sign of stupidity or something, but God it tasted good sometimes. She exhaled, watching the smoke ricochet off the windshield. "How much longer to Sutton, do you think?"

"Maybe a half hour, give or take. Once we get there, I don't have the foggiest what we'll do, other than winging it."

"Well, we just have to find Mac."

"Yes—his operation against Stein may have already started."

She inhaled again, feeling the smoke warm her, knowing on a rational level that it was bad for blood circulation, affected the capillaries and really wasn't warming her at all, but it sure felt as if it were.

She started to say something, when the beast threw itself onto the hood of the truck and she almost dropped the burning cigarette into her lap when she started to scream instead.

"Head down! Eyes closed!" She felt David's hand on the wheel, heard the shattering of windshield glass in front of her and felt the spray of glass against her face and throat and on her hands and heard the pistol shot from close beside her and then the howl of the beast as it was struck. "Open your eyes slowly, very slowly and drive, now!"

She opened her eyes slowly, saw the thing in the moonlight, starting to transform to human shape as it slipped off the hood, a human hand through the windshield, bloodied to the bone, slipping away. She double-clutched and downshifted into third, the pickup getting momentum, then upshifted back to fourth, David shouting to her, "Look out on your right!"

She saw them, but there was no way to turn away, and the werewolves—three of them—jumped toward the pickup from the road just in front of her. She stepped hard on the accelerator, at the same time pulling on the headlights. The creature nearest the vehicle crashed against the hood, the other two falling away in the light.

330

The creature's right front paw hammered through the rest of the windshield, Dannie averting her eyes, keeping her foot to the floor as she cut the wheel right and left and right again, trying to throw the creature off the hood.

David fired his pistol, missed, the werewolf's paw over the dashboard lip now, the creature pulling itself toward her. David fired again, the bullet shooting away the beast's right eye. It fell away, a hideous scream coming from it, half animal, half human.

The other two she had seen bounded along beside the truck as her eyes followed the body of the one David had just shot. And the two jumped and disappeared from sight. In the next instant, Dannie heard them hammering on the roof of the truck cab. "David!"

"Keep driving! There could be more of them!" David pointed the pistol toward the cab roof, fired, fired again, and again. "Keep going, Dannie!" He fired again and again and again and she heard a click, realized the gun was empty. "Don't worry!" He put one of the skinny black things with bullets in it into the handle of the pistol, did something with the top of the pistol, then fired again into the roof.

Dannie screamed, one of the creatures, already transforming, falling across the windshield, half into the vehicle, blood spraying across the windshield so thickly she couldn't see. She found the windshield wiper switch, turned it on, the blood smearing now into something the streakiness and consistency of fingerpaint. She pushed at the washer switch on the wiper control and there was an electrical groaning sound but no fluid. David fired through the roof again.

Through the smear of blood over the windshield, she could see two more of the creatures in the road ahead, bounding toward the truck's lights. David fired through the windshield, missed.

Dannie leaned right, to see to drive where the windshield had been shot away because the glass was hopelessly obfuscated.

And then the truck started to sway, right and left and right and left and up and down and she screamed, "David! What's happening?! David!"

And the truck hit something and she realized it had to be one of the creatures and her steering was gone and she didn't have any control anymore. David fired through one of the holes in the windshield, killed one of the creatures as it sprang onto the hood.

The truck was starting to turn over, going off at a crazy angle to the right, over the side of the road. She tried fighting the wheel, felt David grab for her, pull her head against him. One of the creature's front paws pushed through a hole in the windshield and reached for her and she pulled away as David fired, hitting it in the paw, the creature shrieking from above, the paw turning into a human hand, blood-drenched, groping for her face.

The truck suddenly went, over on its side, rolling, tumbling, Dannie burying her head against David's shoulder.

The truck impacted something — she didn't know what — and stopped rolling, stopped moving.

She was still in the cab, David holding her, David's head thrown back.

In the moonlight streaming through the holes in the shattered windshield she could see a dark stain across David's face. "David!?"

The roof of the pickup truck — claws ripped through it, then again and again and again, peeling the metal back like a little can opener on a tin of sardines, a creature coming at her through the roof.

And another of the creatures lunged through the truck's headlights and onto the roof and as Dannie looked up, she realized that both beasts were fighting, ripping at each other with their claws, one of them tumbling off the roof, the other leaping onto it, going for its throat. One of the creatures was a graying black, the other a deep

332

brown. They fought, jaws snapping, snarls issuing from their muzzles, fangs catching the glow of the headlights, bared, cutting at each other's flesh.

And suddenly they were locked together, but not like animals, like men, rolling, clawing at each other. The dark-brown one had the gray-black one by the throat, but the gray-black one's right front paw swiped across the other's muzzle, ripping away fur and flesh, blood spraying up into the light.

David stirred beside her.

In his hand was the gun.

"David! Shoot! Shoot that one! The dark one. The other one—"

David fired, then fired again, then a third shot, the two creatures falling away from each other, the dark one beginning to transform. David fired as Dannie shrieked, "No!"

His bullet hit the gray-black werewolf and its body fell back, directly into the beam of the headlights.

As the transformation began, returning the creature to human form, Dannie cried, "Richard!"

She pulled away from David as his left hand grabbed for her to hold her back, dragged herself over the dashboard, her dress catching on the glass, ripping it free, falling over the hood of the pickup truck and onto the ground

She crawled along it, forward into the light.

"Richard?"

Behind her, she heard David whisper, "My God."

Richard hadn't died last night. And, she realized, it was the bite of the wolf. By the time Richard had touched the electrical cable between the two buildings to which he'd clung, the poison or whatever it was had reached his system, made him unkillable except by the silver bullet.

Her eyes stared, transfixed, stared at his face.

Bruises almost masked his features to a point beyond recognition, but even as she watched, they began to vanish.

She got to her knees, taking Richard's head into her lap, pressing his face against her breasts. "Richard, we didn't —"

"Dannie."

David dropped into a crouch beside them, saying, "Look, Richard, I —"

And Richard, eyes wide open despite the glare of the headlights, seemed to smile. Dannie touched her lips to his forehead, felt an outrush of Richard's breath against her face.

She just held him as she wept . . .

Small patrols of men in black battle dress utilities identical to the uniform MacTavish had adopted moved about the Sutton campus, armed with M-16 rifles carried in patroling positions under their right arms, ready for instant use.

Commander Tailor beside him, six of the SEAL team personnel around them as the forward maneuver element for the penetration, Mac crouched along the side of the fence. "What do we do, Brigadier? Take them out?"

"Werewolves in military clothing, the only difference. Yes, as we have to. But there'll be more of them. This is a hundred-and-fifty-acre campus, and saturation patrolling would be impossible. The sooner we open fire, the tougher time we'll have reaching our objective." And MacTavish gestured toward the far end of the campus, by the other end of the valley. Low mountains ringed the valley, snowcapped, but higher than any of the other peaks was the one directly ahead across the campus commons and beyond, whiter in the growing moonlight than any of the others, topped by the gleaming white dome of the observatory. Already, other elements of Tailor's SEAL team were circling round the campus, to rendezvous on the other side for the assault on the observatory dome. Sooner or later, one element or another would get into a

334

firefight with the black-uniformed patrols.

MacTavish waited, the music—another element from *The Ring of the Niberlungs*—beginning: *The Valkyrie*.

The armed patrol passed, MacTavish giving the signal to Tailor and the six SEAL team members to move on . . .

David carried Richard's body to the side of the road and into the trees, wrapped in David's coat. David used the big knife that hung from his belt and Dannie used the jackhandle, helping him, digging a shallow grave. David told her, "If we make it through this, I promise we'll come back and get his body a decent burial." The ground was winter hard and they scraped at the earth rather than dug, but kept at it until there was a trench just wide enough for his body and about two feet deep.

She helped David lower Richard's body into it.

And then David recited, "The Lord is my shepherd, I shall not want . . ."

And they mounded the dirt over him and Dannie knelt beside the grave, feeling suddenly guilty for loving David, for not loving Richard more, proud that somehow despite the evil which had overtaken him, Richard's human side had triumphed, that he had fought to save her life.

David brought rocks and piled them atop the grave, she realized not just as a marker but to prevent the grave from being dug up by wild animals and the body eaten.

The moon was full up.

The howling of the beasts filled the night around them.

After a time, her eyes burning with tears, her throat tight, David took her hand, led her off toward the road again.

The truck was useless except as a reference point for finding Richard's grave again.

And it was a long walk to Sutton College . . .

Hugh MacTavish paused, flattening himself flush against the building wall, the seven men with him doing the same. And he realized why the guards patroled the campus.

Not to keep an enemy force out, but to keep the students of Sutton College in.

The dormitories—a dozen buildings, brand-new-looking, multistoried—were ranked on both sides of a long boulevard, the grassy parkway at the center. It was the howling which had brought MacTavish, Tailor and the six SEAL team members here, made them diverge from their path straight to the observatory.

And there in the snow-splotched parkway between the two rows of dormitories, and on the steps leading to the buildings themselves, MacTavish saw the reason for the howls.

The werewolves no longer fed on the cattle kept for them in the agricultural center.

They fed on the student body.

Mobs of the creatures gorged themselves on human flesh, dragging young men and women from inadequately barricaded buildings, ripping bodies limb from limb, sating themselves on human blood.

One of the Navy SEALs wheeled away, vomited into the snow-covered hedgerow.

Tailor hissed, "Belay that, Oglethorpe. We all feel like upchucking."

"Aye, sir," the strained voice came back.

MacTavish was about to speak, but the radio receiver plugged into his left ear began to pick up a transmission. "This is Yankee Doodle One, calling Brit. Over. Yankee Doodle One to Brit, do you read me? Over."

MacTavish took the small teardrop microphone that was clipped to the collar of his BDU and turned it closer to his lips. "This is Brit Leader, reading you Loud and Clear, Yankee Doodle One. Is there word on Dr. Hardy

336

and David Mallory? Over."

"Negatory, negatory, Brit Leader. This is Yankee Doodle Leader. Transmissions across the FM and VHF bands, apparently emanating from objective, contain same signal recorded from your calculator device. We have thousands, I say again thousands transforming all across the Northeast. We will not be able to contain. I have ordered Air Strike on Sutton College radio station coming your way in three minutes; I say again, coming your way three minutes from now. If you are near the station, move to safer location. Over."

"Hit the damned radio station, General. It's coming from the observatory. The dome of the observatory could be reinforced against anything but a direct hit or battlefield nuclear. Do not attack observatory. It may be our only chance to control the transformations. As your aircraft hit the radio station, divert one to the southeast along the boulevard between the dormitories, if possible to make a low pass as diversion preparatory to small unit I am with hitting the werewolves now attacking dormitory students. Suggest burst for effect only with 20mm. Do you Roger that, Yankee Doodle Leader? Over."

"I Roger that and Willco, Brit Leader. Am relaying your request to fighter squadron commander now. Yankee Doodle Surprise standing by. We want to deliver it soon. We are running out of time, Brit Leader Do you Roger that? Over."

"I Roger that, Yankee Doodle Leader. Will advise. Thanks for your patience. Brit Leader Out."

"Yankee Doodle One, Out."

Already, MacTavish could hear the F-15 Eagles approaching from the south, hear the break-off.

"Everybody, listen," Mac ordered. "When that M-61 is fired for effect, it'll get everyone's attention, man and beast alike. We run down the center of the boulevard, killing everything on four legs we can, the dual objective of doing what we can to save some of the student lives and getting to the other side of dormitory row so we can link up with our other elements and hit the observatory. Yankee Doodle Leader wants to hit the observatory. The music—that's why they're hitting the college radio station with the F-15's—is carrying the transmission to metamorphose the affected persons. Thousands of the metamophoses have already taken place. The general can't hold off on the 82nd for much longer. The transmission is being jammed into VHF and FM broadcast bands and getting out everywhere and has to be stopped. I think it comes from the observatory and I want to control it rather than terminate it. So we have to hurry.

"When you fire, make every shot count. Keep the subguns on semi-auto only. One hit with a silver bullet is as good as two or three and we have no idea how many of the creatures we'll find waiting for us at the observatory. Any questions?"

The F-15's were screeching over the campus now.

MacTavish set his Heckler & Koch submachine gun to semi, ready.

There was a deafening high-pitched roar across the night sky, and then a blast from the 20mm multibarrel gun, the werewolves and their victims alike on the ground below stunned for a precious tactical moment. MacTavish ordered, "Follow me!"

He broke into a dead run away from the side of the building, running into the street, shooting a werewolf in the face, dodging the body as it finished the lunge, running across the street now, killing another of the beasts as it grappled with a half-mutilated coed. MacTavish kept running, Tailor on his left now, the other SEALs in a wedge behind him, firing into the werewolves all around them, killing, running, killing.

Toward the center of the boulevard, one of the beasts rose up from the body of its victim, shredded chunks of flesh in its dripping fangs. MacTavish shot out the werewolf's right eye and the beast tumbled back.

MacTavish was ready to use one of the precious silver bullets to put the victim out of its misery, but the girl's right eye was staring upward into one of the streetlights which still burned here, her left eye like the entire left side of her face ripped away.

To the northeast, there was an explosion, then another and another after it in rapid succession, the radio station, then farther off and due north, there was still another explosion, the station's transmitter tower.

But over the howling of the werewolves and the screams of their helpless victims and the shrieks of the F-15's as they pulled out of the missile run were the strains of Wagner . . .

Explosions had rocked the night sky moments ago, and huddled beside David now, high in a rocky promontory over the valley, Sutton and Sutton College below them, David told her, "Our boys, I think. I can't guess the target, but the Brigadier wouldn't have let them hit the observatory, and those planes that passed us flying south to north — F-15's — had to have done it. So the Brigadier isn't into the observatory yet. If we can get down there, near to the observatory, it'll be dangerous, but we'll have a chance of intercepting him."

"Let's do it then."

The aircraft streaked back across the sky and she held her ears against the sound for a moment. But, as she took her hands from her ears, the wind changed blowing toward them now from the observatory. And faintly, very faintly, she thought she heard the strains of classical music.

But then there was the howl of a wolf in the woods near them and she forgot about it.

Chapter Thirty-one:

The Siren Song

The music was the same, but its effect was now radically different.

In the middle of their headlong lunge through the greenway striped down the center of the boulevard between the dormitory buildings, the behavior of the werewolves had begun to change. They abandoned their victims, seemed uncaring of imminent attack by MacTavish and the SEAL Team personnel, merely turned to the north, and began to lope off.

MacTavish stood at the far northern edge of the parkway now, nearly a full thirty-round magazine spent from his submachine gun, nearly thirty of the beasts dead before him.

But how many hundreds more were here on the Sutton campus alone?

And why did they seem mesmerized?

He knew where they were going.

MacTavish activated his radio. "Brit to Yankee Doodle One, over. Brit to Yankee Doodle One, do you read me? Over.

"This is Yankee Doodle Leader, Brit Leader, reading loud and clear. Over."

"The werewolves have ceased attacking the college students from the dormitories and are moving toward the observatory. Are there any reports from the field to indicate similar activity? Over."

"Hold on, Brit Leader."

MacTavish changed magazines in his weapon, took the nearly spent magazine in his left hand and, from a green plastic case in the musette bag at his left hip, with his right hand began reloading the magazine with silver-bulleted 9mm Parabellum ammunition. The werewolves were all but gone from the dormitory area, moving up along the roadway toward the observatory.

"Large concentration of the creatures coming up behind us, evidently intent on intersecting the observatory road near this point, Brigadier," Tailor advised, in contact with the other units of the SEAL Team by separate radio frequency. "I've got reports from almost every element. The same behavior. Wait a minute."

MacTavish clipped two magazines together side by side, substituting these for the single already inserted into the H&K, giving him almost instantaneous access to a second loaded magazine.

"Brigadier, Clancy with Unit Two is telling me he can observe the main road leading into the campus from his position. It's filled with the things as far back as he can see, some of them on all fours, others on their hind legs, moving toward our position, and evidently toward the observatory beyond us."

"Tell them to consolidate on the observatory as per the plan as rapidly as they can." And then MacTavish's radio came back. "Brit Leader, this is Yankee Doodle Leader. I've got reports coming in from the ground and the fighter squadron which hit the radio station as well. Roads are filling up with the creatures. Near Hartford, they're converging on an old factory building. In the rural area around Highcliffe, they're converging on a television broadcast tower. And we've got to act quickly if that observatory is the key to this thing. The music began about two minutes ago, broadcasting from rooftops and vans and abandoned buildings in cities all throughout the Northeast. I've got a report that some of the bridges leading into Manhattan are already filling up with large packs of the creatures, all moving to some central location we're trying to get a fix on. This is bigger than we'd supposed. There must be tens of thousands of them out there. Either you hit that observatory within the hour or we're dropping every piece of conventional ordnance on it we need until it's just a memory. That is a direct order to me from the President who's on the line with me now. Is that Rogered, Brit Leader? Over."

MacTavish looked at his watch.

That left him thirty-four minutes. "You have the Surprise ready to be given, Yankee Doodle Leader. This is Brit Leader, Roger and Out." MacTavish shouted to the men around him, "To the observatory, double time! Move out!"

They started along the road after the creatures, toward the gleaming whiteness of the observatory dome. MacTavish hadn't mentioned this to Commander Tailor, but he wasn't quite certain what he'd do when he got there . . .

Dannie and David witnessed a unit of men in black uniforms stepping aside, not raising their weapons, allowing a horde of the werewolves to pass through the gates into Sutton College, David's arm around Dannie now as he whispered, "They're being drawn toward the source of that music."

"Wagner?"

"Yes, *Siegfried*, one of the pieces that fires the blood of Nazis everywhere. Stein, damn him."

"What'll we do?"

David seemed to consider their options for all of ten or fifteen seconds. "In the event the Brigadier and his unit haven't reached the observatory, or got cut off because of all of this, someone still has to reach that observatory. The regular music must be a carrier for one of the control signals for the werewolves. If we can disrupt it, maybe we can stop them. And I can't leave you here anyway, so we go in."

342

"Just us?" Dannie asked, incredulous.

"Yes."

She thought about her father, and about Richard, too, in an unmarked grave at the side of a country road wrapped up in another man's coat.

The music was beautiful, thrilling, making the blood course the faster just listening to it.

She owed it to her father, to Richard, and to all of the creatures down there filling the road into the Sutton Campus who didn't want to be there, weren't Nazis but victims, owed it to them all to turn off that music. "How do we get in?"

"The guards are too busy watching the invited guests. It's over the fence."

"What if it's electrified?"

"I still have one insulated glove, remember?" And David kissed her right temple, then started down from the treeline, Dannie catching her dress up close around her legs and starting after him . . .

Running through the cultivated woods along the side of the driveway leading to the summit and the observatory which crowned it, they were cutting off distance and avoiding contact with the werewolves filling the roadway.

MacTavish wanted to call a halt, exhausted from the run's duration but fearing that it was his age at fault. But, beside him, Tailor asked, "Sir, can we call a slower step? This has been a long day and we need the men in condition to fight."

MacTavish nodded, trying to control his breathing as he said, "Give the order, Commander."

MacTavish slowed to a normal pace, catching his breath. He was too old for this, and he'd been hearing himself telling himself that for almost ten years. But there was always the thrill of what lay beyond the next moment — there always had been.

But this time there was terror, and the promise that if

343

he was very lucky he'd get his revenge before he died.

The tree cover broke slightly just ahead of them, and, his submachine gun in his hands, MacTavish pushed ahead, reaching it a few seconds before Tailor. "Halt the men, Commander."

Tailor echoed the order.

From here MacTavish could see the observatory clearly. Around its dome there was a walkway, totally circumferencing it, and walking along this were werewolves, as if on guard duty.

The roadway leading to the observatory was choked with the creatures now, just waiting there, those in the front ranks, near the observatory's base, like the faithful waiting in Vatican Square for the blessing of the Holy Father.

For what blessing or charge did the werewolves wait?

"Rest the men for two minutes only. Then we go in, Commander."

"Very good, Brigadier."

MacTavish shot Commander Tailor a grin he didn't feel and a thumbs-up for confidence that signified nothing at all, then dropped to his knees and the ground and took his pulse. So far, so good . . .

She could see the observatory clearly, its gleaming white stone like a beacon against the blue-black night, the moonlight imparting to it a surreal glow.

The fence had been easy enough to cross really, not electrified, and ripping her dress again by now didn't even faze her. Her only concern for her clothing was to get out of it, burn it perhaps, shower forever and shampoo her hair a hundred times and dress in the prettiest thing she could find. She was tired, very tired, of looking dirty and bedraggled and tacky.

They crossed along the farthest edge of the commons and toward the athletic complex, the football practice field spreading before them, only wooden bleachers, a few rows on either side here, and at the far end a gymnasium.

David holding her hand, then running onto the field, toward the gymnasium, and beyond that lay the base of a narrow road leading along to the west side of the observatory.

He slowed down, Dannie grateful for it, exhausted, starving, too. "We'll try and get inside; I'm not quite sure how, but we'll do it. Find that transmitter for the music and how to control it, then either shut it off or, if we can, activate whatever signal it has that will trigger a metamorphosis back to human form. Stein's rallying his creatures around him, for all we know may be broadcasting the same signal all over the Northeast and Canada. We'll —"

"Halt!"

Dannie froze in her tracks. She was mentally set for confronting a werewolf, albeit the prospect terrified her, but who was—" She looked over her shoulder. "David . . . Those men in black uniforms with guns."

"How many?"

"Six."

"Too many. When I shoot, run for the gymnasium. Be ready."

The same voice. "Turn around and place your hands above your heads!"

Her eyes met David's eyes. He winked at her.

They both turned around together, David's hands above his head but his pistol in his right hand still. "We're on our way to the observatory like everyone else, but the transformation didn't work on us," David shouted across the field.

"Throw down your weapon!"

"Be ready," David hissed through his teeth. Then, his voice a shout, "We're here to see Dr. William Stein. He'll be very put out if you don't let us see him."

The six men's heads turned and they seemed to confer for a few seconds; then the one who had spoken before called to them, "Throw down your weapon first. Dr. Stein is at the observatory. We will take you there."

David called back, "Thank you very much!" Then he lowered his right arm slowly, as if starting to toss away his handgun. Instead he fired it so rapidly it was like something out of a movie, a half-dozen or more shots that she could count, two of the guards falling down, a third one grabbing to his leg, the others raising their guns as David shouted to her, "You're supposed to be running, Dannie!"

And she was turning then, David firing another shot over his shoulder.

Across the football practice field, the ground furrowing up around them on either side as gunfire erupted from behind them.

She looked at David, saw him putting one of the things up in the handle again that gave the gun more bullets, running dead-on for the gymnasium, beside her.

More gunfire, David stumbling, shoving her on, beside her again, the gymnasium's nearer wall looming up ahead of them, gunfire impacting it, glass in a side window shattering out, a ripple of bullet holes along the stuccoed wall, David shoving her left, toward the corner of the wall. Dannie ran, David beside her, reached the corner, David pushing her around it, throwing himself against the wall for a second. His neck was bleeding on the right side. "Dive! You're—"

"I'm shot, but I'm fine, just a scratch. Think about it. If it were the carotid artery, I'd be dead, all right? It's just a scratch. Come on!" And he dragged her along the wall.

Double doors, a chain looped around them, a heavy padlock holding the ends of the chain together. "What'll we—"

David pulled her back, aimed the handgun and fired, then fired again, then again, the lock intact-looking but the chain link on one side split. He tore at the chain, kicked at it, the chain breaking away. He threw his body

346

against the doors and they sprang inward, Dannie almost falling inside behind him.

The gymnasium was dark, but moonlight was diffused from the skylights overhead, the skylights filling the ceiling. "Come on! Follow me!" And he started running again, toward the nearest row of bleachers, running up, two at a time, Dannie trying to keep up with him, tripping, catching herself as she started to fall through between seat and footrest, looking back toward the doorway.

Three of the guards were coming through.

Dannie started running again, David at the height of the bleachers, telling her, "Get up here, quickly!" He fired his gun, and there was answering fire, bullets ripping up chunks of the bleachers near her feet.

But she reached the top, David grabbing to the handrail for the track which circumscribed the gymnasium, hauling himself up, flipping over. "Wait!" He fired a few more shots. There was no answering fire.

Then David reached down and grabbed her hands, half dragging her over the rail and onto the track surface beside him.

He was putting another one of the bullet things into the handle of the gun.

She peeked up, looked over the railing.

She could see one of the guards, something to his ear. "My God, David, he's becoming a werewolf!"

"Marvelous! Come on!" He grabbed her hand and started running, but kept low, toward the center of the track. Ahead of them, she saw a ladder, followed it up with her eyes into the brighter light near the skylights above. The ladder led to a catwalk, narrow-looking, the catwalk bisecting the gymnasium across the center. "Up the ladder, you first, then onto the catwalk and keep low!"

"But . . ." She grabbed for the ladder, started climbing, David right behind her. Halfway up the ladder, David stopped, fired at one of the pursuing guards who had followed onto the track, the man not yet transformed.

David's bullet struck him and the man fell, skidding back along the track's surface.

She looked to the gymnasium floor, could not see the one who'd been about to transform.

Dannie reached the catwalk, started out on it slowly, terrified because it was so high and so narrow and if she slipped she'd— "Hurry up, Dannie!"

David was right behind her. She told herself he'd catch her if she started to fall so she started walking faster, afraid to look below her now for the werewolf.

But, as she looked forward, she saw it.

She was about at the midway point across the gym floor, and the werewolf, bigger-seeming than any of the others she'd seen, but that only perhaps because of the catwalk and the beast's looking so out of its element here. But it walked, on all fours, as if it were walking a tight-rope but so adept at doing so that it never once thought of falling.

David told her, "Get down!" She dropped into a crouch, her arms out to keep her balance, more terrified of falling than of the beast attacking. David fired. She saw the bullet strike against the narrow surface of the catwalk, missing.

The beast lay there, like a big furry dog in front of a fireplace, advancing toward them along its belly. David fired again and missed. "I can't shoot past you like that. Get down lower, Dannie!"

Dannie Hardy looked behind her, David weaving side to side with the gun, trying to get a shot.

She lowered her body prostrate onto the catwalk.

As she did, the werewolf darted forward, leaped.

She was screamed out, just shouted, "David!"

There was the crack of a pistol shot, then another, the beast smashing down onto the surface of the catwalk, the entire structure vibrating, Dannie losing her balance, starting to roll over the edge, catching herself as the werewolf rolled past her, tumbled off the edge and fell.

She turned her eyes away.

As she looked up, she saw David, clinging by one hand to the catwalk, sticking his gun into a pocket, then getting his other hand onto one of the rungs, then chinning himself, getting a leg over. He was up into a crouch. Dannie started to get herself more firmly onto the catwalk, hitched up her dress so she wouldn't trip on one of the ragged trailers of fabric, got herself to a wobbly standing position.

She didn't need to be told what to do, just started to walk . . .

On the far side of the gymnasium, through a window there, there were more of the armed guards visible, and the playing field of the football stadium beyond and all the way to the base of the service road was filled with the werewolves. "In here. I saw a sign for the locker rooms for the football team. Sometimes there's a tunnel leading to the stadium. If we can reach the stadium, maybe we can crawl our way along the bleachers and out. Worth a try."

She followed him into the athletic department offices and at the far end of a narrow corridor there was a staircase leading downward. He took the stairs two at a time, the little flashlight in his left hand, the gun in his right, his wrists crossed so the beam from the flashlight pointed in the same direction as the gun.

After three turns at small landings they reached the base of the stairwell and there was another door.

David tried it, the door locked. "Hold these," David ordered, giving her the flashlight and the gun. She was terrified she'd do something and the gun would go off, so she was careful not to move her fingers, just hold the thing.

"Keep the light steady," he told her, so she held it for him as he opened a small case that looked like the sort of carrying case sometimes used with nail files and things, only larger. "Lock picks," David said by way of explana-

349

tion, trying several of the black skewerlike objects, the ends in all different shapes, one even like a tiny corkscrew. At last there was a clicking sound, then David took the gun and flashlight back as he pocketed the lock picks. He tried the door and it opened.

She followed him into the deeper-seeming darkness beyond. "Find a light switch," he told her after a few seconds of moving the flashlight beam around the room. There looked to be various pieces of athletic equipment here. She felt along the wall, her fingers touching at a piece of pipe, then following it down along the smooth concrete to a box with a switch. She worked the switch, squinting her eyes against the light.

When she opened her eyes, what she saw was somehow more horrible to her than anything else she had seen since this all began. There was a treadmill, and suspended over it was a framework made out of pipe. Attached to the pipe was a pair of handcuffs like policemen carried.

And she realized she was standing in the room where her father had died. "That's—"

But David somehow knew, maybe from something she'd said or Mac had told him or maybe he just felt it inside her, because he took her into his arms and just held her tightly, very tightly . . .

Dannie Hardy was still sniffing back tears when David found the entrance to the tunnel connecting the training area to the stadium. Earlier, they had investigated a large, corrugated metal door, something the size for a huge garage of some kind, David telling her that there would be a drive off the service road outside the door, and the door was the means by which the equipment was brought into the training area. There were computers, too, small ones, connected to some of the training machines.

She guessed even physical fitness was getting high tech these days.

They entered the tunnel, David just ahead of her, his

350

flashlight beam scanning the tunnel walls and overhead, not so much ahead of them. "What are you looking for?"

"I don't know but I'll recognize it when I see it, all right?"

She sniffed, grunted in the affirmative, and dogged after him.

At a point that she judged had to be at least halfway along the tunnel's length, David stopped. There was a metal ladder and above it, there was something like a manhole lid, only with a wheel set into it. As she looked more closely, she noticed that the lid was really a round door. David climbed the ladder. "What are you doing? I mean, I can see you're climbing, but—"

"This might be what I think it is."

"What do you think it is?"

"A connection from this tunnel into another one, maybe, maybe leading into whatever's underneath the observatory. So far, we haven't seen any signs of a laboratory or anything where the werewolves are tested, where experiments are conducted. Nazis love experiments," he went on, working the wheel-shaped object at the center of the round door, "so they'd have to have such a place and—"

David stopped talking, pushed up the round door, and cautiously sent his light through.

"Come on," David told her. He climbed up through, Dannie following him, the darkness all around her like velvet except for where David's flashlight penetrated it. He helped her to her feet, shone the light toward the floor, closed the door, turned the wheel, she guessed locking it.

"Which way?"

He pointed the beam of light toward her right. "That way's the only way. We're in another tunnel, and it ends just a foot back there. Made of some sort of pipe, so it was just set in, never actually built. Hold on to my belt and don't let go." He moved her hand to his belt at the small of his back. She locked her left hand around it, determined not to let go. Then, the little flashlight beam the only thing relieving the totality of darkness around them, they started ahead.

As they walked, David whispered softly, "I've got a reasonable amount of silver-tipped bullets, but not enough for what's going on out there. If anything should happen to me, with this pistol all you'd have to do is pull the trigger. Put the muzzle into your mouth and aim upward into the brain and back, then pull that trigger."

Dannie Hardy didn't say anything, because she didn't know what to say. But, she'd do it, because she couldn't end like Richard had ended. And she knew that if she didn't and David had to, he'd kill her.

The thought didn't frighten her; in a way, it was like insurance against disaster.

They kept moving together though the darkness and she never once released her hold on David's belt.

Chapter Thirty-two:

Penetration

There was, almost tritely, a light at the end of the tunnel, glowing dully, a mere pinpoint for the past several minutes. They moved through the darkness toward it.

Twice now, they had discovered a smaller pipe segment branching off from the main unit along which they traveled, and now they found a third. David, as he had done the two previous times, shone the light into it. They saw nothing; they went on.

They didn't speak now, by mutual consent agreeing that there was no way of telling if the tunnel might serve as some sort of whispering gallery, make their words heard great distances away.

Instead, they kept going toward the light, and the comparison to a moth flying into a candle flame was not lost on her; as surely as the moth went to its death, they might be going to their deaths, or worse.

She had always laughed at the concept of a "fate worse than death," but now, confronted with the reality of it, there was nothing humorous. To live the life of one of those bitten and surviving, becoming one of the were-wolves, feeding on human flesh and blood, to be a person locked inside a mindless beast which dominated one's actions, made one perform acts which were repugnant, disgusting, would be a living hell. And, after the episode had passed, to know that it would come again— It was not like Lon Chaney, Jr., waiting for the moon to rise, knowing the evil it wrought on him, because William Stein and his cohort of SS men could bring about the transformation at whim, whenever, wherever, she realized.

There was the true terror.

The light gave the appearance of growing larger, but she realized on a rational plane, of course, that it was not growing at all, that they were merely reducing the distance to it and the light was unchanged. There ought to have been some philosophical meaning to that, she thought, but if there were, it was lost upon her now.

Dannie Hardy was tired, dirty, hungry, scared—and she wanted this to be over, very badly. She was living inside a nightmare and could not wake up until the nightmare's storyline was resolved.

David seemed to quicken his pace ahead of her. She was glad of it.

The faster they reached the light, then maybe the faster this would end . . .

MacTavish found a foothold in the rocks at about hip level, hauled his left leg up, found a handhold for his gloved fingertips, and pulled himself up, Tailor paralleling him in another of the rills. Some of the dirt dislodged and MacTavish slipped downward, spreadeagling his arms and legs, frictioning his body against the dirt and rocks, skidding to a stop, then finding another handhold, another foothold, climbing upward.

He caught a glimpse of the face of his watch. If he had not at least penetrated the observatory within ten minutes, Yankee Doodle Leader would send in his Surprise, the 82nd Airborne. And if the observatory held the key to the transformations—there had to be thousands of the werewolves packing the roadway up the mountain toward the foot of the observatory, spilling back into the football field and surrounding the gymnasium in the distance, and God knew how many thousands more in other parts of the northeastern United States and southeastern Canada.

They could be killed, but how many others were there that had not been activated this night, or had been bitten this night and might naturally transform?

To penetrate the observatory and know its secrets was the only answer—and to make certain that Stein's immortality ended here, forever.

The dirt gave way to rocks, large in size, natural outcroppings from within the geologic formation on which the observatory was set.

MacTavish judged the distance to the top, where werewolves patrolled the walkway circumferencing the observatory dome, as perhaps twenty yards. Keeping his voice as low as he could, he called to Tailor a few feet from him. "Check the other units. We'll go over onto the walkway exactly five minutes from now, and once we've consolidated there, on with the plan. I'm informing Yankee Doodle Leader."

"Aye, sir!"

MacTavish triggered his radio. "This is Brit Leader calling Yankee Doodle One. Over. Brit Leader to Yankee Doodle One, do you read me? Over."

"This is Yankee Doodle Leader, Brit Leader, reading you with heavy static. Are you in position? Over."

"We are in position, Yankee Doodle Leader. I say again we are in position. Order up the surprise." That would give him exactly nineteen minutes before the first chutes would open over Sutton College. "Potentially very hot here. I say again, potentially very hot. Thousands of them surrounding the objective. Is there any word on my colleagues yet? Is Surprise a go? Over."

"Surprise is a go, Brit Leader. No word on your friends Good luck. Yankee Doodle Leader Out."

"Thanks; we'll need it. Brit Leader Out." And MacTavish clicked off his radio.

He signaled to Commander Tailor. Tailor said something into his radio.

And Hugh MacTavish drew his knife from the sheath at his left side. The blade of each man's knife was plated with silver And, just like they'd planned but hadn't had the time to rehearse, they would go over the railing and attack the werewolves, using the knives until they could no longer use them and then the guns. Once the first shot was fired here, there was no telling what would happen; Stein had to know there was an enemy unit on the campus, so why wasn't there more concern already? Was it that Stein was so supremely confident that he just didn't care?

The armed guards on both sides of the road and the thousands who were already transformed to beasts would react, wouldn't they?

He hated the expression, but it truly fit here: All hell would break loose . . .

They were passing another of the smaller tunnels now and without warning, the main tunnel through which they moved took a sharp bend to the left and the light which up until then had still been very small, seemed very distant, was suddenly vastly larger, terrifically brighter.

She was about to whisper something about this to David when she heard something behind her. David must have heard it, too, because he grabbed for her in the darkness, almost throwing her against the curving tunnel wall, her head hitting it, hurting. David's light swept behind them.

One of the werewolves, running straight for them. David fired, the flash of his pistol blindingly bright in the otherwise almost total darkness, the sound of the single shot like the sound of an explosion in the confined space here, echoing and reechoing, her ears, throbbing with it. David fired again.

The creature fell, dead.

From ahead of them, she heard shouts, realizing that if

she could hear them at all they had to be impossibly close. And, as she looked toward the light, she realized that the light itself was moving, toward them. "David!"

David grabbed her, both of them nearly tripping over the already changing body of the werewolf, David stabbing his pistol toward the light that was approaching them. He fired, then fired again and again and again until her eardrums felt like they would explode with the shockwaves.

The light seemed to explode and was gone.

David dragged her on. His mouth was beside her ear and he was shouting at her, but she could hardly hear him. Something about the side tunnels.

They were at the last branch tunnel they'd passed, David urging her up, half shoving her into the opening, then hauling himself up, wriggling past her. The pipe was not tall enough to stand in, nor even to crouch in.

They would have to crawl. David shouted something about the light, and then his flashlight went out.

His left pants leg was oozing a warm sticky substance onto the floor of the pipe. Dannie almost screamed, but David's hand was holding hers now and she had to stretch to keep hold of it as he started crawling.

Dannie crawled after him through the darkness . . .

Mac climbed out onto the framework beneath the walkway circumferencing the gleaming white dome of the observatory. His knife was in his teeth. On the next girder over was Commander Tailor, the other SEALS from their unit around them.

MacTavish studied the luminous black face of his watch, the second hand sweeping toward the inverted triangle that was the twelve.

As the second hand neared it, MacTavish edged slightly forward along the girder, right hand flexing to grab hold of the walkway railing. At any second, the werewolves might smell human presence, attack themselves, preempting any element of surprise MacTavish and the SEAL personnel might have.

The second hand touched the triangle.

MacTavish grabbed to the railing with both gloved hands, saw no immediate sign of the enemy, and swung out, his feet bracing against the girder along which he'd climbed, now pushing him upward as his right hand found the center support and he pulled, his legs swinging free in the air for an instant, then his right leg finding a purchase as he hauled himself up, vaulted over the railing. His right hand grabbed for the knife in his teeth and, as he wheeled around, one of the beasts was lunging for him, a low growl issuing through its bared fangs. MacTavish took a step back, then to the left. He dropped one knee, bracing the knife, ramming the long-bladed cold steel Magnum Tanto up into the creature's underbelly, letting the weight of its body eviscerate it. The creature plopped to the walkway, rolled onto its back, the metamorphosis to human form already beginning.

The SEALs were all over the railing now, most welcome from among their ranks the man with the Barnett Commando Crossbow with its silver-tipped bolts.

MacTavish, the bowman and Tailor moved ahead along the catwalk, toward the breach in the dome through which the telescope would protrude. It had been open as they approached, and MacTavish was willing to bet it had something to do with the broadcast. The music, more from Wagner's heroic retelling of ancient Germanic legend, played on.

As they neared the niche, another of the creatures appeared from around the arc of the dome, and then another; the bowman fired, catching the nearest of the two werewolves through the chest, knocking it down as though struck by an automobile, the second beast lunging for them, the bowman trapped under it. MacTavish and Tailor and another SEAL dove onto the beast, hammering the blades of their silver plated knives into the beast.

As they rolled it away, the werewolf already starting to change back to human form, they saw the young SEAL's throat, ripped out.

MacTavish picked up the crossbow, murmured, "Rest in peace, lad," and grabbed a handful of crossbow bolts from the boy's gear. He braced the nose of the crossbow against the walkway, pushed his knee into the base of the pistol grip, bent back the buttstock, breaking the action, cocking it. He nocked a bolt. "Let's go; someone get his guns and ammunition. Every silver bullet might count."

They moved on, toward the sighting breach in the dome, from behind MacTavish one of the SEALs warning, "Look out!"

MacTavish wheeled around, fired, catching the attacking werewolf in the throat. There was a low growl from behind him, then another and another. MacTavish twisted round, two werewolves hurtling toward them, Commander Tailor throwing himself between MacTavish and one of the beasts, wading in with his knife. MacTavish buttstroked the second beast across its massive lower jaw, deflecting its lunge, the creature slamming to the walkway surface, then up in the blink of an eye, lunging again. MacTavish had one of the crossbow bolts in his right hand, stabbing it through the creature's left eye as it came for his throat, MacTavish's right knee smashing upward into its abdomen to buy a precious second or two. The creature dropped, rolling, growling, shrieking in pain, the transformation back to human form beginning.

At the breach in the dome now, MacTavish recocked the crossbow. A half dozen other SEALs joined them, then in the next second, four more.

Tailor detailed two men through the breach, one of them with a crossbow, the other with a submachine gun readied. A rope was dropped, the crossbowman going first. Another five SEALs arrived, then another six. In all, counting Tailor, there were twenty-six, meaning that four from the original total of thirty men had died reaching the breach in the dome.

MacTavish and Tailor followed down on the rope after the first two men, a small flashlight clamped in Mac's teeth. The dome seemed vastly higher from the inside than it had when viewed as they'd approached it, the walkway which circumferenced it on the outside, Mac-Tavish realized, merely at a level approximately one-third down from its crown, the rest masked by the building's architecture. The experience of entering it now was like roping down from the ceiling of some great and vast cathedral.

And it was a house of worship of sorts, because as his flashlight beam danced along the interior of the dome, there were frescos everywhere.

One depicted Adolf Hitler, his face that of an aesthete, sitting alone and penning *Mein Kampf*. Still another depicted Hitler as he assumed the chancellorship of Germany, still another showing an idealized Hitler, probably more vigorous than the man had been since his brief brush with heroism in World War I, goosestepping along at the head of thousands of Hitler Youth. Nazi symbology was everywhere, the Swastika, the death's head of the SS.

And, as MacTavish looked below, there was a solitary statue, magnificent in its detail and capturing the essence of why MacTavish had come. A lifesize full-figure sculpture of Adolf Hitler, but in his hand a sword, kingly. Kneeling before him, a Swastika armband the only marking distinguishing it from an ordinary beast, was a man-wolf.

The tip of the sword touched at the shoulder of the beast, as though knighting it for some holy quest.

MacTavish looked up, two more of the SEALs roping down just after him.

And above them, he heard gunfire, so much of it that for a moment MacTavish was transported to that afternoon forty-five years ago in the forest in the castle's shadow, the gunfire persisting for several seconds, the sound of an explosion, dust filtering down from the dome above, more gunfire then, then several long bursts, then nothing.

As Tailor dropped from the rope, the SEAL team commander activated his radio. "Edwards, what's happening? Edwards. Answer me, dammit."

There was no reply.

MacTavish touched to the floor, unclipped from the rope, stepped away, the two SEALs who had reached the floor of the observatory first belaying the rope for the other two still coming.

MacTavish, the shotgun in one hand, the crossbow in the other, ran toward the double doors leading into the area beneath the dome, Tailor taking the other side. "They suckered us into a trap. I'm an old fool."

"There was no sign of them, Brigadier. You couldn't have known. And when the 82nd gets here—"

"It'll be a bloody slaughter, Commander—you and I both know that—unless we can somehow get control of the transmission and turn the creatures back to human."

The last two SEALs were down, along with the two who'd belayed the rope joining them on both sides of the double doors "They know we're in here; that's obvious. Stein may want to lead us to him. Let's oblige him."

MacTavish began searching the double doors for any signs of booby traps, the remaining five men doing the same. At last MacTavish kicked at the double doors. They vibrated, but nothing else happened.

"They could be waiting for us on the other side," Tailor said.

MacTavish nodded, half expecting that they would be. "If it's the way of getting us to Stein and his control center, we'll surrender."

Tailor looked at MacTavish, nodded.

MacTavish looked at Tailor, then the four other men. "Whatever happens, be ready to go into action; when it comes down, there won't be any time for thoughtful consideration, gentlemen."

Hugh MacTavish stepped to the doors, handed off the crossbow to one of the SEALs, and, the shotgun in his right hand, opened the doors with his left.

"Good evening, Brigadier MacTavish."

Standing at the center of at least four dozen men in full SS Field Gray, a Luger pistol held almost casually in his right hand, was Standardtenführer William Stein. Each of the SS men had a submachine gun. MacTavish almost laughed. The master race had armed itself with the gun designed and manufactured by the men and women it had deemed subhuman and tried so very hard to exterminate; they carried Israeli Uzis.

"Good evening, Herr Standartenführer," Hugh MacTavish answered.

"If you would care to accompany me, you'll see some wondrous sights, and can even be at my side as I address the multitudes who are the new disciples of the Reich. It would be instructive to you."

"What about my men?"

"We can kill them later; I wouldn't want anything to spoil this for you. After all, MacTavish, you'll be out there with me alone. Perhaps you can kill me," Stein said, looking down at his spit-shined jackboots, then up into MacTavish's face, smiling. "But you must lay down your shotgun and submachine gun. I'm only armed with a pistol. Fair is fair."

"I get to keep my pistol? How nice."

"But my men get to keep your five friends here. It balances off, Herr Brigadier."

Hugh MacTavish took a step forward, unslung his submachine gun, handed it to one of Stein's SS men, handed the shotgun to another of them. "I'm at your disposal."

"Somehow I knew you would be. Come. The hour is late."

MacTavish looked at Stein and smiled. "Indeed."

Chapter Thirty-three:

The Battle Between Good and Evil

David was bleeding badly. As she followed him along through the pipe in total darkness, her left hand became sticky with his blood, and several times she had bumped into him when he had slowed.

"I'm getting ahead of you, David. You keep the gun. Be ready to back me up."

David's voice was very tired. She wished they could risk the light, that she could see his face. "It won't do us any good, Dannie. I fired the last of our silver bullets to kill the werewolf that followed us into the tunnel. The gun is useless to us now."

"Give me your knife. If there's something ahead of us, at least I can fight it."

"It isn't silver-plated like the Brigadier's. It won't do any good, Dannie."

"At least it'll show whoever it is we aren't just going to lay down and die, David."

"All right." He found her hand in the darkness and he pressed the handle of the knife into it. And then he kissed her. "I'm so very sorry this didn't work out, Dannie. I was beginning to look forward very much to being with you."

"We're not dead yet."

"My leg wound, as you may have detected, is a bleeder. I'll be unconscious in another few minutes or so. The blood flow just won't stop, I'm afraid. And a while after that, I'll be dead."

She almost stabbed him as she reached out to hold him, but held on to the knife as she folded her arms around him.

"You go on without me. Maybe, if you find the Brigadier, you can get someone back for—"

"Bullshit, David Mallory! I've heard of men coming up with some crap excuses to avoid the altar, but this really takes the cake."

"The cake?"

"The prize. If you think I'm going to let you just stay in this damn black hole and die while I go on alone and get lost and die, too, well—you're wrong, David."

"I see."

"You keep up with me. If you need to stop, just tell me and we'll stop for a while. But I think we're going to get out of this. And there wouldn't be much point in getting out of this if you were dead, would there?"

"I suppose not, Dannie."

"Then don't waste energy talking; just let's keep going."

"All right."

She kissed his forehead, his cheek, his mouth, wanted to tell him she loved him, felt embarrassed, told him anyway. "I love you."

"I know that; it's my charm, you see."

"Well?"

"Well?"

"Well?"

David said it then, "I love you, Dannie," and she kissed him harder than she thought she could kiss anyone and held him close to her and prayed that he wouldn't die.

That they wouldn't die.

Holding the knife in a death grip, making sure David was behind her, she crawled on through the darkness . . .

There was a very long ramp as wide as a four-lane

road, the ramp sloping gently but decidedly upward, the walls on either side of it and the ceiling high above which completed the tunnel of concrete gleamingly painted, lights set in banks at regular intervals providing enough illumination here to easily read, and making the high polish of the interior that much brighter.

MacTavish walked at Stein's right, since he was the superior officer. Beside him, pacing him, Stein asked offhandedly, "Of course you have silver bullets in that pistol holstered on your hip."

"Of course."

"And you merely wait the chance to shoot me, because you somehow think that will bring all of this to an end, in your favor."

"Of course, Standartenführer."

"Tell me then, Brigadier, how do you propose to deal with the thousands of converts I have made? Not just the ones we will physically address, but all those other thousands all over the planet whom you will not see?"

"Through faith and good works, Standartenführer."

Stein laughed. "You English amaze me, as you did throughout the war. How childish. The odds, the overwhelming technological superiority of the enemy, not even your own feeble strategic or tactical posture will dismay you. You just believe that somehow you will win, that it is destiny."

"Something like that, yes." MacTavish smiled. "May I smoke?"

"But of course. May I have a light?"

"Of course." MacTavish took his own cigarette as Stein took one from a silver case. He recognized the case. It was the one that had belonged to that brave twit Forrestal forty-five years ago. "Nice case."

"War trophy."

"Yes." MacTavish offered his light, Stein pausing in midstride, nodding a thanks, then continuing on as MacTavish fired his own cigarette. "I like your taste in elevator music, Standartenführer; it's usually so bland."

"Thank you very much, but it is about to be turned off." Stein took a small radio set from his belt, spoke into it in German.

Within thirty seconds, the heroic strains of Richard Wagner had trailed off and were gone. "Might I suggest the Beatles?" MacTavish offered. "For a change of pace, of course."

"Somehow British music has never appealed to me, Brigadier MacTavish."

"What a pity."

The ramp leveled off.

They turned a wide corner into a large room that looked like a television broadcast center. Indeed, there were cameras in operation and computers, sound equipment; editing equipment and recording equipment were everywhere. Technicians in headphones, women carrying clipboards, all in SS Field Gray, moved about busily engaged. MacTavish asked, "Are we about to get on the air and ask for donations to save the satellite?"

Stein laughed. "Better than that. And we have a captive audience. They will listen because they have no other choice. Come."

He gestured toward a doorway made of heavy steel, like the vault door of a financial institution. Only there seemed to be no combination lock.

MacTavish walked along beside him.

Stein snapped his fingers to a young Untersturmführer, the officer barking a command in German to a Rottenführer standing before a control panel which looked like an enlarged set of controls for a Concorde. The Rottenführer pressed some buttons, a panel lighting up, then, flipped a switch and MacTavish glanced back toward the massive vault door.

It began to swing open, inward.

As the door finished its circuit and MacTavish drew closer to it, he could see beyond it.

There was a platform of rough black rock, spotlights shining down on it from above, a high lip of rock forming a high barricade around it. It looked as natural as the rock formations around an amusement park ride, and probably was.

"Out there, Brigadier. I wanted you with me, because you are the only one of my original enemies to survive. In a way, this is my tribute to you. You watched the birth of an era, and now you shall see it to its full maturity."

MacTavish stopped walking, looked at Stein. "And then what? Ripped apart by your werewolves or a quick bullet?"

"Only if you wish, Brigadier. I had originally thought to kill you, but why should I? Age will claim you. And no death could ever be so bitter for you as living to see my victory, the triumph at last of the Führer's dream."

"Which dream was that? Killing everybody who wasn't a blond-haired and blue-eyed German?"

"You cannot ruin my evening. This is the dawn of a new era for mankind, a deepening, sharpening of the very definition of humanity. I am giving much of the world immortality, Brigadier MacTavish. Should I be viewed as someone evil when, like the common man's God, I give the promise of eternal life?"

MacTavish looked at him hard. "You're insane; but, of course, you know that."

Stein looked down at his shoes, then up into Mac's eyes and smiled. "You can stand in here, or accompany me outside."

"And what if I shoot you dead?"

"You and your comrades will be torn apart by my werewolves, and what I have set in motion will continue as uninterruptedly as if you had never lived. Join me." He extended his left hand, toward the stone balcony beyond the open doorway.

"Very well," MacTavish told him and walked beside

him . . .

Dannie Hardy's hands felt along the metal door, found the steeringwheellike device. "David? What do you think —"

She touched at David's neck. His pulse was almost gone.

"David?"

There was no answer.

Dannie Hardy knelt there in the darkness and cried. And she talked to the darkness, or to God, or to whomever might be listening. "It isn't fair. It isn't. I love David and he's a good man and he shouldn't die like this. Dammit! It isn't fair!"

She was knotting her hands in her tattered dress.

Now she pounded her fists against her thighs, trying to make herself hurt, tears filling her eyes. "Isn't fair!"

No one answered her. There was only the familiar voice of Dannie Hardy's conscience or whatever it was, telling her to turn the steering wheel and open the little round door and see what was on the other side.

And there was another voice, once she'd never known she had. It told her that maybe on the other side she'd find Dr. William Stein and she could kill him with her knife to punish him for killing her father, killing Richard, killing David . . .

She set the knife under her right knee so she would not lose it in the darkness and began to turn the wheel. It didn't want to budge. She gripped it as hard as she could, threw her weight against it. Nothing. She grabbed up her dress in her hands, putting her hands under the skirt, gripping the wheel through it for added friction. She tried to turn it. Nothing. She inhaled, held the breath, scrinched her eyes almost shut and gritted her teeth and held the wheel as tight as she could and twisted at the wheel as fast and hard as she could.

It moved. She kept it moving, freely now, letting it spin open.

She dragged back on it and the door wouldn't budge. She pushed it outward and it moved so easily she almost fell to her death.

Because, below her, and some distance, too, there was a flat expanse of rock, like a small stage, extending from the side of the mountain. Spotlights were on it. There were microphones in stands and mounted at the farthest forward edge and on either side were television cameras.

Walking out onto the stage was a man in a Nazi uniform, like somebody out of a movie or something. And, dressed all in black, walking beside him, like a friend out for a stroll, she saw Mac.

Dannie Hardy already had the knife in her hand. Her fist balled around it tighter than ever now . . .

Below them were ranked thousands of the beasts, as far back as the eye could see, perched on the rocks on all fours like great dogs, or slumped forward at the shoulders and hunched on their hind legs, but watching, ears pricking as Standartenführer Stein began to speak.

"You have felt yourself compelled, uncontrollably, to come to me. I am your leader, and I control the power which can maintain you forever in your present bestial form or, forever, free you from the lycanthropic state.

"The sun will soon be rising. Most of you realize what you have become and think that the rising of the sun will free you; but it will not today. Only I can free you, only if I so choose. Many of you felt the bite of the wolf last night, lived in pain and fear throughout the day, then when the moon rose, felt for the first time a sensation I first felt four and one half decades ago. I waited for the rising of the moon, though I need not have, so you would feel it as I first felt it, feel the rushing of your blood, the pleasure and the pain and the divine strength."

369

"Your wounds from the previous night miraculously healed. Your vigor increased fivefold or better. Your height, your stamina. And though in the guise of a lower life form, you became the highest form of man, and the ultimate weapon—man himself, but a super man.

"However, many of you were not bitten, and first felt the transformation last night at moonrise. Each of you who did was carefully selected, each of you when news of the recent influenza outbreak—a modest feat of psychological and bacteriological warfare—stepping forward to be immunized. The influenza outbreak passed, but carried in this injection for those select few was what makes you what you are tonight and shall be in order to do my bidding in the name of that immortal spirit so unjustly reviled by the inferior races, Adolf Hitler.

"You are, forever, mine to control.

"You are, forever, the instruments of power."

Hugh MacTavish had his pistol out, but what good would it do? There were not enough silver bullets in the world to stop the man. He slipped the Walther P-88 back into the holster at his belt . . .

Maybe Stein told Mac that she and David were hostages. Maybe Mac was drugged. He couldn't be one of them.

David was unconscious beside her, dying.

But, from the start, this had been her fight, hers and Mac's.

"Don't die, David," she whispered, gripping the knife more tightly.

Maybe, even though it wasn't plated with silver—all the silver bullets were gone—she could open Stein's carotid artery and he would bleed to death before he could transform.

Maybe.

She knelt beside David, kissed his lips. "I love you forever, David Mallory."

And then, the knife clutched in her hand, she started to climb through the doorway and onto the rocks, to climb down, to try to kill William Stein.

Her fight. Mac's fight.

And her father's fight . . .

"With the injection in your system," Stein told the assembled multitude of werewolves below him, "the heightened gravitational effect of the moon—as with the rising and falling of the tides—affected your pituitary gland, to produce a hormone which, in turn, produced a metamorphosis. So as not to reveal my plan prematurally, I waited until the full moon so you could be naturally transformed and those you bit transformed as well. And then I broadcasted my signal, a transmission on conventional AM, FM, VHF, and UHF carrier waves, broadcast from here to an ordinary broadcast satellite and then beamed down across this entire area.

"With this transmission," Stein went on, "I can control the metamorphosis in you, the transmission acting on the pituitary gland to stimulate or retard the production of your hormone. The sun is rising. You will not return to human form this day, but will do my bidding. You will break through the pitiful circle of troops surrounding these counties; you will infect with your bite each person you see and, when the moon rises again tomorrow night, they will join you, to fight beside you. By tomorrow evening, similar broadcasts will begin in all parts of the so-called 'free world,' where the mysterious strain of influenza was inoculated against. The armies of the Reich will grow. Millions will go forth and kill and cannot die. Those who are not killed will join you, swelling the ranks of my army still further, ad infinitum, to the greater glory of the Führer. *Heil Hitler!*"

MacTavish for some reason looked up. Climbing downward along the rocks, a knife in her hand, he saw Dannie Hardy.

"My broadcasts will cover the face of the earth. The impotent mongrel governments of the United States, so-called Great Britain, France, the corrupt puppet regimes of the divided Germany — all will surrender. And only then, when they have surrendered, will I broadcast the signal which will free you from your lycanthrophy. Should there be rebellion, no signal will be broadcast and you will forever be damned to kill and feed on human flesh and blood. Should I die, you will be doomed forever."

MacTavish looked upward again. His eyes and Dannie's met. Stein shouted, "Even those you have bitten tonight, did you not notice them joining you, swelling your ranks in the immortal struggle for the Reich?!"

Hugh MacTavish, his voice almost a whisper, asked, "Stein? Is there a vaccine which will counteract the effect?"

Stein looked down at his spit-shined jackboots for a moment, then over his shoulder at MacTavish and smiled.

"You'll kill me anyway; tell me before I die," MacTavish insisted.

Stein did not look at him, but so that only MacTavish could hear, he whispered one word: "Yes."

As Stein said the word, Dannie Hardy half jumped, half fell on him from the rocks above, the knife in her right hand gouging deep into Stein's right shoulder near the neck, Stein letting out a scream of agony.

MacTavish was beside them, over them in two steps, grabbing Dannie by her clothes, tearing her away, his own knife in his hand, MacTavish falling onto Stein. "The antidote? Where? This one's plated with silver!"

MacTavish held the Tanto poised to strike, but the wind was knocked from him as something hammered into his groin and he fell back for just a second. And then the transformation began to take place. Evidently Stein no longer required even the prodding of one of the calculatorlike devices, could simply transform at will.

As MacTavish rolled to the stone platform, Stein rose up, the knife twisted from his shoulder, the SS Field Gray shredding from his body, his body transforming with a speed MacTavish had not dreamed possible. And Stein grew, unimaginally compared to his initial height.

This was the true William Stein.

The blond from forty-five years ago.

Stein's growl seemed to shake the very rock.

MacTavish drew his pistol, but Stein was too quick, a backhand swipe of one mighty forepaw knocking the Walther P-88 away into the darkness. MacTavish reached for his knife with the silver-plated blade.

But Stein reached for MacTavish first, dragging MacTavish up, shaking him, hurtling him back against the rock wall.

There was a droning sound in the graying night.

MacTavish's sixty-one-year-old body crashed against the rocks and fell, the breath gone from his lungs, the bitterness of loss filling his mouth like bile.

MacTavish heard gunshots behind him, looked past Stein, skyward.

The Surprise.

Parachutes were opening, filling the predawn horizon.

Stein reached for MacTavish, MacTavish hauled up, his feet off the ground, his right foot kicking out. Even a werewolf had testicles.

Dannie moved like a blur at the edge of Mac's peripheral vision, one of the microphone stalks in her hands, driving it downward, into Stein's back.

MacTavish fell, winded again.

Stein shrieked in agony, tearing the hard-chromed metal shaft from his left kidney, hurtling it into the crowd. The werewolves below the balcony were rushing upward, toward them now.

MacTavish dragged himself to his feet.

Stein wheeled toward him, backhanding him across the face, MacTavish feeling bones in his cheek and jaw breaking, his head slamming against the rocks, the blackness of unconsciousness welling up within him.

MacvTavish lay there, shook his head.

Stein was about to lunge for Dannie Hardy's throat. "No, damn you!"

MacTavish was up, throwing himself onto Stein's back, his fists hammering against the creature's head, Stein's body shaking, lurching, MacTavish thrown free, impacting the black stone of the wall again.

MacTavish felt blood dripping into his eyes.

Stein stood over him.

Stein's jaw was open, drool falling from his mouth, his fangs longer than MacTavish had seen on any of the others. There was a low growl from within Stein's chest.

He lifted MacTavish at arm's length, shook MacTavish like a doll, then drew MacTavish toward him.

MacTavish felt the fangs gouge into his left shoulder and the left side of his neck, squeezed his eyes tight against the pain.

So this was death.

MacTavish felt himself falling.

Stein had let him fall, wasn't giving him death, was giving him the living hell of serving the Reich and the forever damned Führer instead.

MacTavish lay there, staring up at Stein.

And then MacTavish moved his right hand, praying now. The calculator. He'd figured out the combination with the help of a computer.

His fingers worked the buttons in series. Simple enough. 1-3-0-1-9-3-3, obvious even.

And Hugh MacTavish pressed the device against his right ear.

With the last of his strength, he shouted to Dannie, "The formula for the antidote must be in the computer inside there, somewhere! Find it and stop the signal to the werewolves. Stop the signal!"

As MacTavish looked back; inside the mountain, there was fighting, Tailor and his SEALs fighting against the Nazis, most of them still not yet transformed but in human form with human weakness.

MacTavish felt a strangeness about his body that he had never known, supposed that it was death.

But as he looked up into Stein's eyes, he realized it wasn't death.

The bite, the transmission from the calculatorlike object.

MacTavish was beginning to transform.

And there was strength flowing through him, godlike, and he knew in that instant the thing which obsessed William Stein, a feeling no ordinary man could ever feel.

MacTavish's body was growing. He could feel as muscles stretched and arteries expanded and watch as skin split, healed, split again, healed.

His head. MacTavish shouted against the pain and the shout was no longer human.

Pain, unlike anything he had ever known, everywhere, consuming him

And his mind was expanding into new directions and down dark paths he had never suspected, anguish and joy and lust and hate and power sweeping through him, corners of his consciousness he had never explored, there, open for him in the light of awareness.

He could feel his own heart pumping, feel the blood course through his veins, feel hair grow on his skin.

His shoulders rose.

The clothing the old MacTavish, the sixty-one-year-old man had worn, tore away from his swelling chest, the pistol belt snapping away from his waist. His organ—my God, MacTavish thought—he was big, bigger than any man, any ordinary man could ever be! And he felt a hardness and power there unlike any he had ever known.

His trousers burst.

The laces on his boots snapped and the seams in the leather tore and MacTavish was standing, a god towering over his fellow man, immortal, the pain only a part of him now, the wonderment replacing it.

His body ached for use.

To never die. Old age had had him, but was forever banished.

This beast before him.

It cowered in the shadow of his might.

MacTavish dropped to all fours, his tongue licking across his mouth, his fangs lusting to pierce the flesh of this creature. And his back arched and he rose up, his hind legs set and his muscles springing as he threw himself at this vile thing he knew somehow the old MacTavish hated and he hated, too.

MacTavish's claws gouged into the beast and the beast's claws tore at MacTavish's neck and shoulders.

MacTavish's muzzle slammed against the other creature's head and his jaws opened and then snapped closed over the beast's throat, but the creature dodged away and MacTavish's fangs bit through the flesh of a shoulder, tearing muscle and sinew, ripping at it.

Pain.

Pain stronger than he had ever known in his side.

Claws.

MacTavish threw his body weight against this beast which fought him. They fell, rolled, jaws snapping, claws raking across each other's body, MacTavish's jaws snapping shut, missing, opening, again, snapping shut, only a mouthful of hair and flesh and the warm salty taste of blood.

Deep inside him, he remembered something. What was it?

Werewolf.

He was a werewolf.

It wasn't so bad, if only he could kill; this thing.

376

What was it?

Werewolf.

He was werewolf and it was werewolf, of course.

How to kill a werewolf?

How?

He remembered.

Hugh MacTavish's jaws snapped, closing over the neck of the beast, and then MacTavish threw his body weight left toward the end of the rocks where the dawn began and there was a cracking sound that was loud and hurt his ears and some of his teeth broke and as MacTavish shook his jaws, the head of the beast was between his teeth and he shook his jaws again and watched as the head of the beast flew into the dawn.

Sound.

It pierced his consciousness, but there was nothing to hear.

Pain.

No. This was strength.

He tried to scream, but words were not words anymore.

Pain.

Cramping in muscles he had not known he'd had, joints twisting, contorting.

Faces around him, distorted, strange, human. Guns pointed at him.

His lungs suddenly ached and around him everything was spinning and there was light and . . .

Hugh MacTavish opened his eyes.

"You should be all right, General."

"Brigadier," he told the man, obviously a medic.

A woman, maybe another medic or a whatever Americans called them—nurses? She had pretty dark hair and smiled at him. He wondered if she had seen him naked and how powerful he was.

MacTavish sat up, a wash of cold sweat over him.

He was not the werewolf. "What the bloody fuck happened?"

He was sitting on a gurney.

Dannie Hardy was standing beside the gurney on the other side.

On another gurney, an I.V. bottle going into him, was David Mallory.

MacTavish felt younger, stronger, healthier than he had for decades.

"I was one of them!"

"You'll be all right," Dannie told him.

"I killed Stein."

Commander Tailor approached and, for the first time, MacTavish looked at his immediate surroundings. He was outside under a shelter of some sort, perhaps a tent. There was a heater going in a far corner. Medical personnel were everywhere, attending wounded and injured.

Tailor said, "You really fought that Stein guy, Brigadier. I've never seen anything like it." MacTavish stared at him, didn't want to say anything to interrupt him. "You were really getting the short end of it, sir, and then he bit you and he was going after Dr. Hardy and you took that calculator thing out. And then, wham! It was like something out of a movie.

"You started growing, your clothing popping off your body and you were this giant gray werewolf. You were bigger than Stein and you could see that Stein was scared shitless—" He looked at Dannie Hardy, adding, "Begging your pardon, ma'am." Dannie dismissed it with a wave, smiled at him, looked at Mac. MacTavish saw a strange look in her eyes, like she was proud of him. "Anyway, it was terrific. The two of you went at it then, you and Stein, Brigadier, and everything he gave you, you gave him better. And then you got your jaws on his throat and threw your front legs back or arms or—I don't know. And you shook your whole body and it

378

shook his body and you—"

Tailor fell silent.

MacTavish supplied, "I bit his head off and threw his head over the side. I remember. And now I'm one of them." He looked at Dannie, at David, David's eyelids fluttering a little as if he were coming round. "Commander. Give me a weapon, with silver in it."

Dannie grabbed Mac's right arm, hugged it, touched her lips to his cheek. "We found the antidote in the computer, and we found gallons of the stuff stored in the observatory. When we shut off the signal, nothing happened. Then Commander Tailor figured we should flip this switch and we did and there was a whole computer menu up. There was a recall message which could change the creatures back. We had to try it. I pushed the buttons and we started the recall message.

"You began changing back just a few seconds after you killed Stein."

"Don't you see, I might—"

Dannie threw her arms around his neck. "We gave you an injection. You've been asleep for ten hours, Mac. You're fine."

"Give me your pistol, Commander."

Dannie shrank back.

Commander Tailor looked around him, looked at MacTavish. "Your pistol."

MacTavish extended his right hand. Commander Tailor drew his weapon, turned it around in his hand, gave it to MacTavish. MacTavish removed the magazine, checked the chamber, replaced the magazine, flipped off the Beretta's safety. "Someone give me one of those calculator things."

Another of the SEALs was nearby, looked at Tailor, got a nod, handed MacTavish the device.

MacTavish announced, "Everyone stand back."

"Mac, it's—"

"I've got to know, Dannie." His fingers tapped out the

379

code, 1-3-0-1-9-3-3, the date Hitler assumed the chancellorship of Germany.

He held the device to his right ear, the pistol tight in his left hand, the muzzle pointed at the underside of his throat, his thumb pressing against the trigger to snap it back.

Nothing happened.

MacTavish sat there for a moment longer, then removed his thumb from the trigger guard, worked down the safety.

He looked at the calculator.

He set it down. "Well, that's better. Now, Dannie, you were about to . . . ?"

Dannie Hardy threw her arms around his neck, her lips touching his cheek, MacTavish folding her into his arms. It was a kiss a daughter would give a father, he knew, but at sixty-one, a man took a kiss from a young girl however he could get it.

Chapter Thirty-four:

Brigadier MacTavish

The "mopping up," as Commander Tailor called, it took four days and Dannie stayed with several of the female personnel in one of the Sutton sorority houses. She was able to shower all she wanted, eat all she wanted and even found some clothing. Things were surprisingly organized, actually, the Sutton students pitching in to help with the grisly task of identifying bodies and also in the task of interviewing the persons who had undergone the metamorphosis. Each person had to be provided emergency clothing, food, shelter and, most importantly, given the injection which would chemically alter the body so that when the next full moon came—

Dannie helped with the work as much as she could, spending her off-time with David, who was recovering very nicely from his gunshot wound in the leg and with Mac, who was sort of in charge of things here.

The computer inside the observatory carried thousands of names, and many of these were thought to be Nazis, part of the conspiracy but based in other parts of the United States and the world.

The President of the United States and the British ambassador and the Canadian prime minister arrived and Dannie was included in their meetings with Mac. The President was very nice, told Mac he was going to personally see to it that Mac received a medal. "That's very kind of you, Mr. President, but the bravery was all on the part of Dr. Hardy and Mr. Mallory and Commander

Tailor and his SEALs. All I did was go along for the ride."

Dannie hadn't realized a man could be possessed of such genuine, self-effacing modesty.

The President insisted about the medal anyway, and the Canadian prime minister, Dannie supposed not to be outdone, promised a medal as well. But the British ambassador outdid them all. When Brigadier MacTavish returned to England, he had an appointment with the queen, a knighthood to be bestowed upon him.

Mac looked honestly flabbergasted.

But he had to fly to Brussels first, to coordinate the roundup of the other Nazis involved in the conspiracy, a joint operation between Nato forces and Warsaw Pact nations, the first of its kind.

She felt good about that.

There were thousands of the werewolves still in Europe, most the unwilling variety, who had to be located and inoculated. And tracking down the Nazis, even with international cooperation, might take a long time.

She had a talk with David. They decided they had not just succumbed to the anxiety of the moment, that they both really did want to get married to each other.

On the morning of the fifth day, Mac received orders that he was to leave for a military airfield by helicopter, and at the airfield he would transfer to an SR-71 spy plane, the fastest aircraft in the world, and fly by SR-71 to a NATO airfield in Brussels. The trail was getting hot and no one wanted to let the Nazis escape.

David walked pretty well now and, helping him a little as she held his arm, his other hand with a cane, they walked out into the Sutton Commons where the helicopter awaited.

As Mac emerged from the dean's offices — he used them as his command center — the military personnel ranked on either side of the admin building and forming a cordon between it and the helicopter came to attention.

Mac stopped at the base of the admin building steps

and took their salute.

He was tall, straight, somehow younger-looking. Maybe it was the effect of the transformation, or just the excitement. He was dressed in his black field uniform, wore a black military beret, a pistol at his hip, but no decorations, no rank.

Instead of walking straight to the helicopter, he walked over toward where she and David stood.

David brought himself to attention, Mac throwing his arms around him. "You get well, lad!" And he held David for a second. He stepped back, a glow of pride in his eyes.

And he looked at Dannie. Dannie threw her arms around his neck and kissed him. "I love ya, Mac. Will you give me away when I marry David?"

"Give you away? I just found you, girl! Yes, of course! You've got your father's courage. His spirit lives in you." And Mac kissed her, held her tight and she loved him so. In a way, it was like he was a new father for her, and she felt that her father would have liked that feeling in her. "Then you'll be joining me in Brussels?"

"Yes, sir," David announced.

Dannie took both their hands, smiled, nodded.

Mac took a step back. "I've gotta keep up a good show, you know, wouldn't want them to suddenly remember I'm supposed to be retired." And he gave them a salute.

She blew him a kiss.

And then Mac jogged off toward the helicopter, with the vigor of a man half his age and a twinkle in his eye.

Dannie Hardy held David's hand tightly and, together, they watched as Mac flew away.

PINNACLE'S FINEST IN SUSPENSE
AND ESPIONAGE

OPIUM   (17-077, $4.50)
by Tony Cohan

Opium! The most alluring and dangerous substance known to man. The ultimate addiction, ensnaring all in its lethal web. A nerve-shattering odyssey into the perilous heart of the international narcotics trade, racing from the beaches of Miami to the treacherous twisting alleyways of the Casbah, from the slums of Paris to the teeming Hong Kong streets to the war-torn jungles of Vietnam.

TRUK LAGOON   (17-121, $3.95)
by Mitchell Sam Rossi

Two bizarre destinies inseparably linked over forty years unlease a savage storm of violence, treachery, and greed on a tropic island paradise. The most incredible covert operation in military history is about to be uncovered—a lethal mystery hidden for decades amid the wreckage of war far beneath the Truk Lagoon.

LAST JUDGMENT   (17-114, $4.50)
by Richard Hugo

Seeking vengeance for the senseless murders of his brother, sister-in-law, and their three children, former S.A.S. agent James Ross plunges into the perilous world of fanatical terrorism to prevent a centuries-old vision of the Apocalypse from becoming reality, as the approaching New Year threatens to usher in mankind's dreaded Last Judgment.

THE JASMINE SLOOP   (17-113, $3.95)
by Frank J. Kenmore

A man of rare and lethal talents, Colin Smallpiece has crammed ten lifetimes into his twenty-seven years. Now, drawn from his peaceful academic life into a perilous web of intrigue and assassination, the ex-intelligence operative has set off to locate a U.S. senator who has vanished mysteriously from the face of the Earth.

Available wherever paperbacks are sold, or order direct from the Publisher. Send cover price plus 50¢ per copy for mailing and handling to Pinnacle Books, Dept. 17-335, 475 Park Avenue South, New York, N.Y. 10016. Residents of New York, New Jersey and Pennsylvania must include sales tax. DO NOT SEND CASH.